New Europe, New World?

The European Union, Europe and the Challenges of the 21st Century

P.I.E. Peter Lang

Bruxelles · Bern · Berlin · Frankfurt am Main · New York · Oxford · Wien

Alfonso Martínez Arranz, Natalie J. Doyle
& Pascaline Winand (eds.)

New Europe, New World?

The European Union, Europe and the Challenges of the 21st Century

"European Policy"
No. 47

This book is funded by both Monash University and the European Commission of the European Union (DG Relex)

© P.I.E. PETER LANG s.a.
Éditions scientifiques internationales
Brussels, 2010
1 avenue Maurice, B-1050 Brussels, Belgium
info@peterlang.com; www.peterlang.com

ISSN 1376-0890
ISBN 978-90-5201-604-7
D/2010/5678/24

Printed in Germany

Library of Congress Cataloging-in-Publication Data
New Europe, new world? : the European Union, Europe, and the challenges of the 21st century / Natalie Doyle, Alfonso Martínez Arranz, Pascaline Winand, [editors].
p. cm. — (European policy, ISSN 1376-0890 ; no. 47)
Includes bibliographical references and index.   ISBN 978-90-5201-604-7
1. European Union. 2. Europe—Politics and government—21st century.
3. European Union countries—Relations—Foreign countries.   I. Doyle, Natalie.
II. Martinez Arranz, Alfonso. III. Winand, Pascaline.
JN30.N4745 2010   341.242'2—dc22   2010006219

CIP also available from the British Library, GB

Bibliographic information published by "Die Deutsche Nationalbibliothek". "Die Deutsche Nationalbibliothek" lists this publication in the "Deutsche Nationalbibliografie"; detailed bibliographic data is available on the Internet at <http://dnb.d-nb.de>.

Table of Contents

List of Abbreviations

ACP	Africa, Caribbean and Pacific group of states
ALP	Australian Labor Party
AMM	Aceh Monitoring Mission
APF	African Peace Facility
APRM	African Peer Review Mechanism
ARF	ASEAN Regional Forum
ASEAN	Association of Southeast Asian Nations
ASEM	Asia-Europe Meeting
AU	African Union
CFSP	Common Foreign and Security Policy
CJTF	Combined Joint Task Forces
CPA	Cotonou Partnership Agreement
DAC	Development Assistance Committee
DM	Deutsche Mark
DRC	Democratic Republic of Congo
EAA	European Armaments Agency
EADS	European Aeronautic Defence and Space Company
EC	European Community
ECAP	European Capabilities Action Plan
ECB	European Central Bank
ECHO	European Community Humanitarian Aid Office
ECJ	European Court of Justice
ECOWAS	Economic Community of West African States
ECPDM	European Centre for Development Policy Management
ECSC	European Coal and Steel Community
EDA	European Defence Agency
EDC	European Defence Community
EDEM	European Defence Equipment Market
EDF	European Development Fund
EDITB	European Defence Industrial and Technological Base
EEC	European Economic Community

EMU	Economic and Monetary Union
EP	European Parliament
EPA	Economic Partnership Agreement
EPC	European Political Cooperation
EPLO	European Peace Liaison Office
ERA	European Research Area
ESDI	European Security and Defence Identity
ESDP	European Security and Defence Policy
ESS	European Security Strategy
EU	European Union
EUMC	European Union Military Committee
EUMS	European Union Military Staff
Euratom	European Atomic Energy Community
FDI	Foreign Direct Investment
FRES	Future Rapid Effect System
GAC	General Affairs Council
GAEC	General and External Affairs Council
GDP	Gross Domestic Product
GNI	Gross National Income
GPS	Global Positioning System
ICG	International Crisis Group
IGC	Intergovernmental Conference
ITAR	International Traffic in Arms Regulation
MDG	Millennium Development Goals
MFN	Most Favoured Nation
MRAV	Multi-Role Armoured Vehicle
NAMA	NATO Airlift Management Agency
NATO	North Atlantic Treaty Organization
NRF	NATO Response Force
OAU	Organization of African Unity
ODA	Official Development Assistance
OECD	Organization for Economic Cooperation and Development
OMC	Open Method of Coordination
PRC	People's Republic of China

R&D	Research and Development
RAND	Research ANd Development (Corporation)
RRF	Rapid Reaction Force
RRM	Rapid Reaction Mechanism
SAP	Swedish Social Democratic Party
SEA	Single European Act
UN	United Nations
UNESCO	United Nations Educational, Scientific and Cultural Organization
USAF	United States Air Force
WEU	Western European Union
WMD	Weapons of Mass Destruction
WTO	World Trade Organization

Acknowledgements

The project that led to this volume grew out of a conference organised jointly by the Monash European and EU Centre and the Australasian Centre for Italian Studies in 2007. We benefited from the generosity and support of the French Embassy to Australia through the Alliance française de Melbourne, the Delegation of the European Commission to Australia, the Grollo Ruzzene Foundation and the Cassamarca Foundation. This book is funded by both Monash University and the European Commission of the European Union (DG Relex). I would also like to thank the Deputy Director of the Monash European and EU Centre, Natalie J. Doyle, who did much of the initial work in getting this conference off the ground, as well as the conference organizing committee, including professors from the Faculties of Arts, Business and Economics and Law at Monash University.

My warmest thanks go to the Administrator of the Monash European and EU Centre, Amanda Crichton, for her devotion and hard work in preparing the conference and to all the students who gave generously of their time to help us. A special "thank you" also to Alfonso Martínez Arranz for having done much of the earlier editing for this book. Finally, I owe a huge debt of gratitude to my husband, Cormac McMahon, for his excellent work in preparing the final manuscript, and to my children for their patience and forbearance.

Pascaline Winand
Melbourne

CHAPTER 1

A New Europe in a Changing World

Challenges and Opportunities

Pascaline WINAND, Alfonso MARTÍNEZ ARRANZ
& Natalie J. DOYLE

Introduction

Over the past few years, the European Union has seen some of the most significant events in its history. Now comprising of twenty-seven countries and with a population of 497 million, it is a key player not only in Europe but also in the world. As a powerful trade negotiator and a leading player in global issues such as the environment, development aid and human rights, the EU is recognized by many as a new force for global security and welfare. It has long played a central role in promoting economic prosperity as well as political stability and democracy in Europe, and this role has been recognized by its partners, including the United States. But does the EU giant have feet of clay?

Eastward enlargement, Turkey's application for membership, the constitutional process and the European Parliament elections have all featured prominently in the recent literature on the EU. The 2004 Treaty Establishing a Constitution for Europe and the 2007 Treaty of Lisbon were both intended to make the European Union work in the context of increasing membership. Yet the French and the Dutch "No's" to the Constitutional Treaty and the 2008 Irish "No" to the Treaty of Lisbon signalled an increasing divide between EU citizens in certain member states and their political class on key issues at both the national and Union levels. The global financial crisis only served to magnify this trend as angry citizens took to the streets to vent their frustration with the handling of the crisis by their governments. As economies further sank into recession and unemployment, some of the new EU member states seemed hardest hit. Meanwhile, Ireland, now equally mired in a severe economic crisis, started to reconsider its vote to the Lisbon Treaty as the EU appeared as "Ireland's safe harbour" in the midst of "the financial storm".[1] Even more recently, the low turnout in the 2009

---

[1] Garton Ash, T., "It takes an Irish poet to remind us of the grandeur of the European project. Seamus Heaney has raised the debate on the Lisbon treaty. A yes vote would

elections of the European Parliament at 43% of the 375 million eligible voters pointed to a lack of interest of EU citizens in the European Parliament, in spite of the constant increase in power of this institution and of the inventive media campaign of EU institutions to attract attention to the elections. A shift of the European Parliament to the centre-right also signalled a disenchantment of citizens with some of the leading political parties. Thus, even though the EU seems to be working well in many important fields such as trade and the environment, there is a widely felt need for reflection on how to enable it to develop into a more successful polity with a coherent and appealing political and social project for its citizens. This in turn has an impact on how the EU is being perceived on the world stage.

This volume intends to contribute to the debate in academic, business, legal, political and cultural circles about the changing face of Europe and the way it works, not just internally, but also with the rest of the world. At a time when regional alliances are very much on the agenda, including in the Asia Pacific region, we are in a unique position to reflect on the many advantages and also on some of the challenges presented by an "ever-closer union". This volume includes contributions from noted international experts from different disciplines and addresses a wide range of current issues relating to the EU as a political and economic space and as a global actor involved in such areas as mobility, culture and identity.

External and Internal Challenges

If the challenges the EU faces today are as varied as they are difficult, it is because Europe has changed and is in the process of re-imagining itself to confront new internal and external forces which could imperil the foundations of its very existence. The EU has transformed itself in response to sweeping European and world events such as the fall of the Berlin Wall, the Balkan crisis and the international actions engendered by the terrorist attack of 9/11 in the United States, not to mention other terrorist attacks in Europe and in the world. In response to shifts in global security, it has adapted its development policy and its instruments for humanitarian assistance to place more of an emphasis on security, stability and democracy through conflict prevention and resolution in Africa and elsewhere. The EU is changing in response to global challenges, such as climate change, which it cannot address on its own, but in which it claims a certain leadership or recog-

---

be good for Ireland and the EU – and Iran too", *The Guardian*, 24 June 2009. The quotation is from the website of Generation Yes, "a campaign organized by young Irish pro-Europeans".

nition in international circles. It is changing in response to the current financial crisis, as it attempts to find common solutions in partnership with key international players, thereby addressing some of the dire difficulties of its own member states, including in central and eastern Europe. The EU is also changing in response to internal tensions. Not least among these tensions is the EU's difficulty in being seen by its own citizens as a political project rooted in popular legitimacy rather than as an economic, institutional and elitist undertaking. The difficulties inherent in European unification also affect the international community's perceptions of the EU.

The EU of today is a different organization to the one that witnessed the fall of the Berlin Wall and is undeniably different from the European Communities of the 1950s when the European Coal and Steel Community (ECSC) took its first fledgling steps, soon to be followed by the European Economic Community (EEC) and Euratom. The end of the Cold War made it possible for Germany to reunify and for NATO and the EC/EU to embark on their most ambitious enlargements ever. As a result, the EU increased in size from 15 to 27 countries and its population jumped from 392.61 million to 495.88 million inhabitants, an increase of 26.3%. This also meant more diversity in political systems and in religious affiliations. In contrast to the secularized societies of the western EU member states which can be said to have been largely post-Christian, many of the new east-central member states experienced a revival of religion, with an organic relation with national identity.[2] Enlargement further meant a higher number of small and middle-sized member states, with the concomitant challenges this posed in terms of representation and votes in EU institutions, in particular for some of the larger member states. Faced with the necessity to embark upon ambitious institutional reforms as a response to enlargement, which included extending the use of qualified majority voting in the Council, large member states soon moved to protect their voting weight in this institution. They proposed to reduce the number of seats per member state in the Commission, while also adapting representation in the European Parliament to reflect their populations. Meanwhile, France experienced at first some difficulty in coming to terms with the prospect of a reunified Germany. During the Nice Treaty negotiations the French pushed to keep the same number of seats as their powerful neighbour in the Coun-

---

[2]   W. Spohn asks whether the growing conflictive role of religion in Europe could potentially endanger the secular-humanist and religious-ecumenical value system of the western cultural integration mode. See Spohn, W. in chapter 4 of this volume.

cil, in spite of a German population now significantly larger than that of France.[3]

Notwithstanding the initial exhilaration of a reunited Europe, the likelihood of increased migration flows from eastern and central Europe was a source of concern for western European governments and populations alike, a concern compounded by further immigration as a result of the Balkan crisis. The new security situation also led to tensions in the Atlantic Alliance. Whilst the relationship between a uniting Europe and the US had remained largely asymmetrical in security terms after the Second World War, the EU now claimed a more autonomous foreign, security and defence policy from the US in the new post-cold war architecture. Washington seemed less likely to play the security role that it had fulfilled in Europe in the past. This new function seemed also, increasingly, to extend beyond Europe.

The necessities of tackling the new security environment and economic and monetary challenges were reflected in a number of new treaties, namely the Maastricht Treaty, the Amsterdam Treaty and the Nice Treaty. The treaties gave the new European Union more responsibilities in home affairs and justice, security and defence, while ushering in a single currency, the Euro, and introducing the concept of EU citizenship. Yet the Maastricht Treaty also seemed to go hand in hand with an increasingly apolitical management of the European economy and the dismantling of labour law or social legislation in a context of growing unemployment.[4]

The 2000 Lisbon Strategy was meant to answer the challenge of globalisation by transforming the EU into a knowledge-based economy, which would make it grow faster while becoming more competitive and more socially cohesive.[5] As the strategy faced some difficulties in implementation, it was later revised in 2006. The emphasis was now on knowledge and innovation, on fostering a better business environment, including for small and medium-sized enterprises, helping people to find

---

[3]   Today's EU comprises very large member states, with a reunified Germany taking the first place with 82.0m inhabitants and France second, with a population of 64.3m, the UK with 61.2m, Italy with 60.0m and Spain with 45.8m. Among the new member states, Poland comes in sixth position with 38.1m and Romania seventh with 21.5m. Other member states range from 16.5m (The Netherlands) to 414,000 inhabitants in Malta, the smallest EU state. Among the new member states the inhabitants of the Czech Republic number 10.5m, Hungary 10.0m, Bulgaria 7.6m, Slovakia 5.4m, Lithuania 3.3m, Latvia 2.3m, Slovenia 2.0m, Estonia 1.3m and Cyprus 797,000 inhabitants (Source: Provisional and definitive statistics from Eurostat, last update 21/1/2010)..

[4]   See Doyle, N.J. in chapter 3 of this volume.

[5]   European Council, *Presidency Conclusions*, Lisbon European Summit, Document No. 100/1/00, 23-24 March 2000.

paid employment and, last but not least, on energy and climate change. The new priorities mirrored the necessary adaptation of the EU to on-going challenges, such as high levels of unemployment, the increase in low-paid jobs, and climate change. In 2008, these priorities were reconfirmed with a recognition that the social dimension of the strategy should be strengthened with the support of a "renewed Social Agenda, addressing Europe's new social and labour realities and also covering issues such as youth, education, migration and demography as well as intercultural dialogue".[6] This renewed, fine-tuned commitment to the Lisbon Strategy implicitly signalled an acknowledgment of the social challenge the EU faced.

Internal crises and external challenges such as energy dependence, global terrorism, organized crime, regional conflicts and the proliferation of weapons of mass destruction made it essential for the EU to redefine itself. Building on previous initiatives and treaties, the 2003 European Security Strategy (ESS), the failed 2004 Constitutional Treaty and the Lisbon Treaty all attempted to deal with these challenges by finding ways of addressing the new threats of the post cold war world while identifying the EU core values. Some of these values were already embedded in the 1993 Copenhagen Criteria which required candidate countries to have national institutions guaranteeing democracy, human rights, the rule of law, the respect of minorities, an operational market economy, and the ability to implement EU legislation.[7] Faced with the prospect of its largest enlargement ever, the EU was forced to reflect on the essence of its identity. The 1997 Amsterdam Treaty focused on much the same values already identified by Copenhagen and specified that the "union is founded on the principles of liberty, democracy, respect for human rights and fundamental freedoms, and the rule of law". In the wake of the terrorist attacks of 9/11, the ESS adopted in December 2003 by the European Council identified the main achievements of a united Europe as having fostered peace and stability within

---

[6] H.E. Bruno Julien, Ambassador and Head of Delegation of the European Commission to Australia and New Zealand, "The EU Lisbon Strategy – Parallels to Australia's Reform Agenda", speech presented to the Committee for Economic Development of Australia, Sydney, 15 October 2008.

[7] On 22 June 1993, EU Heads of state and government gathered in Copenhagen to define entry condition for candidate states: "Membership requires that the candidate country has achieved stability of institutions guaranteeing democracy, the rule of law, human rights and respect for and, protection of minorities, the existence of a functioning market economy as well as the capacity to cope with competitive pressure and market forces within the Union. Membership presupposes the candidate's ability to take on the obligations of membership including adherence to the aims of political, economic and monetary union". See European Council in Copenhagen, 21-22 June 1993, *Conclusions of the Presidency*, SN 180/93, Brussels, Council of the European Communities, pp. 10-15.

its own borders by "dealing peacefully with disputes" and "co-operating through common institutions", thereby spreading the rule or law and democracy. As an inherently peaceful community, both prosperous and stable, based on the rule of law and democracy, the EU seemed also uniquely qualified to spread its model of governance beyond its own borders, thereby promoting democracy, the rule of law and the protection of human rights in the world. To do so, the ESS recommended promoting effective multilateralism by backing international institutions, international law and regional organizations. The EU would play to its strengths. Since it was "the world's largest provider of official assistance and its largest trading entity", the EU would harness economic tools such as development policy and trade to achieve political objectives such as the reform of the international system. But it would also go beyond using economic tools to project its influence on the world stage. It would encourage "a strategic culture that fosters early, rapid and, when necessary, robust intervention"[8] while combining civilian and military instruments in addressing emerging conflicts, and backing the United Nations in crisis management. Did this mean, then, that the EU would be increasingly willing to flex its military muscles, in addition to using its tried and trusted economic tools, to achieve political objectives? Did this change its very nature as a peaceful, essentially civilian power? Was the EU on its way to becoming a great power, or a powerful nation-state writ large?

In the academic community, Ian Manners echoed practical developments in the EU by speaking of a "normative power Europe" characterized by five core norms or values – peace, liberty, democracy, the rule of law and the respect for human rights – and four subsidiary ones – social solidarity, anti-discrimination, sustainable development and good governance.[9] But he soon pondered whether the introduction of the European Security and Defence Policy (ESDP) did not undermine the EU's normative power on the international scene by making it more akin to a large state,[10] a "great power Europe". Such discussion harked back to François Duchêne's description of the European Communities as "civilian power Europe" in the early 1970s. A close collaborator of Jean Monnet – the mastermind behind the Schuman Declaration and the

---

[8]   "A Secure Europe in a Better World", *European Security Strategy*, Brussels, 12 December 2003, http://www.consilium.europa.eu/uedocs/cmsUpload/78367.pdf. See also "Report on the Implementation of the European Security Strategy – Providing Security in a Changing World", Brussels, 11 December 2008, http://www. consilium.europa.eu/ueDocs/cms_Data/docs/pressdata/EN/reports/104630.pdf.

[9]   Manners, I., "Normative Power Europe: A Contradiction in Terms?", *JCMS*, Vol. 40, No. 2, 2002, pp. 235-58.

[10] Manners, I., "Normative Power Europe Reconsidered: Beyond the Crossroads", *Journal of European Public Policy*, Vol. 13, No. 2, 2006, pp. 182-99.

first president of the High Authority of the ECSC – Duchêne argued that the European Community (EC) should not become a "military power Europe" or a "European super-power".[11] The EC was indeed "a large political cooperative formed to exert essentially civilian forms of power". As "a civilian group of countries long on economic power and relatively short on armed force",[12] economic power should be its key role, with military power taking the back seat. In this way the EC would be a force for social justice, democracy and generosity.[13]

The question nowadays is whether the EU has really succeeded in conveying the image that it truly promotes the values that is seeks to project, be it *vis-à-vis* its own citizens or towards the outside world. Is the EU really seen by its own citizens and citizens in other parts of the world as a promoter of human rights, social justice, democracy, development cooperation, environmental protection and multilateralism? Is it perceived as a model of peace and prosperity that can be emulated in other regions of the world? Or, rather, is it seen as a "Fortress Europe", as a club of prosperous countries bent on protecting their own borders from immigrants, and denying accession to new countries to the South and the East? Is the EU perceived as having an exclusive or an inclusive identity?[14] What do its member states, old and new, think of its model for social justice?

Challenges and Opportunities

Unity in Diversity: Values, Culture, Migration and Identity

Part one of this book focuses on values, culture, migration and identity. Several contributors ask to what extent attempts to redefine the EU and identify its core values have been successful. They investigate the key elements of the EU project and what made it distinct from others. Was it common cultural, humanist and religious roots? They ask how EU institutions have addressed the so-called democratic deficit and whether the European integration project is rooted in no more than "a

---

11   Duchêne, F., "Europe's Role in World Peace" in R. Mayne (ed.), *Europe Tomorrow: Sixteen Europeans Look Ahead*, London, Fontana, 1972, p. 37; Duchêne, F., "The European Community and the Uncertainties of Interdependence" in M. Kohnstamm and W. Hager (eds.), *A Nation Writ Large? Foreign Policy Problems before the European Community*, Basingstoke, Macmillan, 1973, pp. 1-21.

12   Duchêne, F., "The European Community and the Uncertainties of Interdependence", *op. cit.*, p. 19.

13   Duchêne, F., "La Communauté européenne et les aléas de l'interdépendance" in M. Kohnstamm et W. Hager (dir.), *L'Europe avec un grand E. Bilan et perspectives*, Paris, Robert Laffont, 1973, pp. 17-45.

14   See Bretherton, Ch. and Vogler, J., *The European Union as a Global Actor*, Oxon, Routledge, 2006.

plurality of nationals with rival and contrasting identities".[15] Do a "European public" and a "united self-consciousness" exist in the EU or should they be fostered, or even, invented?[16] Is something more needed than the "market citizenship" of the Maastricht Treaty and is it possible to go beyond such citizenship?[17] Is Cris Shore right in pointing out that EU legitimacy will always pale next to the historical and social legitimacy of EU nation-states? How should one tackle the growth of immigrant communities in the EU and the concomitant increase in anti-immigration sentiments? One contributor investigates what it really means to be EU citizens for scientists and researchers from southern and eastern European countries, given the varying degrees of development in R&D in these regions, as opposed to Northern Europe.[18] Other contributors question the boundaries of the EU project and its legitimacy. Should only secular criteria for enlargement prevail?[19] Should one reinvent Europe from below and re-politicize the EU to lend it more legitimacy?[20] How should one deal with increasing anti-immigration feelings in the EU and the feeling of an absence of belonging of EU citizens?[21]

In an effort to move away from a European identity that appears excessively focused on the European-ness of Europe and on negative representations of non-Europeans, Giancarlo Chiro and Katharine Vadura argue for the construction of a different kind of European identity which recognizes the many different levels of belonging of EU citizens. In doing so they draw on the Australian experience with multiculturalism, on Ulrich Beck's conception of Europe as a cosmopolitan system on its way to becoming a transnational state with "the constitutional enshrinement of the principle of national and cultural and ethnic and religious tolerance"[22] and on Jürgen Habermas' emphasis on a multiculturalism that allows for the "co-existence of different life forms as equals", with the "mutual recognition of their sub-cultural memberships [...] in a common political culture".[23] They conclude that an inclusive multicultural citizenship in the EU, made possible by policies which foster multicultural coexistence, could contribute to building a new European identity.

---

[15] See Chiro, G. and Vadura, K. in chapter 2 of this volume.

[16] See Chiro, G., Vadura, K., Polonska, E. in chapters 2 and 7 of this volume.

[17] See Chiro, G. and Vadura, K. in chapter 2 of this volume.

[18] See Morando-Foadi, S. in chapter 5 of this volume.

[19] See Spohn, W. in chapter 4 of this volume.

[20] See Doyle, N.J. in chapter 3 of this volume.

[21] See Chiro, G. and Vadura, K. in chapter 2 of this volume.

[22] Beck, U., "Understanding the Real Europe", *Dissent*, Summer 2003, pp. 32-38.

[23] Habermas, J., "Intolerance and Discrimination", *ICON*, Vol. 1, No. 1, 2003, p. 10.

Natalie J. Doyle explains the history of the European Union as a re-action against nationalism that in reality implied an un-reflexive process of cosmopolitan acculturation of European nations to one another, with Franco-German acculturation playing a key role. The dream of a European integration transcending the nation-state, ultimately led to the construction of an a-political Europe constructed from above, with an excessive focus on monetary union and lacking legitimacy from below. She recommends rediscovering the unique brand of social solidarity and democracy which Europeans developed at the level of the nation-state to assert a European political dimension and to reinvent the EU from below.

Willfried Spohn argues for the recognition of organized religion as a key factor in studying the EU in light of the rise in immigration and religious minorities in Europe, and of the increased frequency of inter-religious encounters as a result of globalisation. This is so particularly in the context of the latest EU extension to the East and prospects for future enlargements, with new and candidate member states coming from Catholic, Orthodox Christian and Islamic traditions. The dynamics of the EU enlargement to the East cannot be understood without considering the clashes between a largely secularized Western Europe and a more religious east-central Europe with a lower degree of cultural secularization. Spohn recommends addressing the challenge of reconciling these differing legacies by relying on a "multiple modernities" approach to Europeanisation and religion. Instead of focusing on the secular-humanist western core of European cultural integration and limiting religious diversity, he sees the encouragement "of a form of multicultural citizenship and religious pluralism inside European societies" and including "Turkey as a crucial multi-religious and multi-cultural pillar of European cultural integration and collective identity" as possible solutions. Even though he recognizes that this may be currently unrealistic and that Turkish-EU relations may be confined for the foreseeable future to a "privileged partnership" he does see some advantage in his more inclusive strategy for a better integration of Muslim populations in Europe. As with Giancarlo Chiro and Katharine Vadura, his approach thus encourages the emergence of a more inclusive identity which would fit in better with the diversity of the EU in its current form, and with future prospects for enlargement.

Sonia Morano-Foadi addresses the consequences of EU policies that encourage the intra-European migration of scientists, and focuses in particular on Italian scientists and researchers. She first examines the EU "clustering" policy, which fosters the development of science in those regional areas which allow for inter-linkages between nearby organizations. One of the unintended effects of such a policy, she says, is that the research clusters are located mainly in large cities in Northern Europe, thereby unwittingly contributing to uneven regional development. The problem is compounded by the limitations of EU citizenship, which although it gives EU citizens the full right to move throughout the EU with virtually similar rights in the destination country, does not provide an adequate mechanism to allow highly-skilled scientists to return to their home countries. To make Europe more competitive, the Lisbon Strategy and the Commission's December 2007 Strategic Report on the four priority areas of the renewed Lisbon Agenda strategy identified as a key goal the realisation of a real European Research Area. But what does this mean in practice for researchers from southern European countries, where investment in research is mostly low and prospects for securing permanent positions are even lower? Can scientists return to their home countries after a period of research in Northern Europe? She suggests that there is an internal brain drain in the EU, particularly from the South and East to the North, which undermines overall "brain circulation" in the EU. The solution might be to move away from the soft law, non-coercive tool of the Open Method of Coordination used to implement the objectives of the Lisbon Agenda and to opt for a more regulative system better adapted to the needs of southern and eastern European countries. In addition, there should be better coordination of science and migration policies between the national and European levels. Finally, the EU should promote return policies as part of its citizenship provisions, and perhaps introduce a common selection procedure for scientists. Only then would the free movement of knowledge, the "fifth freedom"[24] really take on its full meaning.

The EU between Soft and Hard Power

The second part of this volume addresses the new role of the EU in world politics. The EU has been grappling in recent years with its geopolitical positioning: "good cop", dormant superpower, power in demise, metrosexual[25] superpower, Venus, normative power. The qualifications are many and pose the question of how strong the EU is seen in terms of hard and soft power by various players on the international stage. In the view of Joseph Nye, military and economic power can be used directly to apply pressure to other actors, even to the point of coercion. But there is a more indirect way of exercising power. "Soft power" as it is called, could be summed up as "getting others to want what you want" and is based first and foremost on the values that a country defends and which are seen in its internal policies and the

---

[24] Julien, B., *op. cit.*, p. 12.

[25] Khanna, P., "The Metrosexual Superpower", *Foreign Policy*, July/August, 2004.

manner in which it acts on the international stage.[26] So can the EU still inspire by its social and development policies? How do other countries view its audiovisual policy? To what extent does the introduction and evolution of the ESDP clash with some member states' commitment to neutrality and development aid? While the ESDP is seen as a necessity for many EU states, the reasons for this necessity are all but homogeneous. For example, the UK aims at better supporting the US while France and Germany would like to see EU actions more independent from American policies. What then is the relation of a constantly evolving European Union to seasoned world players such as the United States and Japan, and new world players such as China and India? How are EU development policies viewed in Africa?

Andrew Scott is confident that much can be learned by "liberal market" economies of the English-speaking world – and this includes Australia – from the success of the "social market" economies of Nordic nations. Their economic success goes hand in hand with responsible environmental and energy policies and socially fair practices. Egalitarian income distribution and a decent minimum income for all, reasonable working hours, family-friendly work policies, low child poverty, high spending on R&D and a generous aid policy all contribute to paint an idyllic picture of Nordic Europe. In spite of the recent election of conservative governments in some of the Nordic countries, the policy legacy of the Social Democrats seems to endure. Andrew Scott is confident that in spite of the victory of Nicolas Sarkozy in France with its potential for undermining the French social model, the French Socialist Party will be strengthened in future by the very economic issues the current French government failed to address. Thus, the situation has striking echoes of when Kevin Rudd defeated Australian Prime Minister John Howard in the 2007 elections, largely because many Australian citizens deemed Howard's industrial relations policy unfair. Scott concludes that the US, the UK and Australia could benefit from gaining a better understanding of the achievements of Nordic Europe and in particular Sweden. In answer to Natalie J. Doyle, Scott thus seems to suggest that the best way of rediscovering the roots of the European social project and its unique brand of social solidarity might be to study Nordic Europe, thereby helping to revitalize the European political project. In turn this would also be a way of projecting a positive image of Europe on the international scene, and of finding some resonance in governments which seem more attentive to economic egalitarianism than their predecessors, as in the United States and Australia. This would be soft power at its best.

---

[26] Nye, J.S., *The Paradox of American Power*, Oxford, Oxford University Press, 2002, p. 9.

Eva Polonska's contribution illustrates the uneasiness in US-EU relations as the two economic giants vie for soft power in the cultural sphere through the audiovisual sector. She also shows the influence of the EU in protecting cultural diversity on the world stage, as an offshoot of its efforts to foster the development of a European identity. Faced with the challenge of creating a "common European feeling" to back the European project, the European Commission sought to achieve political aims by using cultural means "initially with no budget and no legal basis" and by focusing on the economic lines of cultural policy in building a "powerful European culture industry".[27] In the wake of the Maastricht Treaty, the EU intended to foster the emergence of a "People's Europe", European self-awareness and identity in order to back the European project. Keeping European citizens "adequately informed"[28] was to be achieved essentially through the mass media, and particularly television, with an emphasis on trans-national television channels. The EU accordingly was on a head-on collision course with the US. While the EU aimed to protect its audiovisual goods and services industry as a way of strengthening the European identity of its citizens, the US was bent on liberalizing trade in the sector, thereby most likely continuing the US productions' domination of the audio-visual market. The 1989 "Television without Frontiers Directive" lent support for European TV programs and films and introduced quota requirements for European works on television. The EU later extended its quota regime to all audiovisual media services, a policy that resulted in strong growth in European domestic film production. Whatever its successes as a policy, it did not sufficiently encourage the circulation of European films across European countries or the propagation of works from Central and Eastern Europe to Western Europe. On the international scene, the debate on cultural goods and cultural diversity shifted from the World Trade Organization (WTO) to UNESCO. While the EU, together with most other nations, supported the UNESCO approach towards the protection of cultural goods and services as "vectors of identity, values and meaning" which "must not be treated as mere commodities or consumer goods",[29] the US did not. At the same time, by making itself the champion of the "promotion and preservation of cultural diversity" considered "among the

---

[27] See Polonska, E. in this book; Jacques Delors, speech to the European Parliament in 1985, as quoted in R. Collins, *Audiovisual and Broadcasting Policy in the European Community*, London, University of North Press, 1993, p. 14.

[28] "Television without Frontiers: Green Paper on the Establishment of the Common Market for Broadcasting especially for Satellite and Cable", COM(84) final, Luxembourg, OOPEC, 1984, p. 2.

[29] Artiche 8 of the 2001 UNESCO Universal Declaration on Cultural Diversity.

founding principles of the European model",[30] the EU also seems to have imprisoned itself in a set of contradictions. How does it reconcile the image it attempts to project as a defender of global trade liberalization with its image as defender of cultural diversity, also implying a protectionist attitude in the cultural field? The need to foster European identity and to support the cultures of linguistically disparate groups seem to trump the imperative of free and untrammelled market forces here, and, thus Eva Polonska argues that the sector should not be opened to free trade.

Patrick Kimunguyi examines one of the greatest claims of the EU in terms of soft power: its leading role in development aid. He explores the interrelated development and conflict prevention policies of the EU, thereby underscoring both their soft and hard power dimensions. African-EC/EU relations were initially mostly focused on economic development and humanitarian aid. This is no longer the case. As the EU attempts to deal with the security threats of the post-cold war period, it has reframed its development cooperation and humanitarian assistance instruments to include the promotion of security, stability and democracy, without which there can be no sustainable development. In so doing, it has continued to develop political conditionality clauses for the promotion of human rights, democracy and the rule of law, in its development policy. This has increased its influence on recipient states, particularly in Africa. It could also be argued that these values are the very ones which the EU seeks to put forward as part of the European model *vis-à-vis* EU citizens and citizens in the wider world community. Particularly in Africa, but also in other parts of the world, the EU has improved its conflict prevention capacity by developing its instruments for crisis management within the framework of the Common Foreign and Security Policy (CFSP). This has made it a more visible actor on the world scene, while further developing its profile and improving its image in Africa, an image, which the EU has tried to picture as distinct from the colonial past of its member states. This visibility has further been enhanced by the creation of the European Community Humanitarian Aid Office (ECHO) in 1992, which in addition to better enabling the EC/EU to deal with emergency aid situations, has made it possible for the EU to project a highly visible image in the media. Finally, the EU, in redefining its partnership with Africa in 2007, has placed an emphasis on strengthening civil societies in the EU and Africa. This once again underscores efforts on the EU side to reinforce "people-to-people" links in order not only to facilitate the emergence of a "People's Europe" but

---

[30] "Towards an International Instrument on Cultural Diversity", *Communication from the Commission*, COM(2003) 520 final.

also that of the EU as a key international actor, considered as such by non-EU citizens, including in the development field.

Franz Oswald argues that the EU has engaged in "soft balancing between friends" to counterbalance US hegemony in the post-cold war period using non-military instruments such as economic power, and the renegotiation of roles in the international system. While such soft-balancing can be seen as partly *de facto* given the sheer economic weight of the EU in international trade and investment, it has increasingly become more deliberate as the EU has claimed a more autonomous security role *vis-à-vis* the US via "symbolic action and small practical steps". While the Cold War lasted, the growing EC economic weight failed to translate into an increased role in European security. But the economic dimension took a more pre-eminent position with the end of the conflict with the Soviet Union. The introduction of the Euro made it possible for some prominent analysts to think of a "bipolar currency regime dominated by Europe and the United States"[31] instead of the US-dominated regime that prevailed in the past. Yet EU role claims in CFSP were initially not backed by the capability needed to implement them, as demonstrated in the EU's handling of the Bosnia and Kosovo crises. The role claims were subsequently pursued in the development of the ESDP in 1999 and the adoption of the 2003 ESS, with the latter emphasizing the support of the EU for multilateralism. EU efforts to rationalize its defence spending and to develop an integrated European Defence Equipment Market (EDEM) and a European Defence Agency (EDA) were coupled with significant inroads in acquiring military and civilian crisis management instruments. ESDP missions further substantiated the EU's role claims to take on responsibility for its own security. From importing security during the Cold War, the EU also began to export security to the rest of the world to tackle the global challenges of the post-cold war and post-9/11 world such as terrorism, failed states, and the proliferation of weapons of mass destruction.

Rémy Davison further explores the EU's ESDP, while showing the challenges it faces and examining some of its out-of-area operations including in Bosnia-Herzegovina, Georgia, Macedonia and Congo. The ESDP was conceived as a way for the EU to address situations where NATO was not able or willing to act. As part of ESDP, the EU is developing its own combat forces or Rapid Reaction Force (RRF). But the operability of the 60,000-strong RRF, which should be able to deploy within 60 days, has been delayed. Until the RRF is fully functional, missions beyond the EU's own borders have accordingly relied on

---

[31] Bergsten, F., "The Dollar and the Euro", *Foreign Affairs*, Vol. 76. No. 4, July/August 1997, p. 83.

NATO assets and EU defence ministers have opted to form battle groups which can be deployed rapidly. The EU also created the European Defence Agency in 2004. The agency is intended to improve EU crisis management capabilities by encouraging and strengthening EU cooperation in armaments cooperation and enhancing coherence in EU defence procurement. Yet the EDA has been plagued by disagreements by EU member states, thereby also reducing the potential for EU firms to compete with the US in exploiting a lucrative defence procurement market. In addition, some EU member states have preferred to invest in US programmes rather than in European defence projects. The US-British special relationship has also tended to limit prospects for the UK to participate in a significant way in a single EU defence industry. Further, the EU is faced with the competition of former Soviet states in creating an integrated EU market in defence procurement. More generally, Davison shows that there is no single EU view on what the ESDP should do. While France, Germany and the UK mostly steer the agenda, other countries remain on the sidelines or have almost no influence, as in the case of the EU neutrals, Ireland, Finland and Austria. While EU defence expenditures are the second largest in the world, Davison contends that "this does not buy Europe the world's second best military machine". Small defence budgets, a technological and capability gap with the US, and the fragmentation of the EU defence procurement market into small domestic markets make it difficult for the EU to increase its capabilities in crisis management, both in Europe and out-of-area.

Yet, as will be shown in the next section, the EU can be a highly relevant security actor in the world, where there is an increasing need to manage conflict by using both military and civilian means to obtain durable, long-term stabilizing effects.

The EU in the Asia Pacific Region

Part three of this volume examines some of the same challenges as in parts one and two, but with a focus on EU external governance, specifically in the Asia Pacific and on the perceptions of the EU and some of its most visible attributes in this region.

Saponti Baroowa paints a more optimistic picture of ESDP than Rémy Davison. He outlines the success of Operation *Artemis* in the Democratic Republic of Congo. Launched in 2003 in response to a call from the United Nations, this was the first ESDP peacekeeping mission outside Europe. *Artemis* also had the distinction of being free-standing in that it did not draw on NATO assets. It successfully combined military and civilian intervention, thereby contributing not just to manage the crisis in the short-term but also to stabilize the region on a more

durable basis for the future. As Jean-Yves Haine has argued, this signalled that the ESDP was now becoming more than a "tool of crisis
management in the Balkans".[32] In keeping with the newly agreed 2003
ESS, the ESDP was meant to reach out to other parts of the world
beyond the EU and its immediate neighbourhood, thereby endowing the
EU with a more significant role as a global security player as it now
chose its own theatres of operation in the world. The launch of the Aceh
Monitoring Mission (AMM) in Indonesia in 2005 continued this trend
of engaging in a theatre of conflict beyond the EU's own backyard. The
AMM was the first time the ESDP was active in the Asia Pacific. The
mission was also significant in that the EU cooperated with a key regional organization, the Association of Southeast Asian Nations
(ASEAN), to resolve the conflict in north-western Indonesia. This was
in keeping with the EU policy of backing regional organizations as
providers of security and stability in the world, and augured well for the
prospects of ASEAN-EU cooperation in enhancing security in the Asia
Pacific. Saponti Baroova sees a competitive edge for the EU in enhancing security in the region in cooperation with regional actors such as
ASEAN and key individual actors such as India or China. The EU's
experience in conflict resolution and in providing "'soft security' which
uses civilian means instead of military means", would usefully complement its contribution to diffusing tensions on the ground by adding a
multilateral dimension to regional crisis management. In addition,
Australia may well come to play an increasing role in enhancing the
EU's capacity to contribute to security in the Asia Pacific. Indeed,
Saponti Baroova concludes that Australia is uniquely qualified to become "the cementing force in any security and strategic partnership
between the EU and the Asia Pacific region" in light of "its historical
and cultural links with Europe and its geographical proximity to Asia
together with its recent engagements with its Asian neighbours".

The last two chapters focus on the image of the EU in the French Pacific Region and in New Zealand. Yoon Ah Choi examines how the
Euro is perceived in the discourse of major local newspapers in French
Polynesia, New Caledonia and Wallis and Futuna as the introduction of
the Euro is currently proposed in these regions. She concludes that
monetary integration is generally viewed as desirable, while both the
positive and negative consequences of the introduction of the Euro are
outlined in the press media. Natalia Chaban, Sile Sammon and John
Condren similarly analyse New Zealand's public response to the French
and Dutch rejections of the EU Constitutional Treaty by examining the
coverage of key New Zealand newspapers and national "elite" percep-

---

[32] Haine, J.-H., "ESDP: An Overview", *European Union Institute for Security Studies*,
www.iss-eu.org.

tions. Starting from the premise that the failure of the Treaty under-mined internal as well as external perceptions of the EU, they conclude that coverage of the EU in New Zealand increases dramatically when a crisis erupts such as the rejection of the Constitutional Treaty and declines just a dramatically in times of good EU news such as the signing of the Lisbon Treaty. Another finding is that some key member states seemed to steal the show as leaders in the constitutional saga, while EU institutions and officials were generally not in the limelight or were pictured as reactive, all of which had the effect of undermining the image of the EU as a single entity. This could be attributed in part to the kind of European sources which the New Zealand press drew on when covering the Treaty. These sources were mostly British, with an occa-sional reliance on a French press agency. In the wake of the crisis of the Constitutional Treaty, New Zealand policy-makers likewise seemed to perceive the EU as a divided entity, incapable of exerting a leading role on the international stage.

So what can be done to change such an image which is potentially damaging to EU-New Zealand relations, and if such an image also prevails in other non-EU countries, how can the EU present a more unified, cohesive and engaging face to the world? As 90% of EU citi-zens would seem to be keen for the EU to exert a more visible role on the world stage,[33] perhaps a more positive EU global role may serve, in the words of Natalia Chaban, Sile Sammon and John Condren, as a way "to connect the EU with its citizens"?

Conclusion

The picture of the EU that emerges from this volume is that of an in-creasingly important actor on the world stage, not only in economic terms, but also in political, security and cultural terms, with the potential for wielding even more influence if it is able to tackle some of its more pressing internal challenges. The EU will also need to overcome nega-tive external perceptions, notably in the media, while agreeing upon more coherent positions in its external policies based on a credible assessment of its civilian and military capabilities. Indeed, one of the challenges which the EU faces is to redefine what the EU project is about in the wake of its most recent enlargements and in a world fraught with new and not so new challenges such as terrorism, migration and the recent international financial crisis. Perhaps one way of reconnecting the EU with its citizens – beyond using the European media to promote EU identity – may be by rediscovering the European social project, by better

---

[33]   US German Marshal Fund survey, September 2007. Reported in *EUobserver*. See Chaban, N. *et al.* in chapter 13 of this volume.

integrating immigrant populations and by promoting an inclusive multi-cultural citizenship of the EU.

Another challenge with which the EU is confronted is that of over-coming its image as an incoherent and divided actor both in Europe and on the world stage, an actor incapable of capturing the imagination of its own citizens or of presenting a united position in key conflicts such as in the 2003 Iraq war. To be sure, international and external perceptions of the EU are intimately connected, and an EU that is better able to engage its own citizens will also be better able to project a credible and engag-ing image on the world scene. In fact, the EU's external and internal images, policies and actions cannot be separated as they reflect upon one another. Indeed, another way of overcoming the current limitations of an evolving EU may be to capitalize on its recent experience in conflict resolution and crisis management beyond its immediate neighbourhood, including in Africa and in the Asia Pacific.

By continuing to show its willingness to cooperate with regional or-ganizations, the United Nations (UN) and other key players such as Australia, in addressing global challenges such as climate change and terrorism and in preventing and managing conflicts essentially via "soft security", the EU will not only improve its image *vis-à-vis* its own citizens and the international community, but will also continue to build substance behind this image. The image will be that of an essentially, but not exclusively, "civilian power Europe" intent on spreading peace, stability, sustainable development and democracy beyond its own borders, an EU which is not an economic "club of the rich" but rather a force for social justice, democracy and generosity within its own borders and beyond, as François Duchêne hoped would one day be the case.

PART I

UNITY IN DIVERSITY: VALUES, CULTURE, MIGRATION AND IDENTITY

CHAPTER 2

Whither European Integration?

The Impact of Multicultural Identities in a Globalising Context

Giancarlo CHIRO & Katharine VADURA

Introduction

While the project for a united Europe has its roots in the cosmopolitan ideals of figures of the Enlightenment such as Voltaire, Montesquieu and Kant, the immediate historical motives behind the establishment of the European Union (EU) can be found in the aftermath of two world wars. These, at least for Western Europe, brought about the completion of national projects instigated in the previous century. According to Ulrich Beck,[1] cosmopolitan Europe was consciously conceived and launched after the Second World War as the political antithesis to a nationalistic Europe and the physical and moral devastation that had emerged from it. It was in this spirit in 1946 that Winston Churchill claimed, "If Europe were once united [...] there would be no limit to the happiness, to the prosperity and the glory which its four hundred million people would enjoy". For Beck, Europe is a project born of Nazi resistance which was reinvented by statesmen and those most closely identified with the resistance who were able to reach past the mass graves back into the European history of ideas.

Clearly the political and cultural landscape of Europe has changed considerably since those early days. Changing patterns and increasing migration flows, due to market-driven globalising forces in the latter part of the 20th century, security concerns stemming from the terrorist attacks in New York, Madrid and London, and conflicts associated with ethnic and religious diversity in various European cities, all have complicated the notions of belonging, citizenship and integration in the EU. The rejection of the European Constitution in France and the Netherlands in 2005 could have been caused by concomitant concerns regarding multicultural coexistence, the lack of detailed information about the

---

[1] Beck, U., "Understanding the Real Europe", *Dissent*, Summer 2003, pp. 32-38.

political nature of a post-national or trans-national Europe and its consequences for individual nation states.

From its inception, the European Community project has travelled along two intertwining paths: the first leading to the increasing economic and political integration of member states and the second leading to higher levels of individual and national identification with the idea of Europe (promoted initially under the banner of "unity in diversity" and more recently as "united in diversity"). For the greater part of the more than fifty years since the signing of the Rome Treaties, the first project has predominated, concerned as it was with "nuts and bolts" issues, such as achieving an internal market with a single currency and establishing supranational institutions and decision-making mechanisms. The rate of change of the first project appeared to accelerate through the 1990s with the signing of the Maastricht Treaty (1992) and the subsequent treaties of Amsterdam (1997) and Nice (2001), each increasing the powers of the Union over formerly sacrosanct areas of national policy including foreign policy, defence, home affairs and justice.

Whilst pre-Maastricht treaties were overwhelmingly technical in character, the concept of citizenship enshrined for the first time in the Maastricht Treaty and the decision to introduce a single currency instigated widespread grassroots debate across the European Community. The proposed Constitution for Europe went even further, replacing all the existing Treaties with a single text which established the European Union and set out its values, objectives, principles, symbols and fundamental rights. The Constitutional Treaty was preceded by a Preamble which recalled, among other things, Europe's cultural, religious and humanist heritage, and invoked the desire of the peoples of Europe to transcend their ancient divisions in order to forge a common destiny, while remaining proud of their national identities and history. Many of these themes were already present in previous treaties, while others concerning humanism, reason and the national identities of peoples were added. Importantly, the Charter of Fundamental Rights, which previously had no legal force, was integrated in the Constitution.

With the signing of the Treaty establishing a Constitution for Europe in 2004, the stakes for the political unification of Europe rose. The fourteen countries which presented the Constitution to their respective parliaments all ratified the Treaty.[2] Of the countries which chose to follow the referendum method or a combined parliamentary and referendum method, two voted in favour (Spain and Luxembourg) and two voted against (France and Netherlands). Spain recorded the highest Yes

---

[2]   Austria, Belgium, Cyprus, Estonia, Germany, Greece, Finland, Hungary, Italy, Latvia, Lithuania, Malta, Slovakia and Slovenia.

vote with 77% in favour and Luxembourg recording 56%. In the aftermath of the negative results in France (55% No vote from a 69% turn out) and the Netherlands (62% No vote from a 63% turn out), the remaining member states including the Czech Republic, Denmark, Ireland, Portugal, Poland, Sweden and the UK chose to postpone the ratification process.

This was the point in the journey towards European unification where the two paths, the political and the cultural, crossed. Previously the quest for European integration was considered by many observers as little more than an elitist project which had not managed to overly tax the imagination of ordinary citizens of member nation-states. However, since the 1980s, interest in issues of a supranational European citizenship and identity were brought increasingly to the fore by politicians and public servants at both the national and European levels. Indeed, the construction of a European identity appeared to depend more and more on negative representations of immigrant "Others". The rejection of the European Constitution in France and the Netherlands could be seen to stem as much from such concerns as from the lack of detailed information about the nature of an integrated or transnational Europe.

In the end, the Citizenship "chapter" introduced into the Maastricht Treaty was curiously devoid of either rights or duties which citizens of most nation-states would normally expect to see in such a document. Perhaps, as Cris Shore has pointed out, the key rationale for Union citizenship was that of nurturing feelings of belonging. Adopting a "blank banner" or "mobilising metaphor" was designed not so much to generate support for the EU, but to invent the category of a "European public" in the first place. Popularising the "European idea", in turn, is seen as a strategy for endowing the EU institutions with cultural legitimacy, the absence of which is both symptom and cause of the EU's "democratic deficit".[3]

But the success of the unification project will depend on more than the treaties and policies negotiated by national representatives, members of various EU councils and administrative units. It will need more than slick marketing campaigns. Clearly the framers of the integration project as conceived in the mid-1980s, with the enlargement of the Union to twelve countries, could not have foreseen the impact of the collapse of the Soviet Union. Nor could they have foreseen the dramatic rise in asylum-seekers and refugees flowing from the Balkan crisis or more generally, the immigrants seeking employment and a better future driven by trans-national economic forces. Finally, they could not have

---

[3]   Shore, C., "Whither European Citizenship? Eros and Civilisation Revisited", *European Journal of Social Theory*, Vol. 7, No. 1, 2004, p. 31.

predicted the post 9/11 terrorist threat within European states. All of these events, however, have brought the integration process under closer scrutiny from an increasingly suspicious European public, uncertain of how the European Union will impact on their lives in the future. As Habermas has argued,[4] the survival of democratic political systems of advanced capitalist societies rests on popular legitimation in the cultural sphere.

Research on Attitudes towards European Integration

The importance of popular legitimation has been at the core of a growing number of empirical studies which have drawn on Eurobarometer data. In an early study covering surveys held in 1982, 1986, 1989 and 1992, Mathieu Deflem and Fred Pampei found that while an overwhelming majority support European unification,[5] even in those countries that are less enthusiastic, national identification would appear to explain pro-European as well as anti-European attitudes. This suggests that both favourable and unfavourable orientations toward the supranational European Union emanate from national concerns as political citizenship has not been guaranteed on any level beyond nation states. As Roel de Lange argues,[6] the citizenship specified in the Maastricht Treaty is primarily a legally sanctioned economic strategy, a free movement "market citizenship". In spite of the high levels of support it receives, Deflem and Pampei conclude that European unification does not rely on postnational citizens with a united self-consciousness, but on a plurality of nationals with rival and contrasting identities.[7]

More recently, Lauren McLaren examined "cultural threat" as a key variable for understanding reluctance about European integration and found that while large proportions of EU citizens do indeed fear that the EU is threatening their national identity and culture, the effect of this fear on attitudes toward the EU is not that substantial.[8] Other factors such as personal utilitarianism and actual benefits received by one's country have equal or greater impacts on levels of support for the EU integration project, as does the effect of feelings about current national

---

[4] Habermas, J., "Legitimation Problems in the Modern State", *Communication and the Evolution of Society*, translated, London, Heinemann, 1979.

[5] Deflem, M. and Pampei, F.C., "The Myth of Postnational Identity: Popular Support for European Unification", *Social Forces*, Vol. 75, No. 1, 1996, pp. 119-143.

[6] De Lange, R., "Paradoxes of European Citizenship" in P. Fitzpatrick (ed.), *Nationalism, Racism and the Rule of Law*, Aldershot, Dartmouth, 1995.

[7] Deflem, M. and Pampei, F.C., "The Myth of Postnational Identity", *op. cit.*, p. 138.

[8] McLaren, L., "Opposition to European Integration and Fear of Loss of National Identity: Debunking a Basic Assumption Regarding Hostility to the Integration Project", *European Union Politics*, Vol. 8, No. 1, 2007, pp. 83-108.

governments. Thus it appears that while the EU is seen to some degree in terms of its threat to long established national identities, it is perceived far more in terms of the benefits it can provide or the costs it imposes, both to the individual and to the country.

Two further studies have focused on attitudes toward immigration, rather than McLaren's more diffuse notion of cultural threat. In a survey undertaken in Denmark and the Netherlands, Claes de Vreese and Hajo Boomgaarden argued that anti-immigration sentiments tap people's readiness to show negative out-group bias and therefore to oppose further European integration.[9] As such they are not a proxy measure for national identity because personality traits and personal values, as well as perceptions of group competition or a general sense of insecurity, can cause people's hostility towards immigrants. Their results confirmed the hypothesis that in both countries anti-immigration sentiments are the strongest predictor of negative attitudes toward EU integration. Like McLaren,[10] they also found that positive evaluations of the incumbent national governments and optimistic economic assessments were strong positive predictors of support for integration.

These results are supported by Alf Luedtke's study,[11] which investigated the effect of national identity on public attitudes towards EU control over immigration policy. Amid the growing political salience of immigration, which has become increasingly coupled with the terrorist threat after the attacks of 11 September 2001, and the Madrid and London bombings of 2004 and 2005, it is hardly surprising that the "harmonisation" of immigration policy should also appear high on the EU's agenda. If, as Luedtke posits,[12] national identity means self-definition and belonging, then immigration cuts to the heart of this concept. It raises political and cultural questions about how the nation state should be defined, who should belong (and who should be excluded), and establishes the criteria for entrance, expulsion, settlement and naturalisation.

Like McLaren's, Luedtke's analysis shows that identity is a relatively stable and consistent predictor of feelings toward EU immigration policy across most, though not all, member states. Indeed, the inconsis-

---

[9] De Vreese, C.H. and Boomgaarden, H.G., "Projecting EU Referendums: Fear of Immigration and Support for European Integration", *European Union Politics*, Vol. 6, No. 1, 2005, pp. 59-82.

[10] McLaren, L., "Opposition to European Integration and Fear of Loss of National Identity", *op. cit.*

[11] Luedtke, A., "European Integration, Public Opinion and Immigration Policy: Testing the Impact of National Identity", *European Union Politics*, Vol. 6, No. 1, 2005, pp. 83-112.

[12] *Ibid.*, p. 88.

tency across states leads one to speculate about the extent to which public confusion over how Brussels would act in restricting or expanding immigrant rights and freedoms has influenced the findings. Or indeed whether respondents in countries which have been criticised in the past for their less than assiduous control of national borders may actually perceive EU control as a more efficient way of *restricting* immigration flows.

The upshot of such empirical research is to further underscore the importance of understanding the many and sometimes conflicting underlying contextual factors impinging at local, national and supranational levels. For example, national differences, as highlighted in Xenia Chryssochoou's social psychological study of French and Greek nationals,[13] suggest that, within shared theories held about the reasons for European unification and the goals of the new supranational group, the status position of national groups shapes members' feelings towards integration and inclusion. The impact of such national differences on the integration project can only increase with the progressive enlargement of the European Union. The next section of the chapter, considers the impact of the growth of immigrant communities and their struggle for recognition both in European member states and at EU level.

Immigrant Communities

The flows of migration to European countries have depended on a number of circumstances, such as the relationships which individual nation states have had with their former colonies, the recruitment of outside labour during shortages in the post-war era, the proximity to war-torn areas, and increasingly, globalising forces which have contributed to "an exacerbation of existing inequalities in the distribution of the world's wealth and income".[14] The once-poor European countries (Ireland, Italy, Greece, Portugal and Spain) were traditionally countries of emigration, while the former colonial nations to the north (Belgium, France, Germany, The Netherlands and the UK) received a large influx of migrants after the Second World War. Migration traditionally flowed from south to north and from east to west, from under-developed to developed economies. Today, all countries in the European Union have positive net migration, although the patterns of migration remain distinct, with the sources of immigration differing from country to country.

---

[13] Chryssochoou, X., "Memberships in a Superordinate Level: Re-thinking European Union as a Multi-National Society", *Journal of Community and Applied Social Psychology*, Vol. 10, No. 5, 2000, pp. 403-420.

[14] Richmond, A.H., "Globalisation: Implications for Immigrants and Refugees", *Ethnic and Racial Studies*, Vol. 25, No. 5, 2002, p. 717.

Scandinavian countries, Belgium and Luxembourg now receive mostly European foreign migrants. France's migrants have traditionally been from North Africa since the late 1950s and early 1960s and this remains true today (64% of today's immigrants are from outside the EU). Portugal, which only recently began to feel the impact of immigration due to its large emigrant population, has attracted many Cape Verdeans and Brazilians. Germany has experienced the largest increase in absolute terms, due to waves of immigration from central and eastern Europe before German reunification. In spite of these differences, EU countries have been increasingly affected by common factors, such as the Bosnian and Kosovan conflicts, and the rise in asylum seekers. With relatively restrictive attitudes towards legal economic migration, family reunification has gained importance in many countries as a legal means of entry. Furthermore, during the 1990s, people fleeing war-torn Yugoslavia, Albania, as well as Maghreb regimes, continued to expose Italy's and Spain's porous borders.

The emergence of large and dynamic ethnic communities in many European states undoubtedly focused the attention of national governments on immigration policy and citizenship as a means of regulating the flow of migrants and their integration into the receiving society. Prior to the Second World War immigration policies explicitly selected newcomers on the basis of their ethnicity, race or national origins. This was progressively less tenable in liberal democracies after the 1948 UN Universal Declaration of Human Rights and the strengthening of human rights culture worldwide after the 1960s civil rights watershed in the US. In terms of immigration policy, which regulates external exclusions, Christian Joppke argues that the only "restrictiveness" that a liberal state has available today is a reduction of numbers.[15] Whereas public opposition to immigration is usually conditioned by *who* migrates, the liberal state's accommodating response can only be to close *all* immigration, never to close only a *particular* immigration. On the other hand, it is also true that many European states have mastered the art of manipulating immigration categories to favour certain groups such as skilled and business migrants, to the detriment of refugees, asylum seekers and reuniting families.

For Joppke, citizenship policy is even more limited by contemporary democratic logic in the extent to which internal exclusions can be enacted. Most European states now complement their traditionally *ius sanguinis* citizenship laws with elements of *ius soli*, combining non-discriminating admissions and residency-granting procedures, guaran-

---

[15]   Joppke, C., "Exclusion in the Liberal State: The Case of Immigration and Citizenship Policy", *European Journal of Social Theory*, Vol. 8, No. 1, 2005.

teeing that anyone, whatever their ethnic, racial or national origins, can be granted automatic citizenship at birth or optionally at a later stage. Furthermore, Joppke posits that this results in a decoupling of the citizenry from a particular nation or ethnic group, and a weakening of the entire construct of "ownership" of the state by that group.[16]

Whilst immigration and citizenship laws enacted by liberal states may follow a "democratic logic", they have also to be viewed as an elitist construct by vocal members of national majorities who consider immigrants, and especially Muslim minorities, less than favourably. Neo-conservative and more extreme parties across Europe both at regional and national levels have attempted to take advantage of the fear of the immigrant Other. Furthermore, after the publication of Samuel Huntington's *Clash of Civilisations*,[17] the notion of the incompatibility of different cultures has entered the political and public discourse around immigration and citizenship. For example, in the lead-up to the 2002 German elections, Friedrich Merz, a prominent member of the CDU/CSU parliamentary party, launched what became known as the *Leitkulturdebatte*, a debate about Germany's predominant or guiding culture. Pautz argues that the debate functioned as an anti-immigration discourse which worked to construct at the symbolic level a coherent cultural identity in reaction to fundamental social and economic changes that had weakened the nation state and its (old) welfare functions.[18] Most European states now have more tightly drawn citizenship requirements which attempt to define national belonging through an explanation of their core cultural values. The long process of "harmonisation" of European asylum and immigration policies, along with a few human rights safeguards, attempts to gain firmer control of economic migration and refugee flows by tighter administrative measures across all member states and particularly as applied in Europe's "soft under-belly" states.

Immigrants are familiar with the effects of rapidly changing political, economic and social conditions linked to the impact of globalisation. As Anthony Richmond points out,[19] the logic of the global capitalist system requires relatively free movement of labour. Whereas manufacturing moves to the cheapest labour markets and communications workers operate from any computer, wherever located, personal service occupations, management, construction, agriculture and resource exploitation

---

[16]   *Ibid.*, p. 53.

[17]   Huntington, S.P., "The Clash of Civilizations", *Foreign Affairs*, Summer 1993, pp. 22-49.

[18]   Pautz, H., "The Politics of Identity in Germany: the Leitkultur Debate", *Race & Class*, Vol. 46, No. 4, 2005, pp. 39-52.

[19]   Richmond, A.H., "Globalisation: Implications for Immigrants and Refugees", *op. cit.*

"depend on labour mobility".[20] As a result, ethnic communities in Europe and elsewhere have of necessity kept pace with the changing context of immigration and citizenship discourses. As Yasemin Nuhoğlu Soysal suggests,[21] the limits of citizenship are not singularly located in a nation state but also encompass the local and the trans-national. Thus, for example, when Pakistani immigrants in the UK make demands for the teaching of Islam in state schools, or French Muslim students demand the right to wear the veil, or Italian Muslims take civil action to have the crucifix removed from Italian schoolrooms, they do not only mobilise around a Muslim identity but also appeal to a universalistic language of "human rights" to justify their claims.

Multicultural Citizenship in an Integrated Europe?

Whether under the current forms of intergovernmentalism, as a future federation or something in between, all European states will need to come to terms with an increasingly active immigrant presence. The divergence of approaches to integration and the push for enlargement have failed to address one of the issues central to the very construction of a union of European states: the reflexive sense of belonging to a supranational political entity. Within the enlarging EU it is possible to identify different levels of belonging based on a growing number of categorisations linked with nationality, ethnicity, citizenship, immigration, and refugee status. These levels of belonging are mobilised for different political purposes, leading to "insiders and outsiders to political communities being constructed in new ways".[22] To this end, Ash Amin proposes a "new imaginary of European belonging", stating that the European-ness of Europe cannot be the starting point.[23] Instead there is a need to find a new commonality across Europe's diverse communities according to which empathy or engagement with the stranger could become the essence of what it is to be "European".[24]

One suspects, however, that rumours of the imminent demise of the nation state assumed in much of the literature concerning post-national, transnational or cosmopolitan Europe are at best premature. This is especially the case now since the most recent enlargement of the Union includes countries that represent a wide array of national trajectories

---

[20] *Ibid.*, p. 714 (italics in original).

[21] Soysal., Y.N., "Citizenship and Identity: Living in Diasporas in Post-War Europe?", *Ethnic and Racial Studies*, Vol. 23, No. 1, 1994, pp. 1-15.

[22] McNevin, A., "Political Belonging in a Neoliberal Era: The Struggle of the Sans Papier", *Citizenship Studies*, Vol. 10, No. 2, 2006, p. 136.

[23] Amin, A., "Multi-Ethnicity and the Idea of Europe", *Theory, Culture and Society*, Vol. 21, No. 2, 2004, pp. 1-24.

[24] *Ibid.*, p. 3.

from established parliamentary democracies to nations which have only recently established their liberal democratic credentials. In a forceful critique of European citizenship, Shore argues that the factors which gave nation-states their substance and legitimacy are historical and social and are embedded in the fabric of everyday culture.[25] Furthermore, nations and civic institutions have been moulded by the reformist actions of generations of trade unionists, civil rights activists, opposition parties and social movements. As such, Shore suggests that nations have far greater democratic legitimacy and meaning than the remote and elitist ideals of the European Union and its institutions.

Beck,[26] on the other hand, argues that the decline of the nation state is actually a decline of the national content of the state and an opportunity to create a cosmopolitan state system that is better able to deal with the problems that all nations face in the world today: economic globalisation, transnational terrorism and global warming. Since existing European states have already been cosmopolitanised from within, he suggests that Europe must also be conceived of as a cosmopolitan unity that has the capacity to become a transnational state, a more defined and complex variant of what its component nations are already becoming. Further, Beck[27] contends

> Just as the Peace of Westphalia ended the religious wars by separating state from religion, we might consider it the ultimate goal of the European project to separate state and nation. Cosmopolitanism does not mean an abolition of nation, any more than Westphalia meant an abolition of religion. Rather, it means the constitutional enshrinement of the principle of national and cultural and ethnic and religious tolerance.

Cosmopolitanism thus conceived bears a strong resemblance to the several variants of multicultural projects which have developed over the past three decades in several English-speaking countries of immigration, including Australia. Such experience shows that for a multi-ethnic state to survive and develop along multicultural lines, it must incorporate into the political machinery of the state laws and policies which not only tolerate but actively support the cultural diversity of its citizens. It must also cultivate a set of shared, overarching cultural values that extend beyond political structures, reflecting the dominant group's core values, but which also take account of minority groups' aspirations and needs by practising both cultural and political democracy. As Jürgen Habermas argues,

---

[25] Shore, C., "Whither European Citizenship?", *op. cit.*

[26] Beck, U., "Understanding the Real Europe", *op. cit.*

[27] *Ibid.*, p. 36.

Multiculturalism that does not misunderstand its role does not constitute a *one way street* for the cultural self-assertion of groups with collective identities of their own. The co-existence of different life forms as equals also requires the integration of citizens – and the mutual recognition of their subcultural memberships – within the framework of a common political culture. A pluralistic society based on a democratic constitution guarantees cultural differentiation only under the condition of political integration.[28]

Habermas further contends that cultural rights demanded and introduced under the sign of a "politics of recognition" must be understood to be individual rights which guarantee equal inclusion of everyone, irrespective of how marginalised they might have been in the past. Such rights ensure all citizens equal access to cultural environments, interpersonal relations and traditions, to the extent that these are materials for the formation and maintenance of their respective personal identities.[29]

The road to multicultural nationhood is not an easy one. For Jerzy Smolicz,[30] each pluralistic state has to work out its own set of shared values which must, however, remain dynamic enough to reflect that state's changing ethnic composition (whether it is affected by migration or boundary changes), as well as the fluctuating inter-relationships of the collectivities which compose it. Firstly, such a multicultural solution must take into consideration the existence of heritage-based core values of ethnic groups which they may wish to protect and develop within the overarching, shared framework of the commonality. Secondly, account must be taken of the dynamic aspects of the relationship between the shared values and those of the constituent groups and the fact that the equilibrium among the cultures concerned is liable to change. This occurs when individuals construct hybrid identities from a variety of cultural sources, on the understanding that group values can also change as part of the process of cultural interaction in a plural society.

Of course, multicultural policies such as those adopted in Australia have their share of detractors. According to Subhabrata Bobby Banerjee and Stephen Linstead,[31] whilst the multicultural agenda for Australia rejects its assimilation policies of the past and acknowledges the "legitimacy" of cultural pluralism, the power relations between who legitimises and who is being legitimated are not difficult to discern. "The

---

[28] Habermas, J., "Intolerance and Discrimination", *ICON*, Vol. 1, No. 1, 2003, p. 10.

[29] *Ibid.*

[30] Smolicz, J.J., "Nation-States and Globalisation from a Multicultural Perspective: Signposts from Australia", *Nationalism and Ethnic Politics*, Vol. 4, No. 4, 1998, pp. 1-18.

[31] Banerjee, S.B. and Linstead, S., "Globalisation, Multiculturalism and Other Fictions: Colonialism for the New Millenium?", *Organisation*, Vol. 8, No. 4, 2001, pp. 683-722.

acceptance of cultural pluralism is the new assimilation and the message is clear: as long as we do not threaten the dominant ideology, we can be as multicultural as we like". There is, of course, more than a grain of truth in such assertions when one considers recent events in Australia such as the revision of multicultural policies along with the planned introduction of a citizenship test in the aftermath of 9/11 and the war on terror. On the other hand, is it better to revert to the assimilation policies of the past or is the prospect of segregated ethnic communities any more palatable? Multiculturalism can become meaningful when it is supported by the overriding ethos that Zygmunt Bauman[32] has previously highlighted: "giving everyone a chance" (a very Australian value born from trade unionist struggles for "a fair go"). In Bauman's terms this involves a policy of recognition balanced by a distributive justice which subsidises the cultivation of identity.[33]

Ultimately, a successfully balanced pluralist solution within a democratic state can provide a catalyst for regional and global developments. While a single or integral identity is underpinned by feelings of belonging among members of one particular nation or ethnic group, global interculturalism as formulated by Smolicz,[34] rests on the prospect of forming bonds based on cultural experiences which cross existing borders and embrace other groups and other peoples. In this sense, intra-group solidarity, founded upon the principle of the exclusion of "aliens", must be counterbalanced by inter-group solidarity, developed on the basis of the inclusion of cultural Others. One of the most effective means of overcoming mistrust and the fear of difference (whether racial, religious, linguistic or other cultural) is the fostering of intercultural communication – both within the countries concerned, in order to encourage the ethos of multiculturalism, and between them, in the sense of global interculturalism.

Conclusion

Whither European integration? Many nationals currently are in possession of dual citizenship as a result of bilateral arrangements between nation states. In the future, it will become increasingly difficult for individuals to remain a citizen of just one state and a member of just one nation. This is due to the projected increase of cultural diversity within nations and across supranational administrative regions under the impact

---

[32] Bauman, Z., "The Great War of Recognition", *Theory, Culture and Society*, Vol. 18, No. 2-3, 2001, pp. 137-150.

[33] *Ibid.*, p. 145.

[34] Smolicz, J.J., "Nation-States and Globalisation from a Multicultural Perspective", *op. cit.*

of international migration flows and the assertion of local ethnic communities that are able to frame appeals for justice in terms of universal human rights. In this scenario, the protection of ethnic cultural variation and multiple identities may require a "multicultural citizenship" which acknowledges that an individual can belong to more than one cultural community, as well as more than one state. Finally, global interculturalism implies the cultivation of the positive forces of cultural and economic change. This requires a balance between culturally plural nation-states, effective supranational institutions and strong local communities which can develop their own specificities, permitting members to enjoy a multicultural citizenship which in the longer term may well develop into a global citizenship.

CHAPTER 3

European "Integration"
or "Acculturation"?

Natalie J. DOYLE

Introduction

The rejection of the draft constitutional treaty by the French and
Dutch electorates in 2005 brought into full view the self-definition crisis
of the EU. Since the disappearance of the Soviet threat the European
Union has successfully grown, but only in the name of a vision which
now clearly appears disconnected from reality. In the first stages of its
creation, the European Community (EC) was carried by a universalistic
Enlightenment utopia, the abolition of national differences in the pursuit
of a superior, anti-nationalist nation: Europe. The creation of the European Community was understood as a process of integration involving
the harmonisation of national economies, in a way that was ideologi-
cally aligned with the then dominant American evolutionary theories of
modernisation.

As Bo Stråth has argued, this federal vision peaked in the early
1970s with the Werner Plan for economic and monetary union.[1] It was
in part fed by a growing desire on the part of Europe to distance itself
from the United States, a desire which first surfaced with the Vietnam
War and became more pronounced with the crisis of the dollar as the
Americans proved unwilling to accept joint responsibility for the crisis
of the international monetary system. As US Treasury Secretary John B.
Connally famously summarised it: "The dollar may be our currency but
it is your problem". This crisis added urgency to a French-led project
which started to take form in the late 1960s: the project for full economic and monetary union. In its initial conception, the plan aimed for

---

[1] Stråth, B., "The Contours of a European Political Economy: from the Werner Plan to
the EMU" in B. Stråth (ed.), *After Full Employment. European Discourses in Work
and Flexibility*, Brussels, PIE-Peter Lang, 2000, pp. 243-259. Stråth went on to
develop this analysis in a book co-edited with Lars Magnusson and especially in a
co-authored book with J.P. Burgess: "Money and Political Economy: From the
Werner Plan to the Delors Report and Beyond" in Magnusson, L. and Strath, B.
(eds.), *From the Werner Plan to the EMU: In Search of a Political Economy for
Europe*, Brussels, PIE-Peter Lang, 2001, pp. 125-162. What follows draws on both
texts.

the creation of an economic polity in which monetary union was to be kept subservient to the political management of economic growth. However, the crisis after 1975 created a totally new international scene on which the Werner Plan's political project could no longer be sustained.

Globalisation induced a shift in economic thinking away from the synthesis of Keynesian ideas and neo-classical economics which had been enshrined in the Bretton-Woods system at the behest of the Americans.[2] The background to this shift in economic thought was the crisis of the so-called "Fordist" economic model of mass production and mass consumption on which social stability had been predicated in Western Europe since the early 1950s. As the old plans for economic union faltered from the late 1960s onwards, the notion of identity was introduced in 1973 by the European Commission as a desperate attempt to formulate a common response and to translate into a European system of tri-partite economic management the various national systems which had underpinned the successful reconstruction of Europe after the Second World War but were now under threat.[3]

From the Werner Plan to the Delors Report of 1989, the plan for economic and monetary union became dormant. Neither the 1975 Tindemans Plan nor the 1977 MacDougall Report, could breathe new life into it until the Milan summit of 1985. The crucial trigger for its rebirth was the failure of the French socialist government's attempt to implement large scale "Keynesian" policies of public spending and nationalisations. This signalled the triumph of neo-liberal, market-based conceptions of economic management. From then on, François Mitterrand's quest for French greatness, exacerbated by fear of German re-unification, found a new stage: it was reinvested in the construction of Europe and motivated a new project for economic and monetary union.[4] This new project, which led to the signing of the Maastricht Treaty, no longer bore much resemblance to the form of economic union first

---

[2] Purdy, D., "Economic Theory and Policy from the Keynesian Revolution in the Third Way" in L. Magnusson and B. Strath (eds.), *From the Werner Plan to the EMU: In Search of a Political Economy for Europe*, Brussels, PIE-Peter Lang, 2001, pp. 97-124.

[3] Stråth, B., "The Contours of a European Political Economy", *op. cit.*, pp. 250-254.

[4] Verdun, A., "The Political Economy of the Werner and Delors Report" in L. Magnusson and B. Stath (eds.), *From the Werner Plan to the EMU: In Search of a Political Economy for Europe*, Brussels, PIE-Peter Lang, 2001, pp. 73-96. As Amy Verdun points out, authors differ as to the role played by German reunification and the end of the Cold War in the creation of EMU (note 39, p. 86). I agree with her statement that even though the EMU's fundamental architecture was in place before those historical changes, these precipitated a hastened transition to EMU as pushed by the French government.

envisaged by the Werner Plan. For one thing, it gave up any reference to full employment and social welfare now seen as simple by-products of the creation of a self-regulated European market. To this day it remains a mystery how this transformation occurred, especially as it happened under the auspices of the Delors Commission. Jacques Delors – originally a Christian democrat with links to unionism and, later, a minister in two socialist governments – can hardly be suspected of neo-liberal enthusiasm.[5] The international context outside Europe combined with the general triumph of neo-liberal ideas among economists no longer able to offer solutions to the problem of intractable unemployment were probably key factors. Another answer lies perhaps in Franco-German negotiations.

From the start, such negotiations involved the pursuit of national self interest: with respect to the Maastricht Treaty itself, François Mitterrand chose to see in Europe a way to maintain France's standing. A process of *acculturation* seemed to have played a role. Here I use the term "acculturation" not in the meaning it acquired in American anthropology but in the more complex one the French anthropologist Louis Dumont gave to it in his reflection on the progress of modernity in Western Europe from the late 18th century onwards: modernization was a process of cultural interaction between national cultures, in which the more modern – in his terms, "individualistic" – culture first dominated other cultures but then induced them to produce new cultural, synthetic representations drawing on both the dominated and dominant cultures.[6] Lest there be any misunderstanding, I must stress that the way I use the notion of "acculturation" aims at analysing critical moments in the history of European integration.[7] It is not used to argue normatively for a programme of cultural fusion.

The Treaty of Maastricht was the outcome of such a process of acculturation but a largely unconscious one which delivered a dysfunc-

---

5   Milward, A., "Delors Agonistes", *New Left Review*, No. 29, September-October, 2004, pp. 1-4.

6   Dumont first formulated his theory of the genesis of modernity in his *Essays on Individualism: Modern Ideology in Anthropological Perspective*, Chicago, University of Chicago Press, 1986. He developed his analysis of acculturation of German culture to French modernity in *German Ideology*, Chicago, Chicago University Press, 1994, see especially pp. 9-38. Dumont's theory suggests that in the process of acculturation, new representations are created that open up new modes of modernization. These representations have the power to act in return upon the dominant culture and to shape its evolution.

7   By critical moments I refer to those episodes in 20th century history when European countries were confronted with global pressures. The responses which were formulated at a European level can be said to have been attempts to adapt certain cultural legacies to new external changes.

tional hybrid, the current *de facto* a-political constitution of the EU. This chapter will explore the way the EU has developed through such a process of acculturation. This process has become more acute with enlargement and thus demands to be recognised and freed from its original, ideological self-understanding as "integration". Integration is less analytical than normative and implicitly carries with it a teleological interpretation of history. This exploration in turn will allow me to discuss the need to re-conceptualise European integration as a process of acculturation of national cultures, which has not only pacified European nation-states but led them to adopt a cosmopolitan perspective which has not yet become explicit. I will propose that this process of acculturation in its un-conceptualised form has seen the contest of different national configurations of the relationship between the four major components of modernity: the political, the juridical, the economic, and the social. This in turn will allow me to examine briefly whether the cosmopolitan vision of European integration contains lessons for globalisation as some of its advocates argue.

The Straitjacket of the Treaty of Maastricht as Outcome of Franco-German Acculturation

From the beginning, the European project attempted to reconcile two different visions of peace: a French vision aiming at the pacification of Europe and the defence of France's independence through the creation of a new form of polity; and a less political vision, the creation of a liberal economic space linked to the re-construction of a modern socially cohesive German polity. These two visions were reconciled in the liberal Enlightenment's belief in the capacity of trade to deliver peace between nations. This meeting point conditioned the original economic constitution of Europe which, as Christian Joerges argues, clearly established a division of competences: economic management was to be pursued at the international, European level whilst social policy was to remain the preserve of nation-states.[8] The use of this economic lever – later allegedly deplored by Jean Monnet – bequeathed to the European Community a dualism which only revealed its full consequences once the nation-state's capacity for action came under stress as a result of globalisation. Globalisation thus motivated a renewed desire, on the part of the French especially, to acquire more strength, though monetary policy and increased competitiveness, which were thought by people like Jacques Delors to be the key to protecting the cohesion of European societies. This, it was realized, could only be achieved through the

---

[8]   Joerges, C., "What is Left of the European Economic Constitution? A Melancholic Eulogy", *European Law Review*, Vol. 30, No. 4, 2005, pp. 461-486.

creation of a closer union, which opened a new chapter in European integration.

In many ways, the constitutive dualism between supranational economic union and national social policy drew its inspiration from the German Protestant tradition of ordo-liberalism formulated in the 1920s. Ordo-liberalism sought to counter the economic crises and resultant social tensions of post-First World War Germany by formulating a project of "liberal state interventionism" in which the state's main task would be to protect the capacity of the economy to self-regulate. This theory re-surfaced in the post-war context of German re-construction although it cannot claim sole credit for the German economic miracle. Ordo-liberalism left its imprint on German constitutional law but at the level of economic policies, it was tempered by the rebirth under Konrad Adenauer of the aspirations of political Catholicism towards economic democracy, aspirations which motivated the reconstruction and expansion of the German welfare state. The institutions which underpinned the success of the German model of capitalism, the so-called *Sozialmarktwirtschaft* or social market economy emerged from a compromise between protestant ordo-liberalism and catholic neo-corporatism.

However, despite the democratically negotiated pragmatic nature of Germany's economic success, French perceptions of German success in the phase of European integration after the Single European Act (SEA) were captive to an ideological version of German economic success giving first place to ordo-liberalism. This success was interpreted almost exclusively with reference to the strength of the Deutsche Mark. In the lead up to the Maastricht Treaty the French socialist government of Pierre Bérégovoy accordingly pursued most strenuously a monetary anti-inflationary policy based on the alignment of the Franc with the Deutsche Mark, the so-called policy of the *Franc fort* (the strong Franc) with a pun evoking the French name for the German city of Frankfurt, home of the German central bank. This indirect influence of German ordo-liberalism over French perceptions was certainly helped by the fact that as they progressively lost hegemony in Western Germany itself, partisans of ordo-liberalism increasingly saw European integration as the way to fulfil their ambitions, that is to defend a strict economic rationality and put it out of reach of a government they saw as too often captive to partial interest. Ordo-liberalism had evolved new definitions of economic autonomy. From the mid-1970s these found great support in the English-speaking world and gave birth to a new version of economic liberalism: no longer the autonomy of the market under state control but the control of the state by market autonomy. From the start,

Franco-German acculturation as the context of European acculturation also took place against the background American hegemony.[9]

It is clear that the convergence of German ordo-liberal ideas with Anglo-American neo-liberal conceptions profoundly influenced the way French socialists – bereft of their original socio-economic project after the failure of their Keynesian experiment – came to invest their hopes in the project of European integration and to rally the German model of "social market economy" under Mitterrand's leadership. The creation of the EU involved the Europeanisation of the French socio-democratic project born out of the ashes of socialist, "French-style" political voluntarism. This Europeanisation constituted a fundamental paradigm shift for French socialism. It was formulated in reaction to the high social costs of the socialists' conversion to market autonomy, which eventually led them to embrace a policy of competitive disinflation with disastrous results for employment. This reaction triggered a more critical analysis of the place of France's increasingly internationalised economy in globalisation and gave birth to a new socio-democratic economic strategy, which Jospin in 1996 termed *Réalisme de Gauche*.[10]

This strategy encompassed the project for a different mode of globalisation; its high-profile advocate was Hubert Védrine, French foreign minister from 1997 to 2002. As Rawi Abdelal suggests, there is a paradox to this French engagement with globalisation which broke with a tradition of resistance to capital mobility. The globalisation of finance has in fact been backed mostly by influential French figures, such as Michel Camdessus at the head of IMF, Henri Chavranski at the Organization for Economic Cooperation and Development (OECD) and Delors at the European level, supported or encouraged by the general thrust of French policy.[11] These individuals promoted an original stance on

---

[9]   Joerges's discussion of the influence of ordo-liberalism draws on Michel Foucault's analysis of the genesis of neo-liberalism in the lectures he gave to the College de France in the late 1970s. Foucault analysed the way the 1939 Paris Congress of ordo-liberal theorists saw an ideological split as one camp broke away from the classical liberalism which informed original ordo-liberal positions and re-defined the role of the market in history in terms of a new notion of competition. See Ewald, F., Fontana, A., Senellart, M. (eds.), *Naissance de la biopolitique: Cours au Collège de France (1978-1979)*, Paris, Gallimard, 2004. This notion, "Wettbewerb als Entdeckungsverfahren" (competition as process of discovery) was central to the development of neo-liberalism from the late 1960s onwards, in Germany as Joerges shows but also in parallel in the Anglo-American context through Hayek's influence. See "Invasions of the market?" in C. Joerges, "What is left of the European Economic Constitution?", *op. cit.*, pp. 472-473.

[10] Clift, B., *French Socialism in a Global Era: the Political Economy of the New Social Democracy in France*, London, Continuum, 2003.

[11] Abdelal, R., "Le consensus de Paris: la France et les règles de la finance mondiale", *Critique Internationale*, Vol. 3, No. 28, 2005, pp. 87-118.

globalisation that contrasts with the American more *laissez-faire* approach of advocating the need for a governance of globalisation. This stance, in keeping with the French conception of modernity and its emphasis on political sovereignty, does not seem to have been fundamentally abandoned when the Socialists lost control of government in 2005.

All the same, the belated acceptance by the French socialist party, or at least of some of its key members, of the value of economic autonomy, involved some repudiation of deeply ingrained features of French political economy. Jean-Paul Fitoussi argues that this meant a dogmatic, ideological conversion to the values of a market economy which became fused with an equally dogmatic commitment to European integration.[12] In practice, this translated in handing over to the European Commission the role of guarantor of the economy's autonomy from the state and to preserve it from traditional French political voluntarism. The incapacity on the part of French socialists to rethink political action at the national level led to a fateful paradox. The project for a socio-democratic political economy to be pursued at the European level fell victim to the success of the European Union which it helped to create.

It produced a logic of European economic cooperation which, in Fitoussi's metaphor, placed within the European fruit a worm which has been undermining it from within.[13] The need for economic union also became more acute for Mitterrand with the prospect of German reunification after the fall of the Berlin Wall and the fear it reactivated among French elites that Germany would once again go it alone at a time when France most needed Germany's support for its economy. Mitterrand's obsession with securing some control over the German economy meant that the independence of the DM was part of the price Germany had to pay for reunification. In effect, Mitterrand's policies also worked towards assimilating the Socialist Party's conversion to the liberal principle of market autonomy – which in the 1980s took the form of a rigid monetarism – with France's commitment to Europe: any criticism of one amounted to the other. In this respect, the French Socialist Party inaugurated a form of instrumentalisation of European integration: the autonomous agencies of the European Union were given the task of conducting policies which would be unpopular at the national level.[14]

The rejection of the draft Constitutional Treaty by the French electorate in 2005 can in part be seen as having been a form of belated,

---

[12] Fitousssi, J.-P., *La Politique de l'impuissance*, Paris, Arléa, 2005, pp. 28-32.

[13] The metaphor is the title given to Jean-Paul Fitoussi's discussion of the history of EMU in *La Politique de l'impuissance*.

[14] Fitousssi, J.-P., *La Politique de l'impuissance*, *op. cit.*, p. 75.

angry repudiation by the French electorate of this Mitterrand legacy, triggered by the realisation that European integration had not been, as promised, the continued pursuit of French political sovereignty through European means.[15] The new French political project of European integration was handicapped by a crucial flaw: it depended on the guarantee of Germany's economy and it focused exclusively on monetary union as the first step towards economic union.[16] This overwhelming concern with monetary union perhaps put France in a weaker position in the ideological process of mutual acculturation which accompanied the political negotiations towards the Maastricht Treaty and rendered it vulnerable to a German monetarist tradition, which has been obsessed with the concern for inflation. The urgency with which Mitterrand pushed for monetary union and the global influence of monetarist ideas probably led him and his advisers to overlook the question of the status of the European Central Bank (ECB) which was to be modelled on the independent German *Bundesbank*. This occurred even as they pushed for a French director.

The French thought they had won when the Maastricht Treaty was signed but as Joerges points out, it was a pyrrhic victory as the German constitutional court only allowed its ratification on the basis that European integration be understood as strictly economic integration and qualified as a non-political phenomenon occurring autonomously outside the member states.[17] This judgment was formulated to defend Germany's constitutional democracy from the erosion of the nation-state's sovereignty accompanying monetary union. In fact, it amounted to conferring on the European Community's economically liberal institutional arrangements an exclusive legal legitimacy, constraining the nation-states' range of action. From the beginnings of the European Community, a specific economic model was adopted which suited the objective of integration – primarily that of Franco-German reconcilia-

---

[15] The problematic legacy of Mitterrand's "Europeanisation" of French nationalism does not seem to have been resolved by the country as a whole and maintained the French Socialist Party in an ambiguous relationship to the EU. Following Lionel Jospin's ignominious defeat in the presidential elections of 2002 which favoured the National Front's candidate, the ambiguity became an outright division within the French socialist party.

[16] As Amy Verdun point outs, monetary union was already privileged at the time of the Werner plan. See Verdun, A., "The political economy of the Werner and Delors Report" in L. Magnusson and B. Stråth (eds.), *From the Werner Plan to the EMU: in Search of a Political Economy for Europe*, Brussels, PIE Peter Lang, 2001, pp. 73-82.

[17] See Joerges's analysis of the significance of the judgment by the German constitutional court in "Rules vs. politics? Monetary union, the Maastricht judgment and the stability pact" in C. Joerges, "What is left of the European Economic Constitution?", *op. cit.*, pp. 474-478.

tion. Under the influence of new objectives, this model however was extended in a manner that has produced a growing tension between the juridical institutionalisation of norms of economic rationality at the European level and the European tradition of social cohesion which can only be defended at the national level. The judgment of the German constitutional court has the perverse effect of de-politicizing the European Union. As Joerges puts it, it enshrined the definition of Europe as a "market without a state" and reduced its components, the member-states, to being "states without markets". This was most obvious in the area of fiscal policy which ceased to be seen as a political process and was juridified in Art.104 of the Maastricht Treaty and the Protocol "On the Excessive Deficit Procedure and the Monitoring of these provisions by the European Commission".[18] This article was invoked when the need for the "Stability and Growth Pact" was first invoked by the German finance minister Theo Waigel in the mid-1990s. Through the pact's ratification in 1997, Europe as a whole was forced to follow the German model and conform to an economic rule which had acquired the status of law, the 3% limit to budget deficit, which had no political legitimacy and whose wisdom has since come under fire repeatedly. As it turned out, this Stability and Growth Pact became a millstone around the neck of French and German governments. Their being forced to violate it repeatedly in the 1990s considerably weakened their leadership of the European Union.[19]

As Jean-Paul Fitoussi points out, the problem with the Maastricht Treaty was not the introduction of the single currency but the consecration of the internal market's fundamentally a-political institutional architecture in which, as he puts it, "independent agents make political decisions and governments only managerial ones".[20] The Maastricht Treaty created an economic space which by definition prevents any explicit political management of the European economy through the tools of macroeconomic management. The political economy of the EU rests on three elements, the European Central Bank (ECB), the Stability

---

[18] "States without a Market. Comments on the German Constitutional Court's Maastricht Judgment and a Plea for Interdisciplinary Discourses?", *European Integration online Papers (EIoP)*, Vol. 1, No. 20, 1997, http://eiop.or.at/eiop/texte/1997-020.htm, accessed March 2007.

[19] On this question, Joerges points out that the European Court of Justice has shown itself less attached to the principle of legal supremacy entrenched by the Maastricht Treaty, in its refusal to fully support the Commission's request to overrule the Council which had decided to suspend procedures against Germany and France. This judgment implicitly recognised the legitimacy of the Council's political evaluations. See Joerges, C., "What is left of the European Economic Constitution?", *op. cit.*, p. 477.

[20] Fitoussi, J.-P., *La Politique de l'impuissance, op. cit.*, p. 76.

and Growth Pact and the Directorate General for Competition of the Commission. They in fact function as three coexisting uncoordinated autonomous authorities, which only have at their disposal the tool of competition to harmonise national economies. They thus constantly have to push for the dismantling of obstacles to competition in the form of labour law or social legislation. As warned by many economists, the a-political political economy of Europe contributed to entrenching unemployment which over the last 20 years seems to have been tacitly accepted as an adequate means to reach price stability.

As mentioned above, a key factor in the Maastricht Treaty, the French acceptance of German monetary orthodoxy, was probably facilitated by the dominance of neo-liberal economic ideas in French government circles throughout the 1980s. This is not to say this convergence produced a European variant of neo-liberal ideology, as sole source of inspiration for the creation of the EU. Neo-liberalism certainly played a crucial role in the Maastricht phase of the process but the process itself remains ambivalent and polysemic. It is important to consider the longer history of monetary integration from the Werner Plan to the Maastricht and Amsterdam treaties: the emphasis on monetary stability through budget rigidity which came with Maastricht cannot be fully identified with neo-liberal theory despite an apparent affinity. As Stråth shows, one can find evidence in European integration of a socio-political project quite at odds with neo-liberal ideas: the promotion of a European social model with its commitment to citizenship rather than markets or families as the most significant axis of solidarity.[21] This commitment has experienced fluctuations associated with the form assumed by monetary union; a union which is the result of the synthesis of two different traditions of capitalism, that is, of a difficult, historically conditioned process of Franco-German acculturation. Yet, it is clear that this commitment shared by France and Germany has been

---

[21] See Stråth, B., "The Contours of a European Political Economy", *op. cit.*, pp. 254-259; Burgess, J.P. and Stråth, B., "Money and Political Economy: from the Werner Plan to the Delors Report and Beyond" in L. Magnusson and B. Stråth (eds.), *From the Werner Plan to the EMU, op. cit.* Since the creation of the European Union, there has been extensive discussion of the notion "European social model". For the sake of my argument, I am using the term in the way Andrew Martin and George Ross define it in the book *Euros and Europeans*, as a Weberian conceptual abstraction of distinctive and central commonalities that can be derived from the study of the empirical diversity of European societies. The European social model, localised in Western and Northern continental Europe has national variants, which are the product of specific historical and political developments; but despite this, it has a central feature which distinguishes it from the Anglo-American model: its commitment to social citizenship. See "Introduction: EMU and the European Social Model" in Martin. A. and Ross, G. (eds.), *Euros and Europeans*, Cambridge, Cambridge University Press, 2004, 1-19.

severely strained by the a-political straitjacket of the EU's de-facto economic constitution, which the acculturation of the French and German political economies gave birth to.

Crucial to this unsuccessful acculturation was the profound misapprehension of what was involved in the process of European unification and the persistent attachment to the dream of a European identity which transcended national identities and rendered them obsolete. Germany's actions, in the context of reunification, were clearly motivated by the desire to prove itself as good European citizen and to lay at rest the ghost of German nationalism. As it gave in to French demands that it abandon its currency for closer union but wished to hold onto the central tenets of the successful political economy it had forged in post-war period, Germany acquired a special stake in European monetary union, which in fact motivated it even more to reaffirm the vision of a federal Europe. In addition, it seems that French and German cultures faced with the hegemony of Anglo-American political economy in fact retreated into the core values of their own traditions: the creation of a new level of state regulation for the French; a greater emphasis on monetary strength for the Germans. And this, just as the UK with Margaret Thatcher returned to its own distant roots by embracing an even more radical version of economic liberalism than that espoused in the US.[22] Where France and Germany could meet and drag the UK along was in the creation of the European Union through *juridification*.

The Loss of Political Dimension: Juridification, Governance and the Transformation of the European Nation-State

The problem, as Peter Burgess and Bo Stråth put it, is that Germany became too European and I may add, with Joerges, that the EU became too German in its endorsement of the strong monetary bend of the German political economy.[23] This problem is now felt by Germany,

---

[22] Fitoussi, J.-P., *La Politique de l'impuissance, op. cit.*, pp. 24-25.

In this passage, Fitoussi suggests that the UK repudiated its immediate past, that of the post-Second World War era characterised by a high degree of economic collectivisation which had brought it closer to continental Europe in the years immediately following the end of the Second World War.

[23] "The German government has always had to demonstrate its European credibility whereas the French government has always had the pretension of representing Europe, to speak on behalf of Europe. Germany has had to be European, while France has been Europe and told Germany what Europe meant. [...] The problem for Germany, France for Europe is that through its response to the latter crisis [German reunification] Germany became too European" in L. Magnusson and B. Stråth (eds.), *From the Werner Plan to the EMU, op. cit.*, pp. 159-160.

France and Europe as a whole as the absence of any political instruments to coordinate the economic and the social trappings of western European countries in a regime of low economic growth.[24] This loss of political dimension is the ultimate consequence of the *cultural contest* in the process of acculturation which has characterised the progress of modernity in Western Europe since the end of the 18th century and shaped different interpretations of modernisation in Britain, France and Germany. From these diverging interpretations emerged competing political economies and conceptions of democracy. A specific form of acculturation – Franco-German reconciliation – was pursued actively following the near self-destruction of the Western European version of modernity which led to the creation of European supra-national institutions.

This was however within the context of the rise to dominance of the American offshoot of European modernity, the United States. Any assessment of the process of European "integration" thus needs to consider this additional cultural influence. In the case of its last historical chapter – the creation of the EU – I have already indicated the need to look at the convergence of two phenomena: the sustained influence of the German tradition of ordo-liberalism and the re-activation of a specific Anglo-American tradition of liberalism triggered by the crisis of the mid-1970s which promoted globalisation. Leaving aside the role which neo-liberalism played in strengthening the influence which German ordo-liberalism came to exercise over the constitution of the European Union; it is important to note how ordo-liberalism is in fact rooted in a specific political culture which was shaped by the failed attempt in the 1920s to secure liberal democracy in Germany. Ordo-liberalism as a body of economic thought stressing the need to safeguard market autonomy was conceived in response to the lack of legitimacy of the Weimar Republic caused by its failure to implement adequate monetary policies. Its ultimate objective was political: to create a commitment to democracy. The mechanism chosen to achieve this was economic liberalism in accordance with a conception of democracy strongly influenced by the British experience stressing the debt of modern democracy to economic liberalism. The objective was to protect market autonomy from the political interference of party politics. The law was thus called upon to discipline society in the context of political liberalism and the loss of a unified political identity. This was in keeping with a specifically German approach to state-building inaugurated by Bismarck, which paradoxically had first been adopted to counter liberalism,

---

[24] It is clear that the problem concerns the countries of the euro zone and within it, some more than others depending on the specific economic profile of their economies, such as their exposure to intra-European trade.

not anchor it as ordo-liberalism sought to do.[25] This political culture extended its influence beyond Weimar. It also informed the re-establishment of liberal democracy in Western Germany after the Second World War. This can be seen in its juridical conception of citizenship encapsulated in the notion of *constitutional patriotism*. (As Müller has shown, this notion was in fact first put forward under the Weimar Republic).[26]

Habermas first seized on this notion at the time of the Maastricht Treaty to argue for a European citizenship and has developed it in an attempt to counter the crisis of legitimacy of the EU. Associated with French political voluntarism, this notion reactivated the old federal utopia, that of a European constitutional convention which, like the Philadelphia Convention for the United States, would give birth to a new political entity. The result was quite different. The convention gave birth to a laboriously elaborated treaty. It amalgamated institutional innovations designed to give the enlarged EU more capacity for governance with the consolidation of the *acquis communautaire*. As its French opponents argued, this made re-negotiation of previous treaties extremely difficult. As a result, the proposed constitutional treaty only exacerbated the crisis of legitimacy of the EU by frustrating the aspirations for a political project at the European level. Yet this project was essential to address the need to articulate the economic and the social, a need which nation-states no longer can or want to respond to.

Notwithstanding this political deficit, the creation of a unified European market has in fact been a political activity. Just as the invention of market autonomy in early 18th century Britain was part of an alternative vision of society and the attempts in the early 19th century to realise this vision were state-driven, the political dimension has been present also in the European Union but not overtly. To the chagrin of ordo-liberal enthusiasts, the political dimension has resurfaced indirectly through the increasing regulatory role played by the European Commission and the European Court of Justice in a variety of fields from health and work to consumer and environmental protection. From the start, the SEA, which created the Internal Market in 1987, introduced a myriad of rules and measures and constituted, as Stråth describes it, an act of political standardisation and regulation.[27] This role attested to the workings of

---

[25] See Jouanjan, O., *Une Histoire de la pensée juridique en Allemagne. 1800-1918*, Paris, PUF, 2005.

[26] Müller, J., "On the Origins of Constitutional Patriotism", *Contemporary Political Theory*, Vol. 5, No. 3, 2006, pp. 278-296.

[27] Stråth, B., "The Monetary Issue and European Economic Policy in Historical Perspective" in C. Joerges, B. Stråth and P. Wagner (eds.), *The Economy as a Polity.*

normative values transcending the simple question of market autonomy. This regulatory role in turn comforted the vision of a yet to be achieved political union, even if the form of this political union remained hazy. This indirect re-politicisation via juridification, has however grown increasingly problematic as it has merged with the utopia of governance, which seems to have migrated from the world of business to that of public policy and found particularly fertile soil in the EU.

As Alain Supiot has shown, the ideology of governance draws on an imaginary representation of society as a naturally self-regulating body. This representation derives its influence from the retreat of the concern with the authority of power in favour of the question of its effectiveness.[28] Effectiveness became a particularly appealing objective in Western societies following the crisis of the Fordist model of economic growth. As the idea of regulation was transferred from the hard sciences to the social sciences, an ideology formed that fused the two meanings of norm as elaborated in European culture: the juridical norm which derives its strength from the shared beliefs in a common ethical project and the technical norm which derives its strength from scientific knowledge and serves a utilitarian project. As such, governance and the panoply of legal tools it has constructed has been a societal project, centred not on the exploitation of the natural world but on the normalisation of *human* resources. Labour law has thus been its privileged area. The rise of governance has been operative at the level of national states through the retreat of legislative power in favour of collective negotiation overseen by an expert authority. Collective negotiation has come to play a growing role, not only in the elaboration of laws but also in their implementation.[29]

The EU underwent a particular strong turn to governance, perhaps facilitated by the Treaty of Rome's original division of legislative power between the Commission as market authority-cum-executive, the Council representing the member states, the Parliament and the Court of Justice whose judgments can have a legislatively binding dimension. The Treaty of Maastricht made another step in the progress of governance with the creation of the ECB which functions outside of any political control and the introduction of negotiated law in the treatment of

---

The Political Constitution of Contemporary Capitalism, London, UCL Press, 2005, pp. 59-76.

[28] Supiot, A., *Homo Juridicus*, Paris, Seuil, 2005.

[29] Supiot notes the similarities between contemporary governance and feudalism; "[…N]ous demeurons généralement aveugles au fait que le déclin de la souveraineté ne s'accompagne nullement d'un progrès symétrique de la liberté individuelle, car il conduit à une résurgence de la dimension féodale de notre culture contractuelle" in *Ibid.*, p. 250.

social matters. Whilst governance first appeared as so-called "comitology", it assumed an increasingly stronger form after the Prodi White Paper of 2001.[30] Following on the economic convergence criteria and budget discipline which accompanied the introduction of the common currency, voluntary governance or "soft law" has now made inroads into a greater variety of areas in the form of the so-called "Open Method of Coordination".

The Open Method of Coordination (OMC) was first introduced in the area of employment policy and invested with great hopes that it would help reassert the social dimension. Whether it has delivered the benefits anticipated still remains to be ascertained.[31] Regardless of the method's effectiveness, it is clear however that the generalisation of soft law raises some very fundamental questions. The indicators which the European Commission employs are depicted as neutral technical norms which do not need to be submitted to contradictory debates of a parliamentary or juridical manner yet they are in fact the vehicle of a process of social normalisation as is clearly demonstrated in the way the criteria of unemployment rates are defined.[32] As Supiot suggests, this form of governance affects the central principle of democracy: the role of the law as expression and instrument of collective sovereignty. Although it appears to consecrate the victory of one form of law over another (the contract over the statute), in fact, it perverts them both by putting them at the service of an attempt not to establish outright rules but to normalise the behaviour of all legal persons (states, CEOs, trade unions, salary earners …) in a rather surreptitious manner. It does so by binding legal persons within contractual obligations which the individuals in question have not necessarily freely chosen to enter into. The most problematic aspect of this non-governmental form of government is its utopian

---

[30] During his leadership of the European Commission, Prodi launched a program of reform of European governance outlined in his White Paper of 2001. This program advocated the devolution of many aspects of European regulation to lower levels (such as regional). This transformed the nature of the processes used for the harmonisation of the different implementations of European rules across member states, reducing the role of legal oversight carried out by the European Commission's Committee system or "Comitology".

[31] Cohen, J. and Sabel, C.F., "Sovereignty and Solidarity: EU and US" in *Governing Work and Welfare in a New Economy: European and American Experiments*, New York, Oxford University Press, 2003, pp. 345-375. These two authors formulate an assessment of the political deficit of the EU's "deliberative polyarchy" which examines the dangers and promises of what they call the new "anti-constitutional" empirical constitutionalism associated with the OMC.

[32] Salais, R., "La Politique des indicateurs. Du taux de chômage au taux d'emploi dans la stratégie européenne pour l'emploi" in B. Zimmerman and P. Wagner (eds.), *Action politique et sciences sociales*, Paris, Presse de la Maison des Sciences de l'Homme, 2004.

character, the fact that it posits the possibility of pure, immanent intra-subjective harmony which leaves no place for conflict or collective historical action over the direction taken by society.[33] In this respect, the ideology of governance is clearly but a very belated offspring of British Enlightenment liberalism.[34]

In its original appearance, liberalism as a new dimension of Western European societies involved a first fundamental break away from the primacy of the political as expressed in contractual conceptions of society in favour of the belief in society's capacity for autonomous self-regulation and in the power of socio-historical creation which individual freedom unleashed. As Karl Polyani showed, in itself, liberalism how-ever was powerless to coordinate the needs of individual freedom and those of social cohesion. The negative consequences of industrial, technical progress powered by capitalism led to the return of the politi-cal. This return eventually assumed the form of a synthesis of liberalism and democracy but not before it had also given birth to totalitarianism, that is, to attempts to abolish democratic historical indeterminacy, be it in the form of Marxist-Leninism or Nazism.[35] As Alan Milward has argued, European "integration" in fact strengthened this reconstruction of liberal democracy along national lines, which in the context of the paradoxical cold-war peace contributed to an unprecedented period of economic growth.[36]

After the 1970s which were a period of stagnation for European in-stitutions, the creation of the EU was however caught up in a general swing back of the pendulum towards liberalism characterised by a reduction in the exercise of political sovereignty and an acceleration of history in the obvious form of technological change.[37] In this, of course, Europe has not been alone. The US, carried by its absolute faith in the

---

[33] Supiot, A., *Homo Juridicus, op. cit.*, pp. 250-274.

[34] Supiot establishes a similarity between the ideology of governance and totalita-rianism. Governance does circumvent the autonomy of the political and constitutes an attempt to normalise society which institutes a kind of generalised conformism. Whilst this conformism, motivated by the desire to maximise efficiency, does especially bring to mind the productivist ideology of Stalinism, the comparison seems a little overdrawn if one is to consider all the other aspects of totalitarianism, if only the desire to fuse state and society in the form of party dictatorship.

[35] Polanyi, K., *The Great Transformation*, New York, Rinehart, 1944. The legacy of Polanyi's work for an understanding of the political economy of the EU is discussed in J. Joerges, B Stråth and P. Wagnee (eds.), *The Economy as a Polity. The Political Constitution of Contemporary Capitalism*. London, UCL, 2005.

[36] Milward, A., *The European Rescue of the Nation-State*, Berkeley, University of California Press, 1992.

[37] Gauchet, M., "Le Problème européen" in *La Condition politique*, Paris, Gallimard, 2005, pp. 465-493.

presumed laws of economics, have also become ardent believers in governance and globalisation. The difference is that Europeans have done this as part of a pre-existing political project transcending the framework of the nation-state: European pacification, which as it has become secured, has increasingly been seen as the template for all international relations. Until the terrorist attacks of 2001, the US and Europe seemed to converge in this new understanding of international relations but in recent times, the US have reverted back to conceptions of international relations based on power relationships now quite at odds with the European perspective.

The war in Iraq was a crucial moment of divergence between Europe and the US. The pacifistic, cosmopolitan inspiration of European integration became fully visible as European populations – if not all their governments – unified in their opposition to US intervention in Iraq.[38] It revealed the true inspiration of European integration concealed by what Ulrich Beck and Edgar Grande call the EU's *"Lebenslügen"*, that is, the myths which allowed it to proceed but not in full knowledge of what was being achieved. The divergence over the war in Iraq revealed the new orientation taken by Europe after the disintegration of the Soviet Union. No longer could the superpowers contribute to European "integration" by giving it a distant goal to strive for: the creation of a new nation, Europe, to meet the challenge of their confrontation. The exact political nature of this nation to be born had been allowed to remain undetermined, the European Community having evolved along the lines of a compromise between a federation and close intergovernmental cooperation.

Post 1989, the vision ceased to be operative: the enlargement to 25, then 27, killed the myth of a European "identity" to be represented by a super-state. The nation-state was reinstated as the fundamental constitutive unit of the sphere of European pacifism. As Marcel Gauchet puts it, it became clear that the common cliché of early European integration had to be reversed: it was the pacifistic evolution of European countries that had made Europe possible, not the other way round. The European Union started to reveal its original vocation: to be the template of what could be a world federation of nation-states. This vocation, however, clashed to a certain extent with the narrower near-federal framework of monetary union into which the EU had locked itself. The fall of the Soviet Union and the enlargement of the EU triggered a crisis of legitimacy: the EU was shown to be devoid of a clear and accepted framework for public decisions but the creation of such framework could no

---

[38] Beck, U. and Grande, E., *Das Kosmopolitanische Europa, Gesellschaft und Politik in der Zweiten Moderne*, Frankfurt-am-Main, Suhrkamp, 2004.

longer be deferred, could no longer be expected to evolve naturally. The rejection of the Constitutional Treaty by the French and the Dutch electorates brought the crisis into sharp relief but as Beck and Grande suggest, Europe had already manoeuvred itself into a blind alley long before it.[39]

The crisis has paradoxically made clearer the essential vocation of the EU within the greater narrative of European history. As Gauchet argues, this vocation involves the metamorphosis of the modern state as it first took form in Western Europe, a metamorphosis foreshadowed in the difficult creation of the social state at the end of the 19th century but only truly fulfilled in the consolidation of the welfare state after the Second World War. In its first incarnation as fiscal-military state from the late 17th century onwards, the European state had as its first and main *raison d'être* the defence of a clearly defined territory against external threats. As nation-state, it then came to incarnate the identity of society understood as a cohesive body. As social state, it came to assume responsibility for the liberal dream of individual autonomy by providing the means through which this autonomy could be realised (education, work protection). Since 1945, however, it has become so successful in promoting individual autonomy that society has lost its collective identity, depriving it of its representative role. Western European societies now only recognise one supreme principle: the free individual endowed with "natural" and presumably universal rights, even if paradoxically, this is only possible because the welfare state has liberated individuals from almost all their debts and obligations towards the collective.

The universal human rights have in effect become the new religion of Europe and on the basis of the nation-state's prosecution, nationalism, and by extension the nation-state itself, have been identified as the main culprit in Europe's violation of human rights.[40] This has trapped Europe in a self-repudiation which has prevented it from formulating its new identity in any other mode than the negative, the "never again" of colonialism and totalitarianism. Europe is trapped in what Jan-Werner

---

[39] "Europe is in crisis – institutionally, economically and politically. But it would be too simple to blame the failed referendums on the European Constitutional Treaty in France and the Netherlands for the current malaise of the European project. Europe had manoeuvred itself into a blind alley long before that". Such is the opening statement of their article "Cosmopolitanism: Europe's way out of the Crisis", *The European Journal of Social Theory*, Vol. 10, No. 1, 2007, pp. 67-85. This view is shared by Marcel Gauchet in his own assessment of the crisis of the EU following the French and Dutch rejections of the constitutional treaty, "Post-scriptum: la Nouvelle Europe" in *La Condition Politique*, Paris, Gallimard, 2005, pp. 494-504.

[40] Beck, U. and Delanty, G., "Europe from a Cosmopolitan Perspective" in *Europe and Asia beyond West and East*, London/New York, Routledge, 2006, pp. 11-23.

Müller calls moralising "militant politics".[41] Human rights have been an essential motivating force for the progress of the post-national perspective and countered the attempts to lock the EU in a closed, Christian definition. There is however an essential difficulty in trying to build a collective political framework out of individual human rights and a danger in not recognising their "cultural embeddedness".

Cosmopolitan Europe: A New Civilisational Project in a De-politicised Europe

Since the fall of the Soviet Union, a new understanding of the nature of post-1945 European history has become possible. It rebuts all previous theories of European integration divided between inter-governmentalism and functionalism, when in fact these theories address two dimensions of European integration which must be thought together rather than considered as mutually exclusive. As Beck and Grande suggest, the study of contemporary European history must free itself from what they call the false logic of "either or", "either national or supranational" and rethink the connection between the two. Without a doubt, Beck and Grande's 2005 book, *Das Kosmopolitanische Europa*, has been the most systematic and comprehensive attempt at doing precisely that.[42] Their analysis reveals how the history of European "integration" – as misnomer – is in fact the history of European *cosmopolitanism*. However, Beck and Grande's conception of European cosmopolitanism is not just an analysis of the nature of Europe's cosmopolitan evolution. More importantly, it is also a programme for the re-invention of Europe, for a way out of the crisis it is now trapped in.[43] As I have argued above, the notion of cosmopolitanism does offer a new understanding of the logic at play in the creation of the European Union, but can it really be the basis for a political vision? Beck and Grande perhaps underestimate the need for such a vision to be supported by the re-politicisation of the European Union, predicated on that of the nation-states which compose it. Without this, the promotion of cosmopolitan political visions cannot be effective, be it at the European or global level.

---

[41] Müller, J.-W., "A 'Thick' Constitutional Patriotism for Europe? On Morality, Memory and Militancy" in E.O. Eriksen, C. Joerges and F. Rodl (eds.), *Law, Democracy, and Solidarity in a Post-National Union: The Unsettled Political Order of Europe*, London, Routledge, 2008.

[42] For an English translation by Cioran Ciónin, see U. Beck and E. Grande, *Cosmopolitan Europe*, Polity Press, 2007.

[43] This appears clearly in the conclusion of *Das Kosmopolitanische Europa*. The solutions advocated are outlined on pages 515-519 of "Cosmopolitanism: Europe's way out of the Crisis". What follows is based on this.

As Beck and Grande suggest, at first sight the notion of European cosmopolitanism seems to be a rather futile attempt to join together the idea of "world citizenship" and the idea of a continent-wide but still territorially limited political order. By returning to the roots of the notion of cosmopolitanism in late 18th century Europe, one can find a way of conceiving cosmopolitanism that both acknowledges and transcends an intermediate territorially defined identity, that of the nation. This concept of cosmopolitanism provides a new way of dealing with the problem of otherness within societies and among them. Cosmopolitanism as Beck and Grande define it distinguishes itself not only from nationalism and "particularism" but also from a postmodernist celebration of difference as an unbridgeable absolute. Cosmopolitanism seeks to make differences compatible and thus shares with universalism the quest for a certain amount of shared, universal norms. However, it also needs to be distinguished from Habermas's reflexive universalism based on communicative action which being based on individual rights cannot promote the recognition of the other in the form of communities, which they argue is central to cosmopolitanism. Beck and Grande maintain that cosmopolitanism is in fact a form of realism based on the recognition that political action will always be interest-based but also based on the novel insistence that the interests of nation-states be made to take into consideration the impact of their action on a larger community. The affinity between Beck's and Grande's cosmopolitan project and Kantian ethics is self-evident.

In opposition to the banal cosmopolitanism which has accompanied the globalisation of cultural practices, "cosmopolitan realism" is reflexive and implies the construction of an institutional framework to safeguard the principle of cosmopolitan community. In the way it has been experimenting with new forms of political rule beyond the nation-state, Europe has been a kind of laboratory that holds valuable lessons for the extension of the principle at the global level; but as Beck and Grande stress, the spirit of cosmopolitanisation at play in the creation of a new Europe has been stifled by the myth of integration as the abolition of national differences and European unity were confused with uniformity and convergence. In practice of course, to overcome stagnation, many exceptions were made to the principle of harmonisation which defined the so-called "community method" in the 1970s and again in the 1990s, but those exceptions were always conceived as second-best solutions towards the real, superior goal of complete integration.

Beck and Grande argue that this differentiated integration introduced only *de facto* must now be radicalised and extended into formalised principles and methods. In this respect, they refer approvingly to the OMC without addressing the concerns it raises. This is not to say that they are unaware of the problem of a democratic deficit. They in fact make a number of sensible suggestions as to how the EU can be given greater legitimacy. In keeping with their critique of the ambition to turn the EU into a nation-state writ large, they stress that the model of majoritarian rule is insufficient. It needs to be completed by other institutional mechanisms such as Europe-wide referenda, the institutionalisation of minority right at the level of member states in the form of "qualified right of veto" as suggested by Renaud Dehousse and finally the introduction of a "reflexive loop" in decision making proposed by Claus Offe. However valid these suggestions might be – and there is no obvious reason to think that they are not – they only address the institutional mechanisms and do not sufficiently tackle the question of the EU's lack of political vision. As Beck and Grande themselves suggest, the institutional reforms they propose will only contribute to the reinvention of the EU from above if it is matched by its re-invention from below, by a re-engagement of European citizens with the European process but on this, they have much less to say. They conclude their argument with reference to the social effervescence of the 1940s which accompanied the appearance of a pro-European movement within national civil societies and express their faith in the possibility of such popular support being reactivated.

The problem is that the situation is now quite different from that of the late 1940s, which saw a reinvestment of European societies in the collective dimension. European societies have become individualised in unprecedented fashion, something which has become manifest, amongst other things, through the decline of traditional institutionalised religion in a number of Western European countries. The metamorphosis of the state has rendered the collective dimension invisible but the new concern for human rights has not given birth to a new political project of social cohesion based on shared norms subjected to debate. The political deficit at the European level emanates from its counterpart at the national level and can only be solved in conjunction with it. Beck and Grande acknowledge as much in their conclusion but their discussion does not address the challenges posed by the metamorphosis of the European state, which raises the question of the relationship between social cohesion and democratic sovereignty.

The tendency to conflate the nation-state with nationalism, which characterises the discourse of "integration" remains implicitly present in the description of European cosmopolitanism. Authors such as Beck and Grande argue that European cosmopolitanism overcomes the faults of what they describe as the "first modernity" – that which developed with the nation-state according to a logic of exclusion – and opens up a "second modernity" not to be confused with relativist "post-modernity".[44] In other words, the re-assessment of the significance of the European project raises the fundamental question of the role played by the state and the notion of nation in the development of modern liberalism. At this point it is useful to return to Gauchet who formulates a different assessment of the historical connection between the nation-state as political form and the progress of cultural pluralism, which culminates in the new understanding of international relations encapsulated in the notion of cosmopolitanism. Like Beck and Grande, Gauchet's use of the notion of cosmopolitanism refers back to its appearance in the late Enlightenment period and connects it with the phenomenon of the nation-state in a way which rejects the "either or". Gauchet's use of the term however goes further in establishing the essential link that exists between cosmopolitanism and the modern European notion of nation as political and historical society. This is done though an exploration of the historical connection between the appearance of European nations and that of the notion of civilisation in the singular.

The notion of civilisation in the singular, it is clear, has never recovered from its association with colonial imperialism and, apart from the notable exception of the German sociologist Norbert Elias, has more or less disappeared from contemporary intellectual debates. In a rather iconoclastic way and it must be said one that is vulnerable to misunderstanding, Gauchet, however, resurrects the notion to suggest that Europe is now confronted with the need to resolve the tension between the existence of a plurality of European nations and a common ideal of civilisation. The ideal of civilisation, he suggests, was in fact the product of the European notion of nation. It is predicated on the belief in the historical movement of nations towards a form of union which transcends them but to which they each contribute their particularities. It thus relies on a new conception of human communities as historical political actors and entails the belief in their capacity not only to formulate their own rules but also to shape their future. The European modern notion of nation which took form in the early 19th century, however, drew on very old material, on a pre-modern, exclusivist understanding of community. From this, European nation-states inherited the ambition to be the exclusive embodiment of a universal civilisation which fuelled

---

[44] "The negativity of modernity and European awareness of it is not merely a pose, an ideology of the tragic. It reflects the historical invention of a modernity distorted by the nation and the state which has inexorably developed the potential for moral, political, economic and technological disaster like the chamber of horrors of a real laboratory without concern for its own destruction", Beck. U and Delanty, G., "Europe from a Cosmopolitan Perspective" in *Europe and Asia beyond West and East*, London/New York, Routledge, 2006, pp. 11-23.

nationalism and colonial imperialism.[45] At the same time, the notion of nation was by definition plural: European nations defined themselves in contradistinction to other nations in which they recognised legitimate counterparts with which they had to compete for the leadership of Europe, then of the world.[46]

The European nation-state is thus fundamentally ambivalent: it is both a belligerent notion and a pacifying one. The notion of universal community and the cosmopolitan spirit which flourished in the second half of the 18th century is due to its self-assertion. This cosmopolitan spirit drew its inspiration from a new notion of civilisation first fused with the notion of scientific progress as scientific rationality became the new model of universality. The ideal of civilisation matured when the notion of progress gave way to that of history as the notion of popular sovereignty asserted itself: nations became communities of historical destiny and, more significantly, political projects unfolding through history. Through the belief in history, nations and civilisation thus became convergent notions. The era when civilisation was thought to be realised through nationalities as a result of the existence of some kind of natural harmony however only lasted until the mid 19th century to be replaced with that of nationalisms. Nationalisms unleashed the underlying competition between nation-states, now prosecuted in the name of civilisation: the leading European nations each claimed to be the embodiment of universal civilisation and attempted to export it in the rest of the world. The first half of the 20th century saw the disastrous consequences of this appropriation of civilisation by nation-states. In reaction, the ideal of civilisation was reborn in a form which repudiated the historical link to the notion of nation. This was an ideal of civilisation *without* nations or even *against* them. It was not even thought in terms of *civilisation* but in terms of *integration* and was pursued in the name of peace.

---

[45] Gauchet's discussion of European cosmopolitanism must be seen within the context of his general theory of state formation in Western Europe since the high middle ages first outlined in *The Disenchantment of the World*, Princeton, Princeton University Press, 1997. This theory of state formation and evolution situates the invention of modern-liberal democracy within the *longue durée* of state reconstruction in Western Europe following the demise of the Roman Empire and stressed the novelty of the monarchical territorial states which came to supplant the two subsequent carriers of imperial visions – the Catholic Church and the Holy Germanic Empire. These states did not only pursue conquest but, much more fundamentally, intensified control of a well defined territory, in a way which fostered a new relationship to the land and with it a new political understanding of social community.

[46] Gauchet, M., "Le problème européen" in *La Condition Politique*, Collection "Les Essays", Paris, Stock, 2003, pp. 484-491.

As the ideal of civilisation in the second half of the 18th century, the ideal of integration assumed a materialist expression. It was carried by science, industry, technology, exchange, all that which constitutes the modern notion of economy. The civilisational project of integration brought European countries closer but it was not political and in fact necessarily contributes to dissolving the nations as political projects. European cosmopolitanism is an *ethical* project which in fact escapes Europe itself and gives it a global dimension as Beck and Grande argue. This, however, has more to do with the nation-state than these authors are willing to concede: Western European nation-states constituted the laboratories of a new form of social cohesion grounded in the modern notion of democratic citizenship which emancipated itself from cultural conformity. European cosmopolitanism can be regarded as part of a general discovery of cultural pluralism which has unfolded also within national societies themselves. As we saw above, the ideology of integra-tion, however, concealed the debt of pluralism to the notion of nation. European cosmopolitanism itself ultimately relies on the existence of European nations: as Gauchet puts it, the day when there are no longer any nations to want Europe will be the day Europe ceases to be. This must not be taken to be the expression of a more sophisticated form of Gaullism but of the recognition of the interdependence and specificity of the different levels interacting in European cosmopolitanism: the na-tional, the European and the global.

Unlike Beck and Grande, Gauchet does not engage much with the empirical level of institutions and so makes no definite proposals as to how the political dimension can be reactivated at all those levels. How-ever, in his reflexion on the relationship between democracy and human rights, he suggests that the law might paradoxically be the locus of a re-politicisation of European societies in its capacity to force them to debate explicitly their implicit norms and encourage them to formulate agreement as to what constitutes a common European understanding of the finality of collective life.[47] In this, Gauchet's thinking converges with that of Supiot which foreshadows a way out of the mirage of governance. Drawing a parallel between today's situation and that of the late 19th century when civil law was used to create responses to what lawyers could identify as new social problems, in the process giving birth to labour law, Supiot suggests that the law could again play the

---

[47]   See the last section of Gauchet, M., "Quand les droits de l'homme deviennent une politique" in *La Démocratie contre elle-même*, Paris, Gallimard, 2002, pp. 379-395.

same role, be it a European or global level: that of identifying the new challenges to which political solutions must be found.[48]

The very notion of "paid work" which was central to the creation of labour law was the outcome of a process of cross-cultural debate across Western Europe, spanning the traditions of Common law and Civil law, in their various, national-cultural interpretations. Supiot's analysis of the history of labour law points to the inadequacies, in the contemporary context, of this concept of employment enshrined in European law. It shows the need for a kind of social forum to engage in a process of empirical constitutionalisation at the level of the EU, a forum where different, national traditions in the conceptionalisation of work can be compared to foster the elaboration of common norms.[49] It is illusory to believe that the incredible diversity of European social and legal systems can engender one unitary model but all these systems can come together in so far as they face the same problems. They can by the same token open up to the global dimension.

This emphasis on an irreducible but productive cultural diversity links up with Gauchet's main contribution to the debate on European cosmopolitanism. As he suggests, if Europe is to serve as the laboratory of a form of global democracy respectful of civilisational diversity, it first needs to re-discover its *own* civilisational specificity and explore the historical circumstances which imprinted on it a cultural diversity that fed into the invention of modern political society in the form of the nation-state. This means taking the full measure of the extent to which European history produced cultural norms, which far from being universal in fact constitute a kind of anthropological anomaly in the way they challenge the boundaries of cultural identity and proclaim individual autonomy as the ultimate value. This in turn would allow Europe to look beyond its specificity and to approach with realism the fact that even if war between nation-states appears to have diminished, war has not been abolished as many parts of the world still struggle to form viable peaceful, political societies. To put it differently, Europe must come to terms with the fact that the "first modernity" which Europe is now transcending is still far from secure in the rest of the world, as the terrorist events of 2001 demonstrated so dramatically. European cosmopolitanism must emancipate itself fully from the age-old tendency of Europe to universalise its experience.

---

[48] Supiot, A., "Governing Work and Welfare in a Global Economy" in J. Zeitlin and D. Trubek (eds.), *Governing Work and Welfare in a New Economy: European and American Experiments*, Oxford, Oxford University Press, 2003, pp. 376-420.

[49] Supiot, A., "Was is ein Arbeitnehmer?" in H. Kaelble and G. Schmidt (eds.), *Das Europäische Sozialmodell. Auf dem Weg zum transnationalen Sozialstaat*, Berlin, Sigma, 2004, pp. 423-452.

CHAPTER 4

Europeanisation, Religion and Collective Identities in an Enlarging Europe

A Multiple Modernities Perspective

Willfried SPOHN

Introduction

Religion plays a growing and increasingly conflictive role in European societies and politics. There are three interrelated reasons for this. Firstly, along with the breakdown of communism and the re-connection of divided Europe, there has re-emerged the encompassing structural and cultural pluralism of European civilisation. This pluralism is characterised by different forms of religion and secularisation patterns as well as their varying impacts on states, nations, ethnic groups and related collective identities. Secondly, European societies have been transformed into more multi-cultural and religiously more diversified societies due to the impact of growing international migration and immigration. Thirdly, the contemporary wave of globalisation has been accompanied by an intensification of inter-civilisational and inter-religious encounters in cooperative and competitive, as well as, particularly between the Islamic world and the Christian-secularised West, in markedly conflictive ways.

The growing and increasingly conflictive role of religion in Europe challenges the predominant European secularist-cultural integration mode and its extension through the Eastward enlargement of the European Union. At the same time, the predominant approaches in the social and political sciences have been, until recently, rather ill equipped for the analysis, explanation and potential redirection of the cultural dimensions of European integration policy. Most analyses of European integration, in tune with the predominant modernist secularisation thesis, still omit the issue of religion.

In this context, I will (i) outline my multiple modernities approach to Europeanisation and religion; (ii) compare the different relationships of the religious-secular configurations in Western and Eastern Europe to the EU cultural integration mode; (iii) characterise the European and national forms of citizenship and cultural integration regarding immigrants and their minority religions; (iv) analyse the growing impact of religious diversity and mobilisation on European intra-and inter-civilisational boundary constructions and the consequences for the eastern enlargement of the EU; and (v) conclude with a critique of the secular-religious European cultural integration mode from the perspective of religious pluralism.

Europeanisation, Religion and Collective Identities – a Multiple Modernities Approach

Theories of European integration usually do not consider religion as a salient factor.[1] On the contrary, in projecting the modernisation-cum-secularisation thesis of mainstream political and social scientific analysis of the nation-state society on the composite level of the transnational European regime, they presuppose an emerging secular form of European cultural integration, a secular European identity or European civil religion.[2] Against this background, the recently edited volume by Timothy Byrnes and Peter Katzenstein on *Religion in an Expanding Europe* has demonstrated in several assembled contributions the varying positive, ambivalent and negative role of the various national and transnational religious actors, particularly of Catholicism, Orthodox Christianity and Islam in selected European countries for the extension of the EU to the east.[3] In theoretical terms, Byrnes and Katzenstein explicitly reject the mainstream secularisation thesis of European integration theories and subscribe to a multiple modernities perspective that assumes the continuing relevance of organised religion in its multiple forms manifested in Europe.

My own approach will be to follow more strictly Shmuel Eisenstadt's comparative-civilisational framework.[4] European multiple modernity should not be restricted, as the Byrnes/Katzenstein volume is, to the continuing salience of the religious realm in its manifold religious

---

[1] See Jachtenfuchs, M. and Kohler-Koch, B. (eds.), *Europäische Integration*, Opladen, Leske&Buderich, 1996; Loth, W. and Wessels, W. (eds.), *Theorien europäischer Integration*, Opladen, Leske&Buderich, 2001; Spohn, W., "Der Ansatz multipler Modernitäten" in Beichelt, T. *et al.* (eds.), *Interdisziplinäre Europastudien. Eine Einführung*, Wiesbaden, Verlag Sozialwissenschaften, 2006. See also Spohn, W., *Politik und Religion in einer sich globalisierenden Welt*, Wiesbaden, Verlag für Sozialwissenschaften, 2008.

[2] Siedentop, L., *Democracy in Europe*, London, Penguin, pp. 189-214. See also Casanova, J., "Religion, European Secular Identities, and European integration" in Byrnes, T. and Katzenstein, P. (eds.), *Religion in an Expanding Europe*, Cambridge, Cambridge University Press, 2006, pp. 65-92.

[3] Byrnes, T. and Katzenstein, P. (eds.), *op. cit.*

[4] Spohn, W., "Eisenstadt on Civilisations and Multiple Modernities", *European Journal of Social Theory*, Vol. 4, No. 4, 2001, pp. 499-508.

organizations and actors alone. Instead, it should consider its constitutive institutional and cultural role for the secular realm of politics, states, nations and collective identities and accordingly the transnational EU regime and an emergent European identity. Below follow the four main pillars of my multiple modernities approach to Europeanisation, religion and secularisation.

Firstly, from a comparative perspective, the European civilisation is characterised by a specific form of structural and cultural pluralism constituted by multiple political, socio-economic, religious and cultural centres as well as diverse religious and cultural life-worlds and world-views.[5] Of particular importance have been the Greek and Roman institutional, legal and philosophical legacies as well as western and eastern Christianity in its Jewish roots and its exchange with, and opposition to, Islam. On these manifold institutional and cultural foundations, Europe has not been formed as a fixed social entity but rather constructed and reconstructed as a developing social space with changing boundaries and identities. At its core, Europe became historically constituted through the Carolingian Empire and Latin Christianity in opposition to eastern Christianity and Islam, but changed its meanings over time by intra- and inter-civilisational dynamics.[6] The most important historical long-term changes of Europe have been connected to the changing relations between western Christianity, eastern Christianity and Islam; the cultural change of western Christianity through the Protestant Reformation and Enlightenment; the process of secularisation and related oppositions between church and state, clericalism and anti-clericalism or religion and secularism; as well as the geopolitical attempts to unify Europe either in totalitarian or pluralist forms.

Secondly, on the background of the multiple religious roots of the European civilisation, European secularisation should not be viewed as a progressing, though uneven, development from the many religious traditions to secular modernity – secular modernity defined as structural differentiation between the religious and secular spheres, an encompassing expansion of the secular and the privatisation of religion. Rather, European secularisation should be seen as a secularising transformation of the structural and cultural pluralism of the European civilisation without dissolving its manifold religious sources and components.[7]

---

[5] Eisenstadt, S., *European Civilisation in Comparative Perspective*, Oslo, Scandinavian University Press, 1987.

[6] Delanty, G., *The Invention of Europe*, London, Routledge, 1995; Malmborg, M. and Strath, B. (eds.), *The Meaning of Europe*, Oxford, Berg, 2002.

[7] Martin, D., *A General Theory of Secularization*, Oxford, Blackwell, 1978; Martin, D., *On Secularization. Towards a Revised Theory*, Aldershot, Ashgate 2005; Casanova, J., *Public Religions in the Modern World*, Chicago, Chicago University

Structural differentiation between state and church, the development of a secular culture and the privatisation of religion do not represent comprehensive processes. They have been developing in specific configurations depending on their religious foundations, specific cultural forms and secularisation patterns. In addition, these secularisation processes are often accompanied by the sacralisation of the secular sphere particularly in the form of secular or political religions, secular or political ideologies and secularist or quasi-religious collective identities.[8] In other words, within the framework of European multiple modernity, national and European collective identities are not simply secular or post-secular but depend on multiple religious as well as secular components.[9]

Thirdly, on the foundations of European multiple modernity, the different forms of religious development and secularisation patterns in the context of inter-civilisational encounters and conflicts have been accompanied by important changes in the construction of European identities and boundaries. During the Middle Ages, the continuing expansion of Islam at the cost of eastern Christianity laid ground for the connection between western Christianity and Europe. The Protestant Reformation and Catholic Counter-Reformation introduced a basic religious cleavage into western Christianity but also led to the Treaty of Westphalia (1648) attempting to balance national conflicts and contain religious cleavages. The simultaneous western expansion of the Ottoman Empire into Orthodox Eastern Europe sharpened the oppositions between Latin Christianity and Islam but at the same time weakened the religious cleavages between western and eastern Christianity. The Enlightenment, the French Revolution and the following secularist revolutions in Europe further bridged the Catholic-Protestant divide in western Christianity. At the same time, it sharpened the opposition between the "enlightened-modern Occident" and "despotic-backward religious Orient". In the aftermath of the two World Wars, the expanding secularist-totalitarian revolutions in the east contributed also to a bridging of the confessional and religious-secularist divide in western Christianity.

Fourthly, the post-Second World War division of Europe enabled the developing unification of Western Europe on the basis of Latin Christi-

---

8   Press, 2004; Davie, G., *Religion in Modern Europe*, Oxford, Oxford University Press, 2000.

8   Eisenstadt, S., *Vielfalt der Moderne*, Weilerswist, Velbrück Wissenschaft, 2000; Eisenstadt, S., *Multiple Modernities and Comparative Civilisations*, 2 Vols., Leiden, Brill, 2003.

9   Martin, D., *On Secularization, op. cit.* This is not equivalent to the idea of a post-secular Europe, see Eder, K., "Europäische Säkularisierung – ein Sonderweg in die post-säkulare Gesellschaft", *Berliner Journal für Soziologie*, No. 3, 2003, pp. 331-343.

anity and strongly secularising societies in confrontation with communist-atheistic Eastern Europe in the context of the global East-West conflict. The fall of communism restored the structural and cultural pluralism of European civilisation and allowed for the reunification of Europe through the expansion of the western European secular integration project to the east. At the same time, this enlarging process of Europeanisation is accompanied by oppositions and tensions between the western European secular-cultural integration mode and the eastern European revival of nationalism and religion. In addition, the contemporary wave of globalisation with growing immigration and intensifying inter-civilisational interactions is accompanied by an intensifying clash between secularised Latin Christian Europe, revived Christian Orthodox Europe and Islamic civilisation.[10] These cultural-religious asymmetries are at the core of the conflictive dynamic of enlarging European integration to the east.

European Multiple Modernity, Religion and European Cultural Integration

The first major reason for the growing importance of religion for European (cultural) integration has been the restoration of an encompassing structural and cultural pluralism and with it the religious diversity of Europe. European integration was first and foremost based on the formation of transnational economic, political and legal institutions and policies, whereas the issue of European cultural integration and the emergence of a European identity remained, for a long while, rather silent or latent.[11] The original political bases of European integration were Catholic, lay-Catholic and mixed Catholic-Protestant countries as well as social Catholic and Christian Democratic politicians and intellectuals. Yet when the issue of a European identity as a response to the legitimacy deficit emerged, it was framed primarily in secular political-legal and socio-economic rather than cultural and religious terms. This changed only with the confrontation of the western European-based EU by the new member states in the east, their different forms of religion, lower cultural secularisation and strong currents of religious nationalism as well as the contentious issue of the potential incorporation of Turkey with a state-secularist regime but rising mobilisation of Islam. However, the multiple references of the long preamble of the Constitutional Treaty

---

[10] See Axtmann, R. (ed.), *Globalisation and Europe, Theoretical and Empirical Investigations*, London, Pinter, 1999; Delanty, G., *Rethinking Europeanisation*, London, Routledge, 2005.

[11] Kohli, M., "The Battlegrounds of European Identity", *European Societies*, Vol. 2, No. 2, 2000, pp. 113-137; Shore, C., *Building Europe. The Cultural Politics of European Integration*, London, Routledge, 2000.

revealed the difficulties inherent in transposing the humanist-secularist and western Christian-based cultural integration mode to the eastern European new member states and candidates with their differing Catholic, Orthodox Christian and Islamic legacies.

The European cultural integration mode, including its form of religious governance, derives from the converging trends in state-church relations in the original western member states of the European Community. As a corollary to the multi-level regime of the EU, the integration mode formulates, on the European level, the general principles of human, cultural and religious rights in parallel to the national constitutions of each individual member state. Individual nation-states are left to enact those principles according to their own legal, cultural and religious traditions. On the European level, the basic principles encompass particularly the values of religious freedom, union neutrality with respect to world views, tolerance towards different religious and secular orientations as well as equal treatment of religious communities. At their core, these principles are motivated by a humanist-secular and religious-ecumenical value system attempting to overcome the clerical-anticlerical or religious-secularist cleavages so characteristic for most European trajectories of secularisation. On the multiple national levels, the legal, cultural and religious traditions are principally respected. Accordingly, there is a wide space for national forms of religious governance: specific relationships between state and church(es); between church(es) and other religious communities, as well as between the religious and secular spheres.[12]

In institutional terms, there are three types of state-church relations: the strict separation of state and church, the cooperation between state and church, and the preservation of a state-church.[13] These three types are embedded in the historically differing secularisation patterns of Catholic, Protestant-Catholic mixed and Protestant countries.[14] Firstly, the tendency towards a separation between state and church is most characteristic for Catholic countries with a strong anti-clerical-secularist reaction against the traditionally strong bond between the *ancien régime*

---

[12] Koenig, M., "Europeanising the Governance of Religious Diversity – an Institutionalist Account of Muslim Struggles for Public Recognition", *Journal of Ethnic and Migration Studies*, Vol. 33, No. 6, August 2007, pp. 911-932.

[13] Robbers, G. (ed.), *Staat und Kirche in der Europäischen Union*, Baden-Baden, Nomos, 1995.

[14] Martin, D., *A General Theory of Secularization, op. cit.*; Martin, D., *On Secularization, op. cit.*; Spohn, W., "Nationalismus und Religion. Ein historisch-soziologischer Vergleich West- und Osteuropas" in M. Minkenberg and U. Willems (eds.), *Politische Vierteljahresschrift*, Special edition: "Politik und Religion", Vol. 33, 2002, Wiesbaden, Verlag für Sozialwissenschaften, 2003, pp. 323-345.

and Catholic Church. An institutional strict separation between state and church lasted only in laic-republican France. In most other western Catholic countries (Italy, Spain, Portugal and Austria), the clerical/anti-clerical conflicts have been finally overcome by rather cooperative links between state and church. Secondly, the same is true for countries with several confessions like Germany, the Netherlands, Belgium and Switzerland where the conflicts between Catholicism and Protestantism as well as between established state churches and anti-clerical secularism have in the end resulted in cooperative relations between state and churches. Thirdly, state church traditions remain characteristic for Protestant countries such as Great Britain or Scandinavia, though limited by Protestant pluralism and also different degrees of disestablishment. Despite these rather different historical traditions in state-church relations, there are converging tendencies in secularisation. Important elements here are the reduced importance of churches and religion, the decline of clerical/anti-clerical or religious/secularist conflicts and an ecumenical rapprochement between the various religions as well as state loyalty and state support of churches and religious communities. These converging tendencies also define the core of the cultural integration mode and religious governance of the EU.

This cultural integration and religious governance, however, reveals its western European Latin-Christian and secular-humanist bases when confronted with the new, eastern member states and candidates.[15] In these countries, the predominant religions are Catholicism, Orthodox Christianity and their secularisation patterns are with few exceptions characterised by limited secularisation and a strong revival of religion as well as related strong bonds between religion and national identity. In Poland, an institutional separation between state and church exists. However, due to the development of a close organic relation to national identity during communist times, there is typically a strong impact of the Catholic Church on national politics and national identity. The Catholic Church has a privileged role in society against other religions and world views, thus contradicting the European principles of neutrality, tolerance and egalitarian status. South-eastern European Christian Orthodox countries have historically had an even closer caesaro-papist link between State and Church. In addition, due to their peripheral position *vis-à-vis* western and eastern empires, they possess an organic form of nationalism. Both characteristics favour post-communist Christian Orthodoxy against other forms of religion and world views. Finally, in Turkey as the most important non-Christian Islamic candidate, the

---

[15] Pollack, D. *et al.* (eds.), *Religiöser Wandel in den post-kommunistischen Ländern Ost- und Mitteleuropas*, Würzburg, Ergon, 1998; Spohn, W., "Religion und Nationalismus. Osteuropa im westeuropäischen Vergleich" in *Ibid.*, pp. 87-120.

Kemalist revolution removed Islam as the traditional religious core institution of the Ottoman Empire and established, along French lines, a secularist state regulating privatised Islam. However, at the same time, Turkey suffers from a rising mobilisation of social and political Islamic movements against the secularist state.[16]

This religious asymmetry challenges the multi-level mode of cultural integration and religious governance. The originally western European cultural integration mode, based on western European, Latin-Christian and highly secularised societies is in marked tension with the mostly more religious and less secularised East European societies and their forms of cultural integration and religious governance. EU policies of the eastern enlargement have to some extent successfully imposed some of the basic western European standards of religious freedom, neutrality of the state and religious/secular equality. Furthermore, the privileged status of the respective Christian churches in most post-communist countries has triggered a stronger cultural secularisation process. Both tendencies seem to signal a converging movement towards the western European mode of cultural integration and religious governance. However, the multi-level mode of European cultural integration allows for the continuation and preservation of national forms of cultural and religious integration in East-Central European member states that conversely could have a narrowing effect on the humanist-secular and Latin-Christian European cultural integration mode. Regarding the accession negotiations with Turkey, these eastern influences could weaken the western European secular-humanist bridge to the Turkish state-secularist regime and strengthen the European Christian core against the tendencies of Islamic mobilisation and pluralisation.

Europeanisation, Ethnic Minorities and Religious Diversity

A second major factor in the growing role of religion in European integration is the transformation of the historical composition of the structural and cultural pluralism of European civilisation through the increasing impact of international migration on European societies.[17] As a consequence, the weight of immigrant ethnic minorities with different religious and civilisation backgrounds has increased considerably and contributed to a marked transformation of the ethnic composition of European societies and with it a considerable diversification of European religion. Of particular importance is the growing number of Mus-

---

[16] Yavuz, H., *Islamic Political Identity in Turkey*, Oxford, Oxford University Press, 2003; Zürcher, E., *Turkey. A Modern History*, New York, Tauris, 2004.

[17] See Spohn, W. and Triandafyllidou, A. (eds.), *Europeanisation, National Identities and Migration. Changes in Boundary Construction between Western and Eastern Europe*, London, Routledge, 2003.

lims from Islamic countries,[18] but also of members of other world religions such as Buddhism, Hinduism and Evangelical Protestantism.[19] Until 1989, there were markedly uneven European immigration patterns between western European core countries and southern and eastern European semi-peripheries. These patterns parallel the diversification of religion, which was first and foremost a phenomenon of western and northern European societies. Nevertheless, after the fall of Communism with growing immigration also to southern and central-eastern European countries, religious diversification represents a growing tendency in all European societies. As a consequence, the modes of cultural integration and forms of religious governance on the national as well as the European level are also confronted with a changing religious situation.

The modes of cultural integration of non-Christian forms of religion in European societies are closely linked to two institutions: the varied national regimes of religious governance as well as national incorporation modes of immigrants and related forms of citizenship. Through the process of Europeanisation, these varied national institutional frameworks are at the same time influenced by the emerging forms of European religious governance, European immigration policy and European citizenship.[20] Firstly, regarding the national forms of religious governance – primarily a product of managing the religious/secularist cleavages and conflicts between the predominant Christian religious and the secular nation-state[21] – they are now increasingly confronted with growing religious diversification, particularly in the form of Islam. The general institutional tendency is to include other religions into the main legal-moral principles of national religious governance, i.e. religious freedom, religious tolerance, state neutrality and legal equality. At the same time, however, the acceptance of non-Christian religions as equal to the various branches of the Christian faith in European societies is in

---

[18] Esposito, J. and Burgat, F., *Modernising Islam: Religion in the Public Sphere in Europe and the Middle East*, New Brunswick, NJ, Rutgers University Press, 2003; Modood, T. and Werbner, P. (eds.), *The Politics of Multiculturalism in the New Europe*, London, Zed, 1996; Shadid, W.A.R. and Koningsveld, P. (eds.), *Religious Freedom and the Neutrality of the State: The Position of Islam in the European Union*, Leuven, Peters 2002; See also Koenig, M., "Europeanising the Governance of Religious Diversity", *op. cit.*

[19] Madeley, J. and Enyedi, Z. (eds.), *Church and State in Contemporary Europe. The Chimera of Neutrality*, London, Frank Cass, 2003; Shadid, W.A.R. and Koningsveld, P. (eds.), *Intercultural Relations and Religious Authorities: Muslims in the European Union*, Leuven, Peters, 2002.

[20] Koenig, M., "Europeanising the Governance of Religious Diversity", *op. cit.*

[21] Koenig, M., "Politics and Religion in European Nation-States: Institutional Varieties and Contemporary Transformations" in Giesen, B. and Suber, D. (eds.), *Religion and Politics: Cultural Perspectives*, Leiden, Brill, 2005, pp. 291-315.

practice still severely limited.[22] The tendency towards the materialisation of religious freedom, tolerance and equality is supported by the European cultural integration mode and related European religious governance. As a multi-level regime, however, it acknowledges the primacy of the national frameworks of religious governance on the basis of subsidiarity and thus intervenes into the national level only in exceptional cases.

Secondly, the modes of cultural integration of non-Christian religions are primarily linked to the varied national incorporation modes of immigrants and related citizenship regimes for immigrant ethnic minorities and only secondarily to an emerging form of European citizenship. On the various national levels and with marked west-east European inequalities, there are, at present, two general tendencies at work. On the one hand, there has developed a policy to strongly restrict the overall number of immigrants and integrate the immigrant population into the existing forms of civil, political and social citizenship. This predominant "Marshallian" model of citizenship however is abstracted from the different cultural and religious traditions and life-worlds of immigrants and thus is based on a secular notion of incorporation.[23] On the other, the growing presence and public articulation of minority religions, particularly of Islam, has increasingly challenged this secular cultural integration mode, and as a reaction has generated modes of cultural integration including also the status of minority religions. The general direction, here, is to grant the minority religions the same rights as those of the Christian majority religions but to impose the predominant institutional relations between the nation-state and majority churches also on the minority religions. The vaguely emerging components of European citizenship[24] are based on these converging aspects of national citizenship and cultural integration modes without intervening into national immigration and citizenship policies. Within these limits, however, European citizenship attempts to strengthen minorities against particularistic nationalist traditions in the member states and thus also the cultural and religious rights of minorities against the predominant secular-religious regime on the national level.

In the context of the EU eastern enlargement, it has become obvious that the European multi-level cultural integration mode regarding the integration of minority religions faces problems not only in western

---

22 Koenig, M., "Europeanising the Governance of Religious Diversity", *op. cit.*

23 Kymlicka, W., *Multi-cultural Citizenship. A Liberal Theory of Minority Rights*, Oxford, Clarendon Press, 1995.

24 Eder, K. and Giesen, B. (eds.), *European Citizenship*, Oxford, Oxford University Press, 2002; Soysal, Y., *Limits of Citizenship. Migrants and Postnational Membership in Europe*, Chicago, Chicago University Press, 1994.

European countries but even more so in the east-central and south-eastern European new member states and candidates with different types of religious governance and citizenship regimes.[25] In Western Europe, as the original core of the European cultural integration mode, there are three major types of national citizenship regimes linked to the predominant type of religion and religious governance.[26] Firstly, Protestant countries with differing degrees of state-church establishment and religious pluralism prioritise forms of multi-cultural citizenship – so in Great Britain and the Scandinavian countries. Secondly, Catholic countries with differing degrees of state-church separation combine state-church cooperation with a preferential position of the majority Catholic Church *vis-à-vis* other religions and a hierarchical form of citizenship – so in most Roman-Latin countries. Thirdly, mixed countries with a dualism of Catholic and Protestant churches are characterised by forms of corporatist-hierarchical citizenship and other religions – as in The Netherlands, Switzerland, and Germany. In all these cases, there are still tensions and conflicts between the European mode of cultural integration and religious governance and the widespread hierarchical-discriminatory relations between majority and minority religions on the national levels.

In Eastern Europe, by contrast, citizenship regimes and religious governance are still marked by past imperial domination and enduring peripheral dependence. The historical legacies are the intimate post-communist connection between predominant religion and majority nationalism as well as the close cooperation and link between state and majority church. They combine with the discrimination of historical minorities and preferential treatment of the predominant church against ethnic minorities and minority religions.[27] On this historical basis, the sudden influx of immigrant ethnic minorities is met with widespread fear of national disintegration and religious estrangement. Accordingly, the tensions and conflicts with European cultural integration and religious governance exported through the eastward enlargement have been rather high. On the one hand, the EU, through the mechanism of accession negotiations, has tried to weaken the traditional conflicts of ethnic-national relations and support the institutionalisation of citizenship

---

[25] Kymlicka, W. and Opalski, M. (eds.), *Can Liberal Pluralism Be Exported? Western Political Theory and Ethnic Relations in Eastern Europe*, Oxford, Oxford University Press, 2001.

[26] Koenig, M., "Staatsbürgerschaft und religiöse Pluralität in post-nationalen Konstellationen. Zum institutionellen Wandel europäischer Religionspolitik am Beispiel muslimischer Immigranten in Großbritannien, Frankreich und Europa", PhD dissertation, Marburg, Philipps-Universität, April 2003.

[27] Spohn, W. and Triandafyllidou, A., *Europeanisation, National Identities and Migration, op. cit.*

regimes for the growing immigration populations. On the other, it has accepted the many central and eastern European national regimes of citizenship and religious governance. Here, regarding the dominant religion, four main types can be distinguished. The few Protestant Baltic countries have incorporated with hesitations and limitations the (former imperial) Russian and mostly Orthodox ethnic minority. The numerous Catholic countries are now moving, though slowly and reluctantly, to a less discriminatory treatment of ethnic minorities and minority religions. The few Christian Orthodox countries with stronger links between state, majority nation and Orthodox religion are even more hesitant in this regard. Finally, also in Turkey, the secular regime with state-church separation and the placing of religion in the private sphere, goes hand in hand with privileging majority nationalism and discriminating against ethnic minorities as well as the preferential treatment of Islam against other minority religions.

European Enlargement, Religious and Civilisational Boundaries

The third major reason for the growing role of religion in changing the structural and cultural pluralism of the European civilisation is the process of EU enlargement.[28] Emerging after the collapse of communism with the aim to unify the whole of Europe by incorporating the central and eastern European post-communist countries and with it to finalise the territorial-political *Gestalt* of the EU, enlargement has *per se* raised controversial issues about the definition of Europe, European identity and related boundary constructions of Europe.[29] These controversial issues concentrate on the question of the relationship between the boundaries of European civilisation and the European integration project. On the one hand, it is possible to define, on the basis of the historical, cultural and institutional foundations of Europe, a geographically circumscribed European culture area that basically defines the boundaries of any politically legitimate European integration framework. Europe in this sense includes European Russia and Ukraine as well as the European parts of the Caucasus and Turkey. On the other, it is dependent on contemporary geopolitical power relations between the EU member states, European non-members and other nation-states from adjacent civilisations. Both the cultural and geopolitical dimensions determine whether or not and to which extent a congruency between the

---

[28] Mair, P. and Zielonka, J. (eds.), *The Enlarged European Union. Diversity and Adaptation*, London, Frank Cass, 2002; Zielonka, J. (ed.), *Europe Unbound*, London, Routledge, 2001.

[29] Eder, K. and Spohn, W. (eds.), European Identity and Collective Memory. The Cultural Effects on European Integration and Enlargement, Aldshot, Ashgate, 2005.

European civilisation as a European geographical culture area and the European integration project as a specific transnational, political, legal and economic institutional framework will be reached. So, for instance, Russia is not considered as a potential member of the EU, although it belongs to the culturally defined "House of Europe" because it asserts itself as a primarily Eurasian civilisational construction. Turkey belongs to the non-European Islamic civilisation, but thanks to its secular European self-definition, it is regarded at least in principle as a legitimate future member state. In other words, the enlargement of Europeanisation to the East depends, on the basis of the historical and cultural foundations of the European civilisation, on contemporary civilisational self-definitions as well as intra- and inter-civilisational boundary constructions.[30]

In this civilisational and inter-civilisational context, the process of eastward enlargement of the EU has materialised in the accession of eight central-eastern and two southern European countries. It has recently included also Bulgaria and Romania, and foresees the incorporation of some further Balkan states, whereas the inclusion of Turkey, though a candidate, is since the failure of the French and Dutch referendums on the Constitutional Treaty, increasingly contested.[31] The emerging alternative is an associated neighbourhood status that includes special preferences and rights but no full membership and corresponding duties. This associated neighbourhood status is envisioned for most eastern European non-member states such as Ukraine and the Caucasus, but it may also apply to Turkey if the accession negotiations eventually fail.[32] Given this situation, it is very likely that the eastern and southeastern enlargement of the EU will encompass only parts of the broader defined European civilisation.

The reasons for this narrower definition of an enlarged Europe as compared to the boundaries of the European civilisation are political-economic and legal-administrative as well as cultural and religious. The EU and its representatives in managing and negotiating the eastward enlargement within the framework of the Copenhagen criteria have primarily emphasised political, legal, economic and administrative reasons for negotiating and offering EU membership. The successful accession depended primarily on the fourfold guarantees of a stable democratic polity including protection of minorities, a functioning market economy, the administrative implementation capacity as well as

---

[30]   Delanty, G., *The Invention of Europe*, London, Routledge, 1995; Delanty, G., *Rethinking Europeanisation*, London, Routledge, 2005.

[31]   Beichelt, T., *Die Europäische Union nach der Osterweiterung*, Wiesbaden, Verlag für Sozialwissenschaften, 2004.

[32]   Verheugen, G., *Europa in der Krise*, Köln, Kiepenheuer&Witsch, 2005.

the capability to fulfil the obligations of the *acquis communautaire*. In addition, the eastward enlargement also demands the adjustment of the EU institutions to the considerably enlarged number of members. All these criteria are *prima facie* secular ones, but underneath cultural as well as religious criteria in the definition of Europe, its boundaries and the cultural legitimacy of inclusion are also at work. Thus, the eastward enlargement has focused primarily on central-eastern European countries within the orbits of Latin-Christianity. Then, it extended to two other Orthodox countries, in addition to Greece, but the inclusion of Turkey became more contested. This reveals that the historical core definition of Europe as a Latin-Christian civilisation still matters, that its relation to eastern Christianity is still problematic and that the oppositional-conflictive relation to the Islamic civilisation gains a new salience.[33]

In sum, in the expansion of the transnational European regime and its cultural integration mode to the eastern space of the European civilisation in the context of currently intensifying globalisation processes, the reconstruction of particularly three intra- and inter-civilisation cleavages are at work. Firstly, under the growing pressure to define a European identity not only in secular but also in cultural terms and with it to give the European cultural integration mode a moral and institutional *Gestalt*, two religious-cultural cleavages within western Latin Christianity are losing ground. On the one hand, the tendency to bridge the confessional divide between Catholicism and Protestantism has become stronger. On both sides, on the transnational as well as at the national levels, there are increasing attempts to overcome or relativise the traditional theological, symbolic and ritualised differences between the two confessions. On the other, there is a strong tendency to overcome or relativise also the clerical/anti-clerical or secularist/religious divide. Both forms of western European cultural integration contest but also have a transformative effect, in the context of the eastward enlargement, on the east-central European parts of Latin Christianity.

Secondly, a parallel bridging of the rift between western and eastern Christianity is much more ambivalent. The traditional cultural superiority feelings of Latin Christianity, enhanced by European Enlightenment, are still at work. In modern times, Orthodox Christianity had been historically viewed not only as a deviating-inferior but also as a less enlightened and more authoritarian creed.[34] This image was renewed

[33] Byrnes, T., *Transnational Catholicism in Postcommunist Europe*, Lanham, Rowman &Littlefield, 2001; Byrnes, T. and Katzenstein, P. (eds.), *Religion in an Expanding Europe*, Cambridge, Cambridge University Press, 2004; Siedentop, L., *op. cit.*

[34] Neumann, I., *The Uses of the Other: The "East"' in European Identity Formation*, Minneapolis, Minnesota University Press, 1998; Wolf, L., *The Invention of Eastern*

during communist times, emphasising the accommodating arrangements between the communist-secularist regimes and the Orthodox churches in contrast to the western-Christian and particularly Catholic resistance to communist rule. In the post-communist present, Eastern Europe is seen as a secularised space and thus inviting for renewed Catholic and Protestant re-Evangelisation efforts. Conversely, the Orthodox Churches attempted, though only partially successfully, to re-establish themselves as state churches in the caesaro-papist tradition and restrict the missionary efforts of Catholicism and Protestant evangelism. Accordingly, the eastward enlargement is seen as an imperialist expansion of Latin Christianity and western secularism. At the same time, however, in tune with the expansion of the European cultural integration mode, there are some attempts to bridge the traditional divide with western Christianity as well as the still virulent rift between post-communist secularism and the revival of religion in more cooperative-ecumenical ways.

Thirdly, there are two combined reasons for the increasing inter-civilisational cleavage between Christianity and Islam, crystallising in a growing ambiguity regarding the possible accession of Turkey to the EU. On the one hand, the more cooperative-ecumenical attitudes between the western Christian churches and the state and the growing conflicts with political Islam and the claims of immigrant Muslims are supporting also a stronger sentiment against the inclusion of Turkey, seen as a secular-authoritarian state under siege by a mobilising Islam. On the other hand, the revival of eastern Christianity and its impact on revitalised forms of religious nationalism in post-communist central and eastern Europe also strengthens traditional anti-Islamic and anti-Turkish attitudes. Conversely, also in Turkey, the pro-European, pro-accession orientations in its secularist as well as religious-reformist parts are increasingly challenged by nationalistic, Islamic and fundamentalist currents, groups and parties.[35]

Conclusion

There are three interrelated dimensions in which the revitalisation of religion in the contemporary globalisation phase challenges the institutionalised European mode of cultural integration and religious governance and its expansion towards the East. Firstly, the EU eastward enlargement has included and is confronted with differing types of

---

Europe, Stanford, Stanford University Press, 1994; Wolf, L., *The Enlightenment and the Orthodox World: Western Perspectives on The Orthodox Church in Eastern Europe*, Athens, Institute for Neohellenic Research, 2001.

[35] Yavuz, H., *Islamic Political Identity in Turkey, op. cit.*; Zürcher, E. and Linden, H.v.D. (eds.), *The European Union, Turkey and Islam*, Amsterdam, Amsterdam University Press, 2004.

religion and secularisation, state-church relations, religious governance and cultural integration as well as political cultures and collective identities. Secondly, the growing impact of immigrants with different religious backgrounds, particularly, but not solely, from Islamic countries, transform European societies in a more multi-cultural and pluri-religious direction. Thirdly, globalisation in its various economic, political and cultural forms intensifies the interactions between civilisations and religions, enhances the intra- and inter-civilisational boundary constructions within and without European civilisation and thus impinges on the conflictive dynamics of the EU eastward enlargement.

On a cultural integration continuum from "more inclusive to more exclusive" policy strategies, there are two principal ways to respond to these challenges. On the one hand, a more exclusive strategy attempts to strengthen the cultural-secularist integration mode. Here, European cultural integration and collective identity are primarily centred on the received secular-humanist core by limiting religious diversity *vis-à-vis* immigrants and Turkey. This strategy can combine with a stronger emphasis of the western Christian core of Europe and its ecumenical extension to central and eastern European countries. On the other, a more inclusive strategy would attempt to strengthen the multi-religious and cross-civilisational ecumenical bases of the European cultural integration mode. Here, a conscious effort would be made to encourage a form of multicultural citizenship and religious pluralism inside European societies and, as a corollary, to take in Turkey as a crucial multi-religious and multi-cultural pillar of European cultural integration and collective identity.

The first more exclusive path is currently the main tendency. Yet, it might result in a continuing exclusion of Muslim immigrants inside European societies and their potentially growing tendency towards a fundamentalist mobilisation. The second more inclusive path seems to be rather utopian or romantic and currently unrealistic. However, even if the present EU *Realpolitik* would result in reducing Turkey to the status of a "privileged partnership", the more inclusive strategy would strengthen a more pluralistic integration of Muslim populations inside European societies and, at the same time, contribute to a stronger tolerance and pluralisation in Turkish politics and society, both with respect to its ethnic and religious minorities and with potential repercussions on the religious and political conflict zones in the Near East and northern Africa. This cosmopolitan perspective on Europe and European integration however cannot be formulated in secularist terms but would have to develop a secular and ecumenical framework of religious pluralism.[36]

---

[36] Beck U. and Grande, E., *Das kosmopolitische Europa*, Frankfurt/M., Suhrkamp, 2004; Meyer, T., *Die Identität Europas*, Frankfurt/M., Suhrkamp, 2004.

CHAPTER 5

Citizenship and Migration within the European Research Area

The Italian Example

Sonia MORANO-FOADI

Introduction

The European Union (EU) has the stated policy objective of boosting research so that the aim of the Lisbon strategy to make Europe the most competitive place in the world by 2010 can be fulfilled.[1] This objective, the so-called "competitiveness target", has been repeatedly evoked in the Lisbon agenda and in subsequent measures. In order to achieve such a goal, member states are required to enhance their economies, and equally the EU needs to promote balanced growth within its internal borders. The European Research Area (ERA), a space of research with virtually no barriers for scientists on the move within the EU, was created as a vehicle for the achievement of the "competitiveness target". The EU has focused its attention on promoting excellence by encouraging and funding clusters, which can potentially attract the best talents in Europe. This so-called "clustering policy" aims at developing science in regional areas with a high concentration "of agglomerations where interlinkages between the organizations located in proximity to each other exist".[2] The interlinkages are considered important factors in attaining competitiveness and innovation. Research and Development (R&D) clusters "are generally built on inter-organisational networks, such as inter-firm alliances and university/industry links, and are often supported by regional economic development agencies".[3]

Within the EU, significant science clusters are mainly based in northern European cities and areas, such as Munich, Paris, Stockholm-

---

[1] European Council, *Presidency Conclusions*, Lisbon European Summit, Document No. 100/1/00, 23-24 March 2000.

[2] Millard, D., "The Impact of Clustering on Scientific Mobility – A Case Study of the UK", *Innovation: The European Journal of Social Science Research, Special Issue, Scientific Mobility in the European Research Area: Promoting Balanced Growth*, Vol. 18, No. 3, 2005, p. 346.

[3] Millard, D., *op. cit.*, pp. 346 and ff.

Uppsala, Oxford and Cambridge.[4] Scholars have observed the close link between the migration of highly skilled academics and workers and uneven regional development.[5] It would thus appear that EU clustering policy works against balanced growth in Europe. Empirical research shows that researchers "are apparently not only attracted to the European regions which invest most heavily in R&D, or those where the major R&D clusters are located. Prestige and networks are particularly important factors in the location decision".[6]

In a context of intra-community migration, donor member states, which invest less in R&D, are deprived of their elite of intellectuals who contribute to the progress of their nations. The Commission acknowledges such a risk. It reports that

> within the Union regional cohesion will be pursued by taking due account of the necessity for less developed regions to attract researchers in order to allow for their own R&D-driven, long-term development strategies and to avoid that less-developed regions suffer from increased competition for highly qualified researchers.[7]

Although the problem of internal brain drain in the logic of balanced growth is affirmed and economic theories focus on the impact of long-term and permanent migration on the host and home states,[8] the EU has failed to introduce effective policies in order to avoid unbalanced internal growth. It has limited its intervention to statistical analysis and collation of data collected by each member state. Issues such as internal brain drain have not been considered on the European agenda, as the EU aims to strengthen its position on the world stage as a bloc in competition with the US and Japan. Moreover, the ERA aims to create an area which could attract talent from abroad and where national research policies are coordinated and conform to the European research policy. In practice, the ERA management is left mainly under the responsibility of the member states. As research is a policy area where both the Community and member states have competence to act, the principle of subsidi-

---

4   Millard, D., *op. cit.*, p. 342.

5   Mahroum, S., "Scientists and global spaces", *Technology in Society*, Vol. 22, 2000, pp. 513-522; Meyer, J.B. *et al.*, "Scientific Nomadism and the New Geopolitics of Knowledge", *International Social Science Journal*, Vol. 168, 2001, pp. 309-321; Williams, A.M. *et al.*, "International Labour Mobility and Uneven Regional Development in Europe: Human Capital, Knowledge and Entrepreneurship", *European Urban and Regional Studies*, Vol. 11, No. 1, 2004, pp. 27-46.

6   Millard, D., *op. cit.*, 2005, p. 342.

7   European Commission, *A Mobility Strategy for the European Research Area*, COM(2001) 331 Final, Brussels, 20 June 2001.

8   Lowell, B.L. and Findlay, A., *Migration of Highly Skilled Persons from Developing Countries: Impact and Policy Responses*, Geneva, International Labour Office, 2002.

arity plays a role in determining which actor has competence. To overcome the lack of action of certain national governments in the research sector and given the objective of balanced growth within the EU, the balance should shift in favour of the transnational level (Community intervention).

Highly skilled migration can have very negative consequences for the donor country if there is no return. This is true for European and non-European donor countries alike. Still the European governance perseveres in paying particular attention to brain drain from third countries. As stated by the Commission "making Europe more attractive for researchers, special attention needs to be paid to prevent new forms of 'brain drain' from third countries with less developed research capacity [...] The present strategy should strengthen and develop a symbiotic collaboration with these countries, thus encouraging them to build up their own research capacity".[9]

Within the EU, balanced-growth logic is altered by unbalanced migration fluxes. Clear negative knock-out effects are present when there is highly skilled out-migration with no return and no highly skilled in-migration. Some donor states, such as Italy, to cite one example, either attract low-skilled migrants or highly skilled migrants from third states who are not in a position to find a proper job in their field.[10] Consequently this has contributed to the country's competitiveness loss. In Italy a number of problems in relation to the academic system defined as anachronistic and based on a feudal logic contribute to the brain drain.[11] Whilst in theory the system of academic appointments based on public competitions (*concorsi*) is open to everybody, in reality outcomes are often known in advance. Obviously, this does not always mean that those who get the job are not worthy;[12] but the problems experienced in the Italian academic environment are a clear obstacle for scientists who wish to move to Italy. The question here is how to limit the effect of the Italian brain drain and it is connected to the types of conflicting interests to be protected. These are the will of EU scientists to move and return home, of the EU to be seen as a coherent organization and the interests

---

[9]   European Commission, A Mobility Strategy for the European Research Area, *op. cit.*

[10] In 2006 the ISTAT produced statistics of foreign nationals employed in Italy per economic sector. For further details see http://www.istat.it/salastampa/comunicati/non_calendario/20060327_01/

[11] Hellemans, A., "Beating the European Brain Drain", Nature, 22 November 2001, pp. 1-2; Di Giorgio, "Cervelli in fuga negli USA. La UE parte al contrattacco", La Repubblica, 16 January 2004.

[12] Jappelli, T., "L'immobilità dei docenti universitari", 10 September 2002, http://www.lavoce.info/articoli/pagina97.html, accessed 30 October 2008.

of the individual member states. The introduction of European citizenship has not been helpful for return migration.

This chapter is divided into three main sections. Firstly, the EU governance in relation to the ERA is questioned. In particular, the Lisbon objective of competitiveness, focusing specifically on science, and uneven regional development are explored. The extent to which the EU clustering policy feeds unbalanced growth and internal brain drain as opposed to "brain circulation" is also considered. The second section outlines the conceptual bases of EU citizenship relevant to the discussion and argues that EU citizenship in its current conception does not assist in maintaining balanced growth. The last section, based on the findings of empirical research,[13] considers the link between EU citizenship and return migration, looking at a case study of Italy.

Economic Balanced Growth versus Uneven Migration Fluxes within the ERA

In the last few years the ERA has been transformed from a theoretical concept to a practical policy embodying many different dimensions. It was reinforced in 2000 by the Lisbon European Council which re-launched European competitiveness and identified research as a key factor in business competitiveness, employment and quality of life.[14] To achieve competitiveness the Lisbon conclusions encouraged benchmarking of national R&D policies through an Open Method of Coordination (OMC).[15] In 2005, the Lisbon strategy was revamped with the aim of setting policies to deliver growth and employment. The strategy was not making enough progress toward the competitiveness goal.[16] Since the ERA's creation, a new policy context has emerged, to face economic, social and environmental challenges such as rising unemployment, an ageing population and global warming. Although the policy context has evolved, the ERA core objectives are still the same. Initially, its aim was to find ways to improve the efficiency and effectiveness of fragmented research efforts and systems in Europe, and to get a better return on investment. Since then, the focus has encompassed "the need for more public and private investment in research", and "the necessity for im-

---

[13] This chapter is based on a completed research project entitled "Mobility and Excellence in the European Research Area" (the MOBEX Project) funded under the ESRC's Science in Society Programme Project, Reference: RES-151-25-00, http://www.sci-soc.net/SciSoc/Projects/Economics/Mobility+and+excellence+in+scientific+labour+markets.htm, accessed 30 October 2008.

[14] European Council, Presidency Conclusions, 2000, *op. cit.*

[15] *Ibid.*

[16] *Council Conclusions*, Document 7619/1/05 REV1, 22 and 23 March 2005, pp. 2 and ff.

proving coherence and synergies between research and other EU policies in order to achieve the renewed Lisbon strategy".[17]

Within the ERA there is still a different spectrum of research policy and the R&D market is heterogeneous. Traditionally, southern European countries under-invested in research, attracted fewer scientists from abroad, and failed to secure permanent positions for those who are in science. This is due to a number of factors such as poor research infrastructures, poor career perspectives, both in the private sector and in the public sector, along with poor social security benefits. Most researchers derive their support from grants for a long period of time, due to scarcity of jobs in science. The lack of research positions compels researchers to move abroad. Industrial research is at its embryonic stage and private companies under-invest in the research and development sector. In Italy, Spain and Portugal, there is a "feudal-like system" where individual professors build up their respective research groups and secure research contracts for those who work within the group.[18] Under this model, researchers see few, if any, prospects of returning to their own countries.

Those who have experienced mobility often speak of a feeling of having "fallen out of the system" due to difficulties on their return or during the (re)integration phase. Southern European member states are not the only ones to suffer from this particular problem. Eastern European countries are also known to exhibit these same difficulties, although this is mainly due to the scarcity of funding available and additional problems specific to these member states.[19]

Central and northern European countries witness greater incoming mobility flows due to the large number of fixed-term contracts and post-doctoral fellowships available. The UK, for example, has been described as a "post-doc paradise".[20]

In terms of investment in R&D, there is a marked North/South divide, with the Nordic countries, notably Sweden and Finland, leading in terms of R&D intensity, followed by other northern European countries,

---

[17] European Commission, Staff Working Document Accompanying the Green Paper "The European Research Area: New Perspectives", COM(2007)161 Brussels, 4.4.2007 SEC(2007) 412/2, p. 8.

[18] Morano-Foadi, S., "Scientific Mobility, Career Progression, and Excellence in the European Research Area", *International Migration*, Vol. 43, No. 5, 2005, pp. 133-162.

[19] Gill, B. and Ackers, L., *Researchers in the European Research Area*, James Martin Institute Working Paper, No. 7, 2007, pp. 3 and ff.

[20] Balter, M., "Europeans Who Do Postdocs Abroad Face Re-entry Problems", *Science Magazine*, Vol. 285, No. 5433, 1999, pp. 1524-1526.

with the four southern European countries at the bottom of the "investment league".[21]

As for the private sector, the EU still lags behind the US and Japan in terms of business R&D spending. Regarding overall performance of the European research system, there is still much to do. Not much progress has been made towards the EU R&D investment target of 3% of Gross Domestic Product (GDP) (two thirds of which is to come from private sources) since this objective was set in 2002. The deficit in R&D activity in the EU compared to that of the US has not been reduced – on the contrary – and current trends suggest that China will catch up with the EU-27 by 2009, in terms of its share of GDP devoted to R&D.[22]

The problem lies in the fact that the 3% objective set in the Lisbon and Barcelona agendas was based on a soft law tool, i.e. the OMC. This instrument involves an exchange of information and best practice; fixing European guidelines and translating them into national and regional policies; establishing indicators and benchmarks; periodic monitoring, evaluation and peer review organised as mutual learning processes.[23] Its aim is to ensure satisfactory progress in policy areas which are primarily within member states' competence. Although, in principle, the OMC tool would assist in the complex research and innovation field, perhaps a more regulative system would be more suited to southern and eastern European states.[24] As the core of the strategy is cooperation and exchange of best practice among member states and their commitment to the Lisbon agenda is essential for the achievement of the competitiveness target, the Lisbon strategy has not had a very strong impact as it is based on voluntary and non-coercive tools.

Regarding the competitiveness concept, there is no single definition of competitiveness at the European level, as it is primarily related to selected key indicators. The *European Competitiveness Report 2006* refers to competitiveness as "a sustained rise in the standards of living of a nation or region and a level of involuntary unemployment as low as possible". By contrast, in an industrial sector, the concept is related to

---

[21] Millard, D., *op. cit.*, p. 342.

[22] European Commission, Staff Working Document on "The European Research Area", *op. cit.*

[23] CREST Expert Group, Encourage the Reform of Public Research Centres and Universities, in Particular to Promote Transfer of Knowledge to Society and Industry, Final Report presented to CREST, 6 March 2006.

[24] For more details on this point see Morano-Foadi, S., "The Missing Piece of the Lisbon Jigsaw: Is the Open Method of Coordination Effective in Relation to the European Research Area?", *European Law Journal*, Vol. 14, No. 5, September 2008, pp. 635-654.

"maintaining and improving its [sector's] position in the global market".[25]

These definitions evoke a commitment towards balanced growth in the European area by the EU. Article 3(3) of the Lisbon Treaty on the European Union reinforces the EU commitment to "the sustainable development of Europe based on *balanced economic growth* and price stability, a highly competitive social market economy, aiming at full employment and social progress, and a high level of protection and improvement of the quality of the environment.[26] The article then emphasises the need to "promote scientific and technological advance" which is also one of the priority actions outlined in the reform agenda proposed by the Spring European Council of 2006.

In particular, the ERA project highlights the importance of the clustering and the concentration of scientific expertise in Centres of Excellence as the basis for competitiveness.

Whatever the accepted definition of competitiveness is, mobility and skills balance are both essential to scientific growth and competitiveness. The debate on whether regional specialisation is more conducive to innovation and growth still shows no immediate signs of abating in the literature.[27] Despite that, it can be argued that the EU strategy of regional specialisation and scientific clustering has amplified the problem of the uneven nature of scientific personnel flows within the ERA. These ERA policies are in conflict with the commitment to "balanced growth", in that they encourage the relocation of scientists to Centres of Excellence (typically located in the economically stronger regions) thus potentially reducing the ability of weaker regions to regenerate.

Whilst the circulation of talent is considered positive for competitiveness and scientific excellence, problems arise when the rates of return are low and also when the country or region fails to attract scientific talent from outside. In Europe, there is a need to coordinate science and migration policies at European and member state level to enhance the attractiveness of European host countries and facilitate the return of scientists to their home nations. The European Commission should strengthen its approach toward return migration and adopt measures to encourage intra-community mobility. There are still a number of limitations in most of the return grants available at EU level. Eligible candi-

---

[25] European Commission, *European Competitiveness Report 2006*, COM(2006) 697 final.

[26] See Fredman, S., "Transformation or Dilution: Fundamental Rights in the EU Social Space", *European Law Journal*, Vol. 12, No. 1, 2006, pp. 41-60.

[27] European Commission, *European Competitiveness Report 2003*, SEC(2003) 1299, Brussels, 12 November 2003, p. 143.

dates are those who benefited from an EU grant and very limited fund-ing is available.[28] At present, nothing is available for scientists who leave their country without EU funding.

In addition to regional disparities, there is concern around the issue of inequality in terms of individual opportunity. At the individual level, the emphasis on mobility potentially generates differential opportunity, as more "footloose" scientists are able to respond to these challenges whilst others, perhaps with family or caring commitments, are less able to do so.[29] Although this is an important issue, as certain groups of scientists might be disadvantaged and their ability to progress might be restricted, this topic is not within the scope of this chapter.

Citizenship: What Implications for Highly Skilled Migrants?

The corollary of EU clustering policy is constituted by the "expecta-tion of mobility" in science careers, which is country and discipline specific. "Brain circulation" is one of the milestones of the ERA as scientists are required to visit laboratories and research groups for skill acquisition and knowledge transfer.

Ideally, EU scientists would have the right to circulate freely within the ERA. The right to free movement has been described as "the core and the origin of Union citizenship. Mobility is the central element around which other rights crystallise".[30] Thus citizenship and migration are strictly connected. This means that almost all of the rights conferred by EU citizenship are contingent on residence in another member state other than the one of one's own nationality.

Citizenship is a topic that has attracted increased attention in recent years. As an integral part of the debate on European citizenship, scholars have devoted much effort to the definition of citizenship in general and citizenship in Europe in particular. The term citizenship has been rooted in a rich variety of contexts and has taken various aspects.

---

[28] European Commission, *FP7 – Tomorrow's Answers Start Today, Seventh Frame-work Programme*, http://register.consilium.europa.eu/doc:12032/06.

[29] Stalford, H., "Parenting, Care and Mobility in the EU. Issues Facing Migrant Scientists", *Innovation: The European Journal of Social Science Research*, Special Issue, Scientific Mobility in the European Research Area: Promoting Balanced Growth, Vol. 18, No. 3, 2005, pp. 361-380.

[30] D'Oliviera, J., "Union citizenship: pie in the sky?" in A. Rosas and E. Antola (eds.), *A Citizen's Europe: in Search of a New Order*, London, Sage, 1995, p. 65.

In 1974, Raymond Aron suggested that "there are no such animals as European citizens".[31] This idea arose from a concept of citizenship that was strictly linked to the notion of the nation-state. The nation has generated the ancient concept of citizenship, which described rights and duties to belong to a social entity.

In theory, all European citizens should have the same rights, enjoy the same opportunities and be subject to the same obligations. However, the concept of European citizenship that has been proposed is not similar to the concept of national citizenship.

Citizenship of the Union is more political rhetoric than legal and social reality.[32] Although the traditional concept of citizenship guarantees equality, implying a range of rights for everybody,[33] the EU citizenship concept, stated in Article 17 EC, is relevant only if linked with migration. This is because the concept of EU citizenship does not cover national or internal situations that do not have links with Community law.[34] The scope of the article is limited to situations that trigger recourse to Community law. In order to apply the free movement provisions, a person has to migrate between two member states. Even in a migration context, there is a hierarchy of social status deriving from a person's economic contribution and family status. "Citizenship of the Union", as suggested by Article 17 of the Treaty establishing the European Community, does not substitute national citizenship but it does "complement" it. The details relating to the right to free movement have been regulated by secondary legislation that has added "meat to the bones" of the Treaty. This legislation refers specifically to migrant workers to overcome difficulties and financial and social obstacles which have hindered their free movement. In a migration context, at the apex of the hierarchy stands the Community worker or the self-employed person and his/her family. This includes the children and relatives in the ascending line of Community workers and his/her spouse or partner. Scientists and highly skilled workers are considered "top class citizens" as they represent a gain for the host state.

The European Court of Justice (ECJ) jurisprudence and Directive 2004/38/EC have contributed towards the achievement of a full right to

---

[31] Aron, R., "Is Multinational Citizenship Possible?", *Social Research*, Vol. 41, No. 4, 1974, pp. 638-656.

[32] Cleinmay, M., "Citizens Arise? Europe and Social Citizenship" in M. Kleinman, *A European Welfare State?*, Houndmills, Palgrave, 2002, p. 191.

[33] Davies, G., "Services, Citizenship, and the Country of Origin", *Mitchell Working Paper*, Edinburgh Europa Centre, 2007, p. 2.

[34] Craig, P. and De Burca, G., *EU Law: Text, Cases and Materials*, 4th edition, Oxford, Oxford University Press, 2007, p. 847.

move throughout the EU for each EU citizen.[35] The Directive codifies in a single instrument the complex legislative corpus and the rich case law on free movement and residence.[36] This legal instrument has made these rights clearer and more transparent for Union citizens and for national administrations. The directive creates a single legal regime for free movement and residence within the context of citizenship of the Union while maintaining the acquired rights of workers. It also facilitates the exercise of the right of residence by simplifying conditions and formalities, creating a permanent right of residence and reinforcing the rights of family members.

In the Fourth Report on Citizenship (2001-2004) the Commission affirms that:

> the introduction of this new directive marks a major step forward in terms of freedom of movement and residence in relation to the existing situation in line with the expectations expressed by citizens. It will also encourage mobility of Union citizens across the European Union, which in return will have a positive impact on the competitiveness and growth of European economies.[37]

It is still too early to comment on the impact of this directive on EU citizens, as it only entered into force in April 2006. However, the main problem in relation to highly skilled migrants is not in terms of diminished rights in another EU country. These should virtually be the same for both national and European workers. The difficulty primarily relates to the possibility of return to the home country after a period spent in another member state. The implications for returnees are related to the complexity of the academic or research systems of their home country. Despite progress made to remove obstacles to mobility, no intrusions into internal policy areas such as those in relation to employment, healthcare or education are possible. EU law generally protects migrant workers and their families, in the sense that it guarantees no discrimination with nationals in the host country. Although free movement and citizenship provisions apply to returnees, they do not impact on policy areas that are under the domestic domain. Most of the ECJ jurisprudence has tried to balance the rights of the individual to a family life and concerns of the member states over immigration in relation to third country nationals as opposed to EU citizens. An example is the Singh

---

[35] Carrera, S., "What Does Free Movement Mean in Theory and Practice in an Enlarged EU?", *European Law Journal*, Vol. 11, No. 6, 2005, pp. 699-721.

[36] The Directive amends Regulation (EEC) No. 1612/68 on freedom of movement for workers and repeals nine directives. It also replaces Commission Regulation (EEC) No. 1251/70.

[37] European Commission, *Fourth Report on Citizenship of the Union (1 May 2001 – 30 April 2004)*, COM(2004) 695 final, Brussels, 26 October 2004.

case,[38] which demonstrates that EU migrant workers can rely on at least some rights for their spouses and families against their home member state when they return. The present case regards an Indian citizen (Mr Surinder Singh) who had married an English national in 1982 and moved with her to Germany. In 1985 he returned to the UK to open a business. In 1988 their marriage broke down. The UK authorities wanted to deport him but the ECJ held that on his return to Britain, Singh was entitled to claim his rights as a spouse under EC law.

However, case law in this area has developed piecemeal, and there is a need for secondary legislation to address "the tensions in this area and consequent difficulties in identifying the proper boundary to workers' rights".[39]

The main problem, as far as Italian scientific migration is concerned, has less to do with the proper boundaries to workers' rights and more with the impact of internal policies of member states, such as, for example, the organization of the academic system.

While the EU is promoting the idea of mobility and circulation of talents to strengthen the ERA in pushing toward a European science model, it is failing to provide a mechanism that allows EU highly-skilled citizens to return to their country of origin. Differences in national research markets push scientists to migrate and the lack of return policies often forces them to follow a pattern of consecutive moves within the ERA or outside Europe. EU funding foresees return schemes for scientists who have been awarded an EU mobility grant. However, these EU return grants are highly competitive and limited in number. Consequently migrant scientists have to apply for national return fellowships (if available).

Moreover, those scientists who did not apply or are not granted EU funding for their research in a country other than their own cannot rely upon EU return grants. The EU citizenship concept is of little help in this respect as it fails to overcome internal policy areas regulated by national law. Member states are free to introduce return policies to call back their highly skilled migrants and no centralised policy is envisaged to preserve balanced growth within the European Union.

---

[38] R v. Immigration Appeal Tribunal, *ex parte* Secretary of State for the Home Department (case C-370/90).

[39] Steiner, J. *et al.*, *EU Law*, 9th edition, Oxford, Oxford University Press, 2006, p. 419.

The Need for a Strict Return Policy
to Reverse the Brain Drain from Italy

The Italian political agenda refers to its scientific diaspora as a permanent loss of brains rather than an outflow having temporary implications. Newspapers, policy makers and academics in Italy have adopted the expression "brain drain" (*fuga di cervelli*) as coined by the Royal Society to describe the outflow of scientists and engineers to the US and Canada in the 1950s and early 1960s.[40] This contradicts what recent research seems to suggest, particularly in the EU context. Some scholars support the idea that there has been a shift from "brain drain" to "brain circulation".[41] It has been argued that modern migration, "has lost some of the traditional features that led it to being characterised as a brain drain", as there are new types of mobility which are temporary, rather than permanent, multidirectional rather than unilateral and of a global nature, i.e. affecting developed, as well as developing, countries. Contrary to previous experience, modern migrants interact at a distance and maintain links with their region of origin.[42] This thesis is supported by the belief that highly skilled professionals generally do not transfer completely, as they often retain links with their country of origin, reinvest, send remittances and sometimes migrate back to their country of origin.[43] Discussions around the "brain drain" phenomenon date back to the 1960s and relate mainly to the contentious North-South debate.[44] Later on, as a result of economic recession, interest in the topic declined. Recently this topic has returned to the public agenda, because of growing attention to the so-called global knowledge-based economy. Although this controversial concept has framed discussion on the move-

---

[40] Cervantes, M. and Guellec, D., *The Brain Drain: Old Myths, New Realities*, OECD Observer, 2002, www.oecdobserver.org/news/fullstory.php/aid/673.

[41] Ackers, L., "Promoting Scientific Mobility and Balanced Growth in the European Research Area", *Innovation: The European Journal of Social Science Research*, Special Issue, Scientific Mobility in the European Research Area: Promoting Balanced Growth, Vol. 18, No. 3, 2005, pp. 301-317; Meyer, J.B., "Policy Implication of the Brain Drain's Changing Face", Science and Development Network, Policy Brief, 2003, http://www.scidev.net/en/policy-briefs/policy-implications-of-the-brain-drain-s-changing-.html, accessed 30 October 2008; Johnson, J. and Regets, M., "International Mobility of Scientists and Engineers to the US Brain Drain or Brain Circulation?", NSF Issue Brief, 1998, pp. 98-316; OECD, International Mobility of the Highly Skilled, Paris, OECD, 2002.

[42] Meyer, J.B., 2003, *op. cit.*, p. 2.

[43] Vincent-Lancrin, S., *Building Capacity through Cross-border Tertiary Education*, March 2005, p. 32.

[44] Carrington, W. and Detragiache, E., "How Extensive is the Brain Drain?", *Finance and Development*, Vol. 36, No. 2, June 1999, pp. 1-7.

ment of highly skilled professionals until early 1990,[45] the Italian media are still making extensive use of this expression. A huge number of articles have reported issues relating to the exodus of Italian scientists. Many of these focus on the fact that the researchers leave, not just to broaden their experience before continuing their career in Italy, but leave, never to return. There are limited statistics on the real extent of the phenomenon.[46] However some sources refer to about 30,000 outward bound and only about 3,000 in-coming researchers.[47] This means that significant resources are being invested in the training and education of researchers that the Italian system is then unable to retain. It is but one paradox of these movements that Italy, which is among the most industrialised countries in the world, should nonetheless suffer so heavily from "brain drain". Incidentally, this confirms Mahroum's thesis that the direction of brain drain and brain gain, unlike in previous decades, is now more varied: North-North, North-South, South-North and South-South.[48]

The discussion and conclusion in relation to Italian scientific migration is based on the findings of a research project (the MOBEX Project)[49] on the Italian-UK flows and two discipline areas, i.e. physics and life sciences. The empirical work carried out in the project consisted of fifty-two interviews conducted with Italian researchers working or having previously worked in the UK and key informants' interviews. The questions asked mainly related to the scientists' career history, family-formation and employment decision-making within households including migration and also policy issues, such as, for example, UK/Italian science strategy, scientific clustering and family-friendly policies. Return schemes, and national policies were also explored. Interviews with key informants covered many aspects of migration and employment policy, including: equal opportunities, flexible working,

---

[45] Meyer, J.B., 2003, *op. cit.*, p. 2.

[46] Becker, S., Ichino, A. and Peri, G., *How Large is the Brain Drain from Italy*, CESIFO Working Paper, No. 839, University of Munich, 2003, http://ideas.repec.org/p/ces/ceswps/_839.html, accessed 30 October 2008.

[47] http://www.rientrodeicervelli.net/, accessed 30 October 2008.

[48] Mahroum, S., "Highly Skilled Globetrotters: the International Migration of Human Capital", Institute for Prospective Technological Studies, Joint Research Centre of the European Commission, Document DSTI/STP/TIP (99)2/FINAL, Seville, OECD, http://www.oecd.org/dataoecd/35/6/2100652.pdf, accessed 3 September 2008, p. 168.

[49] See "Mobility and Excellence in the European Research Area" (the MOBEX Project) in which the author was co-applicant, funded under the ESRC's Science in Society Programme Project, Reference: RES-151-25-00, http://www.sci-soc.net/SciSoc/Projects/Economics/Mobility+and+excellence+in+scientific+labour+markets.htm, accessed 30 October 2008.

family-friendly policies, mobility schemes and policies in relation to the attraction, support, retention of migrant scientists.

Although it might be true that Italian scientific migration often begins as a temporary phenomenon, it seems evident that it often leads to a permanent move as there are very limited return policies in place. Consequently, Italy fails to benefit in any way from the experience and know-how of its small army of Italian-trained scientists working worldwide. Even more unfortunate is the fact that no serious return policy is envisaged. Scientists are constantly torn between the need to move, particularly when no employment opportunities are available in their home country, and the risk of being forced to remain abroad for good, or even obliged to follow a consecutive migration pattern. Mobility typically proves to be something of a "double-edged sword": mobility fellowships present an opportunity to leave to work in another country but they are not coupled with a secure way to return home. At best they represent a one-way ticket out of the home country. Except for the international outgoing fellowships, which foresee a compulsory return phase back to the fellows' country of residence, the return phase is not part of any of the other intra-European schemes. At the end of their grant period, scientists who are awarded Marie Curie funding (EU funding), must apply for an EU reintegration grant to return home.[50] However, the success rate is very low. In general, the interviews show that life is not so easy in a foreign country and Italian scientists are not so keen to live all their lives abroad. Even if they value their overseas experience highly, they feel they should be given the opportunity to return home at some point in their careers, should they wish to do so. Brain drain is often the unintentional result of short moves, and the true costs and benefits of working abroad only emerge over time. It is often too difficult to migrate with families and children and so the researcher prefers leaving his/her family behind, particularly if the move is temporary. In this case, the scientist requires a high level of motivation to survive in the host country. However, elements such as a patriotic sense of belonging to Italy, an attachment to their families, friends and cultural environment play a strong role for most of the researchers interviewed.

Encouraging the return of the highly skilled seems to be the most broadly accepted way to address the brain drain. Some analysts have advocated strict imposition of return at the end of fixed-term contracts,

---

[50] See CORDIS web site for more information on the Seventh Research Framework Programme, http://cordis.europa.eu/fp7/dc/index.cfm?fuseaction=UserSite.FP7 DetailsCallPage&call_id=168.

especially among the highly skilled.[51] Dustmann and Weiss question the reasons why immigrants should return and conclude that "return migration may be triggered either by higher preferences for consumption in the home country, or high purchasing power of the host country currency in the migrant's home country, or by accumulation of human capital in the host country in a learning by doing way that improves productivity back home".[52] Therefore, imposing return after every contract and even discouraging pathways to residency or citizenship may not be the optimal solution when one of the previous conditions is not fulfilled or there are no equally good employment opportunities in the home country. Moreover, imposing a return to EU migrant scientists constitutes an obstacle to mobility and as such, constitutes an infringement of EU provisions on free movement and citizenship. However, the point is that researchers working abroad should be given the chance to return to their home country at the end of their period employment.

In 2001, the Italian Government attempted to promote the return of Italian researchers and attract foreign scientists to work in Italy, through a programme called *"Rientro dei Cervelli"* (loosely translated, *brain-return*).[53] Candidates for this award had to be in an academic or scientific research post abroad for at least three years prior to making the application. Their demand needed also to be submitted by a particular university interested in hosting the candidate. Those selected as fellows then had to sign contracts with these universities. These were initially three-year contracts, but were extended to four years.[54] They were proper full-time employment contracts involving both research and teaching. The aims of this programme were to allow Italian scholars and scientists to carry out research in their home country, to re-establish professional contacts which had been lost, to make themselves known to the Italian scholarly and scientific community, and to transfer knowledge to their colleagues and students.

---

[51] Findlay, A., "From Brain Exchange to Brain Gain: Policy Implications for the UK of Recent Trends in Skilled Migration from Developing Countries", *International Migration Papers*, No. 43, Geneva, International Labour Office, 2001.

[52] Dustmann, C. and Weiss, Y., "Return Migration: Theory and Empirical Evidence from the UK", *British Journal of Industrial Relations*, Vol. 45, No. 2, 2007, pp. 236-256.

[53] Italian Ministry of Universities and Scientific and Technological Research, Ministerial Decree, D.M. 26 January 2001, No. 13, http://www.miur.it/atti/2001/dm010126_13.htm.

[54] Italian Ministry of Universities and Scientific and Technological Research, Ministerial Decree, DM 20/3/2003, http://www.miur.it/0006Menu_C/0012Docume/0015Atti_M/3274Rientr_cf2.htm.

In 2005 the Moratti Law,[55] confirmed the programme and allocated funding to it. By 2006, approximately 500 scholars in various subjects, mainly scientific disciplines but also law, architecture and philosophy had returned to Italy from abroad.[56]

Notwithstanding some positive signals emerging from the programme, there are still a number of limitations in relation to the funding and also to the length of contracts available. The posts are based on fixed-term contracts, which are not renewable. The *Rientro dei Cervelli* programme ought to help alleviate the brain drain problem, but without providing long-term opportunities for returning scholars, it seems destined, by and large, to fail.[57]

Empirical findings raise doubts in relation to the government approach towards the brain drain problem.[58] The main reason lies in the type of appointments and the transparency of the system. They suggest that if the Government had any interest in retaining its scientists and calling back those who moved away it should rework the foundations of its academic system, starting from admission procedures. The academic system is based on a cumbersome admission procedure through public competition, the so-called *concorsi*. Scientists interviewed in the research argue that the whole idea of public competition should be drastically changed. Concerns were raised in relation to this impenetrable selection process, notably its complexity and bureaucratic nature. In particular, the difficulties associated with passing written and oral exams, taken in Italian, make it difficult for Italians, never mind foreigners, to obtain a permanent contract. This is because often the recruitment process is not entirely related to merit. Even in those cases where a job is secured, the working environment and the conditions in which research is being carried out may play a negative role. With such working conditions, Italy cannot hope to attract brains from abroad.[59] Moreover, since 2003, the Government has frozen academic admission procedures to permanent positions and therefore those who returned after their contracts expired have to secure another short-term contract.

---

[55] Law 4/11/2005, No. 230, the so-called Moratti Law on the reform of the university system. A new university reform has now modified the Moratti Law. See http://web.camera.it/parlam/leggi/08133l.htm, accessed 30 October 2008.

[56] A list of people is available at http://cofin.cineca.it/cervelli/finanziati.html.

[57] The Decree 30 April 2008 Prot. No. 99/2008 which provided for a fund to promote the return of Italian scholars and attract foreign academics. The new reform (Law 133/2008) has further decreased research funding, http://www.miur.it/0006Menu_C/0012Docume/0015Atti_M/7084Decret.htm, accessed 30 October 2008.

[58] See Jappelli, T., "L'immobilità dei docenti universitari", *op. cit.*

[59] Morano-Foadi, S., "Key issues and causes of the Italian Brain Drain", *Innovation: the European Journal of Social Sciences*, Vol. 19, No. 2, 2006, pp. 209-223.

This scheme, recently abolished by the new Centre-Right Government, has not guaranteed a more stable career to returnees or foreign scholars. The brain drain has not been reversed by such a policy, as scholars, at the end of their contracts, are faced with the choice of moving abroad once again or being unemployed. Other European countries have had more success with schemes similar to the *Rientro dei Cervelli* programme which, crucially, offered researchers permanent employment.[60] By contrast, the whole Italian return policy seems inappropriate, and the funding allocated to the scheme has done little to boost competitiveness.

Conclusion

The creation of the ERA, with the stated aim of enhancing competitiveness in the EU, has intensified intra-EU movements of highly skilled scientists and researchers. Indeed, the increasing number of researchers leaving some European countries (Italy, for example) is a worrying phenomenon.

The Italian Government's claims to the contrary notwithstanding, spending on research has not, in fact, increased; nor has Italy succeeded in attracting researchers from abroad. Consequently, the country is facing a fall in its productivity and competitiveness.[61] This, in turn, feeds the brain drain from Italy and produces unbalanced growth within the ERA. A spill-over effect of the clustering policy inherent to the establishment of the ERA is the increasing loss of key scientists and thus competitiveness of poorer regions within the EU. The inertia of donor member states could be compensated for by EU schemes promoting return migration as part of the free movement/citizenship provisions. Migrant scientists are keen to cite EU law to protect their right to seek employment in other member states but its applicability is limited to the non-discrimination principle and it does not cover situations which are considered "internal". The EU should take responsibility for the collateral effects of its policies. In the context of internal mobility, "brain circulation" (as opposed to "brain drain"), which also includes return migration, should be promoted. Proper EU return policies should benefit the poorest regions and make funds available for migrant scientists to set up research groups back home. One option would be for the EU to introduce common rules for academic careers within the ERA. A common selection procedure for scientists based on publications and scien-

---

[60] Giannaccolo, P., *Brain Drain Europe* 2006, http://www.webalice.it/mvendruscolo/giannoccolo_braindrain_europe_2006.pdf, accessed 30 October 2008.

[61] See *IMD World Competitiveness Report*, 2007. A copy of the report can be purchased at the IMD web site, http://www.imd.ch/wcc, accessed 30 October 2008.

tific excellence where mobility occupies an important role should be considered. Mobility should be promoted, even for a short-term period, being based on academic exchange and considered as one of the promotion criteria. Scientists who wish to return home should be offered the possibility of being transferred from a university to another within the ERA, retaining the same position. Such a system involving selection and promotion procedures based on accepted common guidelines, comparable qualifications and exchangeable academic or scientific posts should operate under the direct control of the European Research Council.

The empirical work conducted by the author suggests that an effective strategy is necessary to redirect patterns of migration and reverse the brain drain.

PART II

THE EU BETWEEN SOFT AND HARD POWER

CHAPTER 6

Nordic Europe's Policy Leadership[1]

Andrew SCOTT

Introduction

The release of a pamphlet in 2005 extolling the merits of social democratic Sweden by the energetic Compass grouping in the British Labour Party[2] came at an important time, given that Prime Minister Tony Blair would soon step down and the precise policy stance of his successor, Gordon Brown, was yet to be determined. The Compass grouping has since issued quality publications calling for a new approach to political economy;[3] and critically assessing the short-comings of the Blair government in reducing inequality.[4] Various studies demonstrate the continuing extent of social policy provision and achievement in particular parts of continental Europe.[5] These suggest that there is much that Anglo-Saxon "liberal market" economies can learn and borrow from the success of the northern European "social market" economies, particularly in tackling inequality.[6] The EU and many of its continental member countries, especially in Scandinavia or Nordic Europe, continue to pursue substantially different economic and social policies from the market liberalism which predominates in the English-speaking world. This chapter explores aspects of this policy distinctiveness, its context and its significance.

---

[1] Parts of this chapter have been previously published in my contribution to Langmore, J., *To Firmer Ground: Restoring Hope in Australia*, Sydney, UNSW Press, 2007, pp. 117-120.

[2] Taylor, R., *Sweden's New Social Democratic Model: Proof that a Better World is Possible*, London, Compass, 2005.

[3] McIvor, M. and Shah, H. (eds.), *A New Political Economy*, London, Compass in association with Lawrence and Wishart, 2006.

[4] Compass, Closer to Equality? Assessing New Labour's Record on Equality after 10 years in Government, http://www.compassonline.org.uk/publications/.

[5] For example, see Castles, F., *The Future of the Welfare State: Crisis Myths and Crisis Realities*, Oxford, Oxford University Press, 2004, pp. 89, 171, 181.

[6] For example, see Pontusson, J., *Inequality and Prosperity: Social Europe vs. Liberal America*, Ithaca, Cornell University Press, 2005, *passim*.

Scandinavian Policy Achievements

The nations of Scandinavia, or Nordic Europe, provide particular and living proof that economically successful, socially fair and environmentally responsible policies can succeed. The four principal Nordic nations (Sweden, Norway, Denmark and Finland) are consistently assessed as among the most economically efficient or "competitive" nations in the world by the World Economic Forum. They also consistently rate as the most equitable nations in terms of income distribution. Sweden, which has the largest population of the Nordic nations, is much more equal than Australia and Britain and twice as equal as the United States, according to the Luxembourg Income Study.[7]

This mix of strong economic performance and relatively equal income distribution makes a big and positive difference in many facets of life. While there is a strong work ethos and commitment to "productivism", working hours remain within reasonable limits for work/life balance. In 2005, workers in Australia worked on average 1,811 hours a year, compared with 1,360 hours in Norway, 1,551 in Denmark, and 1,587 in Sweden, according to Organization for Economic Cooperation and Development (OECD) data. These countries also pay attention to the working environment. Positive environments, in which workers have reasonable variety and the chance to work in teams, maximise employees' morale, commitment and output. Particularly successful Nordic corporations such as Volvo and Scania are associated with innovative workplace design and a high quality of management, which involves proper consultation with workers.

The Nordic nations are notable for driving child poverty down to unparalleled lows and enshrining the rights of children; comprehensively tackling housing and health inequalities; improving gender equality and providing family-friendly workplace arrangements, including twelve months' paid parental leave, a minimum of two months of which must be taken by fathers; fostering knowledge through high levels of private and public investment in research and development; being generous aid donors to the world's poorer nations and taking in asylum seekers at relatively high rates; adopting a thorough and serious approach to democratically tackling long-term policy issues in a way which involves the different sections of society; leading the push within the EU for action to cut greenhouse gas emissions by 20% by 2020; and developing renewable sources of energy (Denmark, in particular, is a world leader in the use of wind power). There is much that Australia and other countries can learn from the Nordic nations' successes in these fields.

---

[7] Assessed via the ratio of the disposable money income of people in the top 10% to the disposable money income of people in the bottom 10%.

While there were setbacks to the Nordic nations in the international economic recession of the early 1990s, they have continued to hold on to values such as universalism, full employment and equality. These values have helped rather than hindered these countries resume their strong overall economic, social and environmental performance since that time.

As Swedish scholar Dr Jenny Andersson writes (specifically in relation to Sweden), most people there continue to emphasise the interdependence of growth and security. The Swedish word for security, *trygghet*, has a broad meaning that goes beyond issues of material concern and refers to notions of comfort, wellbeing and belonging. In Sweden, security is still regarded as a precondition of change, whereas in the United States, Britain and Australia, the greater dominance of economic liberalism requires individuals to be induced and coerced to accept change as a precondition of security. This is a very important difference. The international evidence is that the Nordic approach is more beneficial socially than elsewhere.

The four main Nordic nations have the world's highest labour force participation rates for women. In all four nations, the labour force as a proportion of the population is higher than it is in Australia. Unemployment, including hidden unemployment, is still a problem in the Nordic nations, as in Australia. However, mainstream political and policy debate in these countries goes beyond the narrow official measurements of unemployment to confront the broader problem of joblessness. This confirms the quality of the democratic discourse and the breadth of policy ambition there. Those who are not employed in Nordic countries benefit from far more comprehensive and higher quality skills training than do Australian unemployed people at present. These countries, moreover, do not suffer the serious vocational skills shortages which have emerged in Australia as a result of a decade of inadequate public and employer investment in training.

The universal approach to welfare provision in Nordic Europe also guarantees a decent minimum income for all and prevents the spiralling hostility towards some categories of welfare recipients which occurs in countries with more selective and minimal welfare arrangements. There continues to be widespread public support in the Nordic nations for equality, for a strong welfare state and for taking the "high road" to prosperity. The resilience of these distinctive nations rebuts claims that "globalisation" is eliminating all policy options for nation states.

In three of the four main Nordic nations – Sweden, Finland and Denmark – manufacturing for export continues to be economically important and supported. The Norwegian economy, by contrast, is like Australia's in that it relies much more on resources. However, unlike

Australia, Norway uses its present resource riches wisely, building up reserves to ensure that it will be able to benefit from those resources in the much longer term. Norway aims to sustain its national inheritance, in line with the legacy of its former long-serving Prime Minister, Gro Harlem Brundtland, who led the preparation of the landmark 1987 international environmental report entitled *Our Common Future*.

Many other EU continental member countries are more advanced than English-speaking countries in important policy areas, too. One clear example is the extent to which workers' rights to participate are embedded in formal arrangements across almost all of the continent.[8] Germany, meanwhile, is the world leader in developing solar energy despite having much less sunlight than, for example, Australia. Even the Business Council of Australia, in a recent policy statement on innovation,[9] has acknowledged the success of the "Nordics", in marked contrast to its critical response to a major Australian trade union report on Scandinavian policy achievements in 1987. These findings are relevant for both the British Labour Party, and the Australian Labor Party, to consider.

Demographic Challenges to European Social Democracy

However, soon after the Compass pamphlet on Sweden was published, the Swedish Social Democratic Party (SAP) suffered a rare national election defeat. Despite this defeat in 2006, and challenging demographic and political developments which lie ahead, there are good grounds for thinking that Sweden and the other Nordic nations have a future of continuing to be a social democratic alternative to market liberalism.

The defeat of the Social Democratic Party in the 2006 Swedish national election was newsworthy precisely because it is so unusual for one of the most successful political parties in the world to lose an election. Having governed for 65 of the preceding 74 years, the SAP built up an egalitarian, welfare-orientated society in Sweden which also performed very strongly in economic terms. The extent to which its opposing parties had to concede policy ground to have a chance of beating the Social Democrats and its allies shows how left-of-centre parties can, with clear ideas and purpose, set the terms of policy in developed nations.

No other party has governed for more than two consecutive terms in Sweden since 1932. The last such government held office for just one

---

[8] See Pontusson, J., *op. cit.*, pp. 115-118, and http://www.etuc.org/a/2841.

[9] Business Council of Australia, *New Pathways to Prosperity: A National Innovation Framework for Australia*, Business Council of Australia, Melbourne, 2006.

term, despite coming to power in an atmosphere of serious economic crisis. This was not the situation in 2006. Four parties had to come together in 2006 in a new so-called "Alliance for Sweden" to very narrowly defeat Göran Persson's government after 12 continuous years in office.

Many people changed their vote because they were tired of the party leader. In addition, the Alliance parties tactically outperformed the Social Democrats in policy areas in which social democracy has traditionally been strong, such as employment policy. Voters did not, however, reject the fundamentals of the welfare state and of equality.[10]

The new (Reinfeldt) government has quickly slipped up and lost support. On past precedents and present performance the new centre-right Government seems unlikely to achieve major changes to Sweden's distinctive combination of economic prosperity and social equality.

The Swedish Social Democratic Party has very strong reserves of participation on which to draw to reverse this unusual setback in its electoral fortunes. These include the 80% of the Swedish workforce in trade unions, which is exceptionally high by world standards. This, of itself, is likely to help the SAP to return to government sooner rather than later and to resume its leading and progressive policy role. Mona Sahlin, the new leader, is now energetically reconnecting the Party with its grass roots and leading renewal of its policy agenda; and at the time of writing the SAP holds a substantial poll lead over the Reinfeldt Government.

Whatever the term "Swedish model" really means, and however much the model may have declined since its golden days, the fact remains that Sweden is still playing an important role of international policy leadership. It is true, as Jenny Andersson points out in her recent book, that "much of the international literature surrounding the ideological change of contemporary social democracy has tended to see Sweden as a kind of resilient, inherently welfare statist society, built on corporatism, social consensus and a persistent *folkhem* ideology".[11] In part, this is because "Swedish social democracy has not developed a third way discourse to the same extreme as Britain has [but has] instead [...] held on to values such as universalism, full employment and equal-

---

[10] Two incisive discussions of the 2006 Swedish parliamentary election are provided by Jenny Andersson, in "On the Problem of Being Proud and Satisfied", *Renewal*, Vol. 14, No. 4, 2006; and N. Aylott and N. Bolin, "Towards a Two-Party System? The Swedish Parliamentary Election of September 2006", *West European Politics*, Vol. 30, No. 3, May 2007, pp. 621-633.

[11] Andersson, J., *Between Growth and Security: Swedish Social Democracy from a Strong Society to a Third Way*, Manchester, Manchester University Press, 2006, p. 15.

ity".[12] However, as she also correctly writes, "whereas this is true in the *relative* sense, that is, in comparison with the more radical changes in social democratic ideology that have taken place elsewhere, it is not true that Swedish social democracy has not changed nor that Swedish welfare policies have not changed in the last decades".[13]

There were indeed serious changes to traditional Swedish social democratic ideology going on in the early 1980s. There was a turn to neo-liberalism then, which did involve "an Anglo-Saxon discourse historically alien to Swedish political thought".[14] It "contained unmistakeable traces of the incentives discourse put forward by the Swedish right"[15] and it "seemed to mark almost a complete turn around in Swedish social democracy's outlook on social policy".[16] These changes paralleled – although they did not go as far as – changes which were occurring under a Labor Party government in Australia at the same time.

Yet, nevertheless, as Jenny Andersson has also pointed out, "in the late 1990s and early 2000s, the SAP tried to reconnect to its historical articulations and break with the legacy of its third way experiment. Once again, party rhetoric contains echoes of post-war discourses".[17] This attempted reconnection has not removed all ambiguities in Swedish social democratic ideology. Clearly the party did not convince many of its former supporters in the 2006 election of where it wanted to take the country in the future. However,

> Sweden has emerged on the other side of the 1990s as a fairly solid welfare state. The Swedish third way was a hesitant experimentation with a new social democratic language around economic and social affairs based on choice, cost efficiency, and individual responsibility. It never went as far as, for instance, its British equivalent.[18]

Nor did it go as far as Australian Labor's acceptance of neo-liberalism, for that matter. The Australian Labor Party (ALP) did not find it possible until 2007, with its assertion of the needs of "working families", to reconnect with important elements of its traditional philosophy and to step back from the neo-liberal turn which it took in the 1980s.

---

[12] *Ibid.*

[13] *Ibid.* Emphasis added.

[14] *Ibid.*, p. 119.

[15] *Ibid.*, p. 121.

[16] *Ibid.*, p. 123.

[17] *Ibid.*, p. 9.

[18] *Ibid.*, p. 132. Emphasis added. See also Andersson, J., "The People's Library and the Electronic Workshop: Comparing Swedish and British Social Democracy", *Politics and Society*, Vol. 34, No. 3, September 2006, pp. 431-460.

This contributed to the length of time it spent out of government and the four consecutive election losses it suffered from 1996.

The Swedish people have not voted in favour of more inequality of the kind which exists in the United States and in other parts of the English-speaking world. Swedish social democracy has achieved things which are worth preserving. A majority of the Swedish people want to preserve them. The SAP now needs to articulate more clearly its vision of how to preserve those achievements for the future.

In the other Nordic countries, a conservative government was re-elected in Denmark in 2005 and 2008 (very narrowly). Under Prime Minister Anders Fogh Rasmussen it has enforced strict anti-immigration measures with the support of the far-right People's Party. In Finland, meanwhile, the Social Democratic party became, after the 2003 election, the junior partner in a coalition led by the rural Centre Party, having previously led the preceding Coalition government. It subsequently performed poorly and left government altogether following the 2007 election.

These trends have led to suggestions that traditional characteristics of the Nordic nations may be undergoing significant change. Norway, however, returned to left-of-centre rule in the 2005 election. While the Social Democrats are currently out of power in Denmark and Finland their policy legacy and approach persists there, as it does in Sweden.

French Political Developments

Among other political developments which may affect the future of European nations continuing to provide some social democratic alternatives to market liberalism was the Socialist Party's improved showing but eventual defeat in the 2007 French Presidential election.

In that election, the Socialist Party's candidate made it through to the second ballot but was then defeated. The campaign by Nicolas Sarkozy against "illegal migrants" and their children, designed to court former Le Pen voters, is reminiscent of former Australian prime minister John Howard's moves against asylum seekers in 2001. These actions were undertaken to win back people who had voted for Pauline Hanson's One Nation Party in Australia in 1998.

The French Socialist Party's opposition to the measures was muted in the same way the ALP's in Australia was, due to its discomfort about possibly alienating its traditional supporters. Under Ségolène Royal, the French Socialists even for a time seemed to be trying to match and thereby neutralise Sarkozy's push for Le Pen supporters.

French Prime Minister Lionel Jospin's Socialist Party, in office from 1997-2002, had not moved to the right to the same extent as his British counterpart Blair had. It must be recalled that François Mitterrand as president from 1981-95 had already overthrown the left's traditional economic policy approach in France, much as Bob Hawke and Paul Keating had done to Australian Labor in much the same period (1983-96).

One of the parallels between Australian and European politics since the 1990s has been the rise of support for far-right parties and policies hostile to immigrants and refugees.[19] Economic policy changes made by the mainstream left-of-centre parties (the Socialist Party in France, the Labor Party in Australia) when in office in the 1980s and 1990s may have contributed to the subsequent rise of support for far-right "populist" parties including among blue-collar voters, and to the adoption of hostile policies towards immigrants and refugees by established right-wing parties to the continuing electoral detriment of the mainstream left.

The negative EU constitutional referendum outcomes in France and The Netherlands are comparable with the rejection in 1999 of the referendum for a proposed constitutional change towards an Australian republic. In all three cases, normal voting allegiances fragmented and odd political bedfellows found themselves arrayed on the Yes and No sides, each with subterranean political concerns. What they all shared was a grievience that stemmed from the imposition of an "elite"-determined proposal, with these feelings proving decisive in the outcome, more than the formal question being put.

Charles Sowerwine, an Australian-based historian of France, has suggested that the class-based politics of France in the 1980s has now given way to race-based politics with the incorporation of France's previous "other": the Communist Party.[20]

Natalie Doyle argues that the vote to reject the new European Union constitution in 2005 in France occurred partly because of a fear that "a new Europe has been created and the French electorate feels it was not consulted": in particular, it feels railroaded by the attempted imposition of neo-liberal EU arrangements based on an "Anglo-Saxon" model which does not satisfy the desire to preserve France's social model.[21]

---

[19] These are discussed for example by R. A. DeAngelis, "A Rising Tide for Jean-Marie, Jorg and Pauline? Xenophobic Populism in Comparative Perspective", *Australian Journal of Politics and History*, Vol. 49, No. 1, March 2003, pp. 75-92.

[20] Notes made from Professor Charles Sowerwine's speech to The University of Melbourne Contemporary Europe Research Centre (CERC) Roundtable: "A New Era for France? National and International Consequences of the 2007 French Elections", 14 August 2007.

[21] Notes made from Dr. Doyle's speech made to The University of Melbourne's CERC conference when presenting her paper "The Significance of the French Electorate's Rejection of the Constitutional Treaty", December 2005.

Doyle has further argued that the vote to reject the new European Union constitution in 2005 in France,

> whilst still reflecting the views of traditional opponents of European integration [...] also manifested a new kind of opposition from the young and the educated: pro-European hostility. Faced with what it perceived as the arrogant assumption by its political elites that to be pro-European could only mean voting 'Yes', the French electorate, as in the presidential elections of 2002, sent a strong message to its political leaders. This message expresses profound dissatisfaction with the failure of French political elites to address national problems and their tendency to use the European Union to escape responsibility.[22]

A wave of riots in disadvantaged urban areas of France in November 2005 had highlighted that nation's continuing failures to give immigrants from different racial backgrounds sufficient opportunities. Another wave of riots in France, by students on campuses in Paris and throughout the nation during March and April 2006, were specifically against moves to remove employment protection for young workers. These moves were seen as part of the imposition of an "Anglo-Saxon" economic model and hence were vigorously and successfully resisted.

French President Jacques Chirac, in response to criticism of higher unemployment in his country than in Britain, explicitly rejected the notion that the British model is one that France should envy: "Certainly, their unemployment is lower than ours. But if you take the big elements in society – health policy, the fight against poverty [...] spending involving the future – you notice that we are much, much better placed than the English".[23]

Whatever his motives may have been, Chirac was factually correct in pointing out that France spends significantly more of its annual income than Britain does on education; and that British children are more than twice as likely to live in poverty than French children.[24]

Charles Sowerwine wrote two consecutive newspaper articles in Australia previewing the 2007 French Presidential election. These pieces drew pithy parallels between French and Australian politicians and cast the French political scene of the time as a re-enactment of the 1998 Howard vs. Beazley Australian election. He memorably described Nicolas Sarkozy as "John Howard with a charisma implant" and his opponent in the presidential elections, Ségolène Royal as "Kim Beazley

---

[22] *Ibid.*

[23] Reported in *The Weekend Australian*, Sydney, 16-17 July 2005.

[24] These facts are confirmed in the comparative statistical Tables assembled by Tiffen, R. and Gittins, R., *How Australia Compares*, Cambridge, Cambridge University Press, 2004.

with a policy implant, plus an extreme makeover". On the question of image, Sowerwine draws attention to the importance of Sarkozy's promise to a public meeting in a poor Paris suburb in October 2005 to clean out the "scum", "gangerine" and "thugs". When two young men, who were hiding from police, were electrocuted in an electricity sub-station two days later, riots broke out. As his piece explains:

> Sarkozy thrived on accusations that his comments had provoked the riots. He repeated the words on television. Like Alan Jones [a highly controversial Australian radio journalist] during the racial riots in Cronulla, Sydney, he was, as Howard put it [...] just articulating "what a lot of people think". His approval rating shot up 11 points.[25]

Although the Socialist Party protested that Sarkozy's dismantling of community policing initiatives contributed to the riots, his "tough" image won voters from the National Front. Sarkozy may not have put forward much specific policy, but he made his intentions clear, indicating a direction that:

> the French call neo-liberal and we would call Thatcherite [...]That many French contemplate such a rupture suggests a crisis of confidence. France has undergone a series of shocks, leading to questioning of the "French model" [... yet] the French remain attached to the social achievements of the 20th century and the model of a strong state with a solid welfare base. Anglo commentators often point to high unemployment [...] and high taxes, but most French have jobs and love their security; all French love their efficient public transport, high-speed trains running like clockwork at 320km/h, efficient urban planning, fine health services and excellent state primary and secondary schools.[26]

Sowerwine goes on to list many of the achievements of the French social model, such as accessible and affordable child care, five weeks of annual leave and of course, the 35-hour week. He notes that working-age French people are placed eighth in the OECD for workforce participation. This compares favourably with New Zealand, Britain, the US and Australia, which is ranked in twenty-second place. Drawing conclusions from these observations, Sowerwine cites a Deutsche Bank Research report that makes an explicit link between "supportive state policies" and higher-than-average female workforce participation. Bringing these disparate elements to bear on his analysis of the failure of the EU Constitutional Treaty referendum in France, he explains: "The strong state that provides all this is under threat in a globalised world and a European Union that [to some extent] pushes Thatcherism, a main

---

[25] *The Sunday Age*, Melbourne, 22 April 2007.
[26] *Ibid.*

reason why the French voted 55/45 against the EU constitution in 2005".[27]

Sowerwine further analysed Nicolas Sarkozy's election victory, concentrating on his ability to "garner" the right wing and, more particularly, the extreme right wing vote in France. This was done by being seen to "[talk] tough against those of North African origin" while promising "never to sink into the demagogy of apologising for colonialism". These two elements were sufficient to secure for Sarkozy the votes of the eliminated far-right candidate, Jean-Marie Le Pen. This is, in essence, a "dog-whistle" racially based political discourse and parallels John Howard's description of refugees as "that kind of people".

Turning his analysis to the use of the media, Sowerwine notes that

> Sarkozy has been pilloried in the equivalents of the [Australian] Fairfax Press [and] likened [...] to the wolf in Little Red Riding Hood.[...][He] speaks to dissatisfied people on commercial media, as John Howard speaks through the Murdoch press and talk-back radio; [Ségolène] Royal speaks through other media. Comments on pedophilia or colonialism cause Sarko[zy] trouble, but only in the media he does not use.[...] But [even if] people under 24 do need jobs and aren't getting [and] would [arguably] benefit from the Anglo policies Sarkozy represents, [...] how many French believe the young would benefit enough to make up for insecurity after age 24? Expect trouble if he wins. [...] Gaullism is dead and no one knows what will replace it.[28]

After Sarkozy won, Dr Philippe Marlière, senior lecturer in French and European politics at University College London, in reviewing the election result, wrote about how

> An eclectic coalition cheered the election of Nicolas Sarkozy [... seeing him as] the man who will introduce a good dose of Thatcherism in France [...] proponents of the Anglo-Saxon "free market" model hope that Sarkozy will put the Left in its place. And who knows, maybe he will convert the French to the neo-liberal agenda that, so far, a majority of them have stubbornly rejected.

Marlière notes that French workers have succeeded in maintaining the French social state in the face of concerted attacks over the last 15 years. Sarkozy's victory points to the inherent contradictions associated with an election victory based on a populist appeal to the right wing. Which part of the right-wing agenda will the French President seek to make his own, and how will he square it with French egalitarianism? A right-wing nationalist and anti-immigration voter is not necessarily an enthusiastic supporter of free-market liberalism, after all.

---

27 *The Sunday Age*, Melbourne, 6 May 2007.

28 *Ibid*.

Will Sarkozy emulate Margaret Thatcher and tame the French trade union movement? Will he manage to undo French labour laws or undermine the right to strike? Will he, in short, break the strong egalitarian ethos of French society? And, if he is successful, will the Socialist Party finally cease to be "socialist" altogether and come into line with Britain's post-Thatcherite New Labour?

It is too early to answer these important questions. However, [...] Sarkozy's politics are totally at odds with the more egalitarian, secular approach of mainstream French politicians [...] Sarkozy has appealed to large sections of the working class (some of them being former National Front voters) [... yet] it seems unwise to jump to the conclusion that popular support for the right represents an adherence to Sarkozy's free-market policies.

It is clear that Sarkozy's strong stance on immigration, law and order and national identity has appealed to working-class voters. It is far less obvious that the same voters would approve of the policies of economic deregulation, or back the dismantling of the social state. Sarkozy shrewdly talked about the "right to work more and to earn more", an indirect attack against the 35-hour week implemented by the Socialists.[29]

Australian Prime Minister John Howard promised when first elected in 1996 that "no Australian worker will be worse off" under his Government. His rhetoric about wanting Australia to feel more "comfortable and relaxed" and his conservative cultural policies all gained some workers' support. However he fell badly behind in opinion polls as soon as Kevin Rudd became ALP Leader and he then lost the 2007 national election, in large measure because of his Government's introduction of an industrial relations policy which heightened insecurity and reduced fairness. Marlière goes on in his analysis of the French Socialists' 2007 defeat to argue that "Royal did not consistently attempt to underline the correlation between free market policies... [and] social insecurity [... while] the sectarianism of far-left parties that failed to unite in the first round played an important part in demoralising left-wing voters".[30]

The French Socialists nevertheless rebuilt their standing compared with the 2002 Presidential election when the Party failed to even make it into the second ballot. Sarkozy's victory was only by a few percentage points. The Socialist candidate polled 47% in the second round of the 2007 Presidential election.

Sarkozy started off as President in a very inclusive fashion. He appointed Bernard Kouchner, a person with a left-wing humanitarian background as his Foreign Minister, and put forward Dominique Strauss

---

[29] *The Age*, Melbourne, 9 May 2007. (Originally published in *The Guardian*, London, 7 May 2007.)

[30] *Ibid.*

Kahn, a socialist, as France's nominee to head the International Monetary Fund (IMF). However, he suffered early setbacks in local elections in March 2008 in which the Socialist Party performed strongly. It is likely that Sarkozy will take steps which seriously undermine France's "social model", and which threaten French workers' rights and conditions, as Howard did in Australia. If and when he does so, France's Socialist Party can expect support to return to it as economic questions again become more central for voters. This will particularly be the case if differences between the main parties on these questions become more clearly articulated.

Economic Inequality and Politics

This brings us back to the Nordic nations. Sweden stands out as one European country in which a far-right party opposed to migrants and refugees has not developed to the same degree as other countries, including France. Although the Swedish Democrats Party does show some characteristics of far-right parties elsewhere and its potential to grow further should not be underestimated (a matter, in itself, of some concern), nevertheless it has not become strong in Sweden at the national level as similar parties in other countries have.

There is interesting evidence that strong welfare states reduce the likelihood of far-right parties arising.[31] Jens Rydgren meanwhile has highlighted how in Sweden the continuing salience of class-based economic issues and a clear divide between the parties on those issues has in the past prevented a far-right party gaining ground on cultural questions.[32] Therefore, re-establishing the Social Democrats' traditional credibility on employment issues becomes a crucial priority not only for the party to win back office but also to prevent the further escalation of ugly racism in politics.

A European Commission Vice-President, the Social Democrat former Swedish Social Affairs Minister Margot Wallström, in the wake of the French and Dutch votes to reject the proposed new European Union constitution during 2005, called for the EU to become more democratic.[33] Wallström also stated that an obstacle to creating a better connection between the EU and Europe's citizens is a lack of any "common narrative" about the actual nature of European integration:

---

[31] As found by Swank, D. and Georg-Betz, H., "Globalization, The Welfare State and Right-wing Populism in Western Europe", *Socio-Economic Review*, Vol. 1, May 2003, pp. 215-245.

[32] Rydgren, J., "Radical Right Populism in Sweden: Still a Failure, But for How Long?", *Scandinavian Political Studies*, Vol. 25, No. 1, 2002, pp. 27-56.

[33] Reported in *The Age*, Melbourne, 15 October, 2005.

"the real problem in Europe is that there is no agreement or understanding about what Europe is for and where it is going".[34]

It is appropriate that initiatives for the EU to become more democratic should be made by a Swedish social democrat. Sweden was a late and reluctant entrant to the EU because of the assumption in Social Democratic circles that Sweden had little to gain from integration: "Not only was it richer than the [then] EC, [but] the latter was also characterised as 'conservative, capitalist and Catholic' – that is, incompatible with Swedish Social Democracy's fiercely rationalist egalitarianism".[35]

In 2003, in their referendum, Swedes rejected adoption of the euro because of their desire to maintain the *higher*-than-EU standards which had been achieved in their country.

Their record on aid donation and rate of acceptance of asylum seekers tends to counter suggestions that the Nordic nations' egalitarianism is linked to their ethnic homogeneity. Approximately one million of Sweden's population of nine million were born overseas, concentrated in particular centres like Malmö. The proportion of immigrants and their children is growing and will continue to grow. It is an important question as to whether social democracy can be as strong in a Sweden which is becoming more multicultural than Sweden has been in the past. In my interviews during 2007 with Social Democratic political and trade union officials in Sweden and Norway I found them to be very committed to ensuring that the growing numbers of migrant workers in those countries receive proper wages, conditions and union coverage.

In Sweden, to the extent that there has been public defiance of an "elite" imposed agenda it has been to resist moves to erode the strong welfare state and Scandinavia's distinctive high road to prosperity and equality.[36]

The bi-partisan approach taken in Sweden in response to the financial crisis of the early 1990s to intervene and restore stricter regulation is also now being discussed as instructive for the United States to emulate in response to the September 2008 crisis on Wall Street which resulted from excessive financial deregulation.[37]

---

[34] Wallström, M., Vice-President of the European Commission responsible for Institutional Relations and Communication Strategy, "Communicating a Europe in Stormy Waters", Speech, Brussels, 28 June 2005.

[35] Aylott, N., "The Swedish Social Democratic Party" in R. Ladrech and P. Marlière, *Social Democratic Parties in the European Union: History, Organization, Policies*, Basingstoke, Macmillan, 1999, p. 201.

[36] Widfeldt, A., "Elite Collusion and Public Defiance: Sweden's Euro Referendum in 2003", *West European Politics*, Vol. 27, No. 3, May 2004, pp. 503-517.

[37] See for example Carter Dougherty, "Can the U.S. Learn any Lessons from Sweden's Banking Rescue?", *International Herald Tribune*, 22 September 2008.

Conclusion

Barack Obama has now become the 44th American president, historically overcoming racial barriers in that nation and strongly criticising the extent of America's economic inequalities and the effects of financial deregulation. Many have expressed hope that Obama will play a rebuilding role similar to that which Franklin D. Roosevelt played in response to the Depression of the 1930s. The success of Sweden as a genuine, substantial social democratic "middle way" between unrestrained market liberalism and undemocratic Communism inspired great interest among Roosevelt's supporters. It can now provide similar inspiration to supporters of Barack Obama.

The US, Britain, Australia and other countries can benefit greatly from closer study of the achievements of Nordic Europe, which continues to provide crucially important policy leadership to the world.

CHAPTER 7

The WTO and Cultural Industries

Is Free Trade Good for Europe?

Eva POLONSKA-KIMUNGUYI

Introduction

In June 2007 the World Trade Organization (WTO) trade talks held in Germany ground to a halt – again. The official reason was agriculture. Since the protests in Seattle, USA in 1999, it has been clear that global free trade is not regarded as a benefit by all WTO members and compromise has proved elusive. This time around, if it had not been for agriculture, the audiovisual goods and services sector would surely have brought the negotiations to a standstill. The recent Doha Round was expected to establish a benchmark for trade in cultural products but, as in agriculture, it failed to do so.

This chapter argues that free trade in the audiovisual sector would not serve European interests well. The arguments about protection of tradition and media pluralism advanced by Europe at the close of the Uruguay Round in 1994 have been joined by one more: that of the media being perceived as a main tool in generating "European-ness". Free trade in the media and audiovisual sector would allow foreign productions to flood the European market to the detriment of the European project. Starting from a brief overview of the trade in media since the Second World War, the chapter will discuss the various policy positions adopted by Europe and the US. It will outline their different conceptions of markets and culture and propose one possible solution to the controversy.

GATT 1947

In the audiovisual field, the first sector to be affected by international rules on trade was that of cinematographic films. The General Agreement on Tariffs and Trade (GATT) of 1947 included films as tradable products. The GATT aimed at combating trade restrictions on imports and subsidies for exports. It introduced two basic rules in order to meet its goals: multilateralism and progressive liberalization (in rounds). Each round of negotiations dealt with new industry sectors and countries – members of the GATT were, and still are, expected to make commitments according to the schedule of the round. Each state has the option to apply a more deregulated system than that set out in the schedule. Crucially, members do not have the option of putting in place a less deregulated system. Article IV of the GATT allowed countries to maintain screen quotas on cinema exhibition to protect local industries and to ensure that local productions would find their way to the picture theatres. This proved extremely important in a devastated post-war Europe that wanted to rebuild its film industry to pre-war levels. Countries had to agree, however, that quotas were temporary and that they would be reduced and eventually eliminated. There were no tariffs or limitations on imported films; quotas were imposed only for exhibitors, not distributors. Subsidies for cinema production were also allowed. In cases when one country felt that subsidies "threatened" its products, it could demand that they be discussed but not removed.[1] Strange as it may seem, no-one was sure whether television was included or not. In the 1940s, television was still in its infancy. Many countries had no television industry to speak of and the main focus of the audio-visual sector was undeniably the cinematographic film.

The GATS (1986), Media and the Problem of Definition

By the 1980s television had become a major business, creating not only films but also series, comedies, sit-coms, quizzes, shows of every description. Because the TV industry now produced more programs than cinema, and because people spent more time viewing the small screen in their sitting room than the big screen at the cinema, trade liberalisers saw no reason why television should be omitted from negotiations. In 1986, the Uruguay Round put quotas and subsidies on the table, as they were now considered serious barriers to free trade. The television industry was doing well, so there was no reason to offer it the sort of protection it had received during the post-war recovery period. At the same time, it was also decided that it was not just films that counted as products under the Round, but each step in the process of film creation, that is to say, people's work and talent that could be traded. Under the new regime, technology provided concerns for classification of films and TV programs. Where previously films – printed on reels – physically crossed borders on their way to another country, the media content was now supplied in the form of a signal sent by a satellite, or even later, a file downloaded through a computer. So films could no longer be treated as goods – they became *services*. The long discussion as to whether or not television fell under the ambit of GATT was now brought to an end. But the changing nature of audiovisual industry output and the rapid

---

[1]   Given, J., *America's Pie: Trade and Culture after 9/11*, Sydney, University of New South Wales Press, 2003.

technological developments it has undergone, still pose significant problems of classification and demarcation if characterized as a service. As Ming Shao explains:

> Three characteristics commonly distinguish services from goods. First, production and consumption must be simultaneous in the case of services but not goods. Second, unlike goods, services are impossible to store. Third, services are intangible, while goods are tangible. Although the above criteria work well in distinguishing activities like haircutting from conventional goods, they have not proven very useful in classifying audiovisuals.[2]

The feature of service transactions requiring the simultaneous presence of both consumer and producer is already outdated in many other sectors and is now seen as a legacy of earlier days. In the media field, this is because production and display of a movie or a television show involve a chain of services: script-writing and production set-up, of necessity, come before acting, editing, composing music and sound effects, marketing and ultimately, transmission of the film or distribution to cinemas. Only once *all* the sequential services have been performed can the film or program be considered ready for consumption. The technology that brings films and television programs into existence has now superseded two further characteristics of the above definition of a *service*: it now allows for the *storing* of those services and thus, has made them *tangible*. It also allows the consumer, by renting a DVD or recording a program from television, to decide the most convenient time of consumption.

To regulate trade in services, the Uruguay Round, which started in 1986, created a new agreement – the General Agreement on Tariffs in Services (GATS). It dealt with television and other sub-categories in the creation of movies or TV programmes: 1) motion picture and video tape production and distribution, 2) motion picture and projection services, 3) radio and television services, 4) radio television transmission services, 5) sound recording and 6) other. Since the establishment of GATS, uncertainty about the very notion of audiovisual services and their categorization has increased.[3] With digitization, convergence and the emergence of new electronic media, coming soon after the GATS was concluded, many of the categories listed above soon proved to be too vague or too narrow. For instance, the possibility of streaming radio or television content over the internet was not covered under any sub-category. The United States questioned the classification, objecting that

2 Cited in Goff, P., *Limits to Liberalization: Local Culture in a Global Marketplace*, Ithaca, Cornell University Press, 2007, p. 133.

3 Messerlin, P., Siwek, S. and Cocq, E., *The Audiovisual Services Sector in the GATS Negotiations*, American Enterprise Institute for Public Policy Research, Washington, D.C., AEI Press, 2004.

it did not cover certain services, such as exhibition of films, the operation of cinemas, or direct-to-home satellite services.[4] With more and more services falling under the category of "Other", future conflict seems inevitable. A clear distinction between services distributed through traditional broadcasting networks and those distributed online no longer seems possible. As Patrick Messerlin, Stephen Siwek and Emmanuel Cocq[5] argued, the term "audiovisual services" as the main category, however, is broad enough to accommodate any form of emerging technology.

Since 1995, both the GATT and the GATS have been administered by the WTO. GATS members are not obliged to "schedule" all services sectors. A government may not want to make a commitment on the level of foreign competition in a given sector. In this case, the government's only obligation is to be transparent in regulating the sector, and not to discriminate against foreign suppliers. The WTO is feared by many, as the price for falling foul of its rules can be high. According to Seán Ó Siochrú, the WTO is currently "the most powerful global trade institution ever created. Its members – governments from around the world – have given it enormous powers to deliver sanctions should they breach its rules, sanctions strong enough to hurt even the most powerful government".[6] This fear stems from the fact that "when countries do sign, sometimes with a period of grace for poorer countries, there can be no going back – the 'ratchet effect' means that no country is permitted to backpedal on its agreement or to renegotiate its terms, under threat of very severe sanctions".[7]

What is at Stake in the Media Business?

By the time GATS was being negotiated in the mid-1980s, the audiovisual sector had grown to become one of the most important sectors in the US economy. The US audiovisual industry is increasingly dependent on exports.[8] While few countries made any kind of commitments on audiovisual services, many more reserved their right to pursue national cultural policy measures. Audiovisual services were affected in two ways. First, member states accepted new obligations about the kinds of government measures they could impose covering services, invest-

---

[4]   *Ibid.*, p. 3.

[5]   *Ibid.*

[6]   Ó Siochru, S., Girard, B., Mahan, A., *Global Media Governance. A Beginner's Guide*, Lanham, Rowman & Littlefield, 2002, p. 51.

[7]   *Ibid.*

[8]   Siwek, S., *Engines of Growth: Economic Contributions of the US Intellectual Property Industries*, Washington, D.C., Economists Incorporated, 2005. See also UNESCO, "International Flows of Selected Cultural Goods 1980-98", Paris, 2001.

ment and intellectual property. Next, the consequences of failure to comply with those obligations were now made more severe under the new dispute settlement mechanism, as New Zealand and Canada were soon to find out.[9] Those cultural policy measures, seen from the perspective of the GATS, constitute barriers to free trade:

- content laws (quotas) infringed the Market Access rule (as the market is not open when quotas do not allow foreign productions to enter);

- cooperation agreements infringed the Most Favoured Nation (MFN) clause (as they gave privileged access to one market only to a chosen few);

- subsidies for production infringed the National Treatment rule (as subsidies for national producers can make their product cheaper than an imported one).

The public sector, as was established, was excluded from liberalization and subsidies for public television were allowed under Article 3(b). In the case of the European Union, television quotas, imposed by the "Television without Frontiers" Directive, attracted particular scrutiny. This directive required broadcasters to devote a majority of their qualifying transmission time[10] to European output,[11] national language quotas in EU member states, subsidies,[12] domestic subsidies in member states, screen quotas in various countries (e.g. France, Spain), dubbing licenses (Spain) and regulatory licensing and ownership restrictions.

Europe and America: at Opposite Ends of the Spectrum

At the time of Uruguay talks, the European Union was itself divided and could not present a united position. The Commission proposed that cultural concerns be recognised explicitly in the preamble to the GATS. France went a step further in its demands, and asked for "cultural exception" of audiovisual goods and services, as they were culturally significant. Ultimately the Commission supported France's stance and the Uruguay negotiations stumbled on two completely opposite blocks:

---

[9] Goff, P., Limits to Liberalization, *op. cit.*

[10] Qualifying transmission time (QTT) is the time after excluding news, advertising, teleshopping and games from overall broadcasting time.

[11] Articles 4 and 5 of Directive 97/36/EC of the European Parliament and of the Council of 30 June 1997 amending Council Directive 89/552/EEC on the coordination of certain provisions laid down by law, regulation or administrative action in member states concerning the pursuit of television broadcasting activities, also known as the Television without Frontiers Directive.

[12] MEDIA Programs – EU subsidies for the development, distribution, promotion of European works and training of professionals; Eurimages – the Council of Europe's initiative providing grants and loans for the co-production of European works.

- "exceptionists", represented by the European Union, Canada and Australia, wanted to protect the countries' right to conduct national policies aimed at supporting domestic cultural industries and maintaining public aid strategies for art and culture;
- free-trade advocates, notably the US and Japan, joined by Mexico and Brazil, which considered cinema and audiovisual works as entertainment, and rejected any idea of protecting the industry.

The Americans, the largest global exporter of cultural goods,[13] supported by Japan, were reluctant to concede special recognition of culture because of the precedent such a move might set.[14] For them, all cultural goods and services constituted an important export sector (in the US, audiovisual goods are, after transport, the second largest-earning international industry).[15]

The "Solution"

At present the GATS does not have any specific provisions for the cultural sectors. This means all sectors are treated equally and are subject to liberalization. With no agreement between the two opposing blocs on the language recognising special characteristics of audiovisual services, the European Community did not make any concessions in this area of negotiations in 1994. As a result, many other countries withdrew their audiovisual industries from liberalization commitments. Of 105 states present at the close of the Uruguay Round, only a few decided to open their film industry to foreign competition. The idea of opening the television and radio markets attracted even fewer takers.[16] Two states, the US and the Central African Republic, were prepared to fully open their markets in all six categories of audiovisual services, the former being a leviathan, the latter a minnow in media production. The majority of participants chose to keep various forms of protection in their audiovisual sectors. After marathon rounds of negotiations, causing delays in closing the Uruguay Round, the audiovisual sector was eventually omitted from the WTO deal. Cable and satellite television were also kept out of the telecommunications agreement.

---

[13] UNESCO, "International Flows of Selected Cultural Goods 1980-98", Paris, 2001.

[14] Goldsmith, B., "Cultural Diversity, Cultural Networks and Trade: International Cultural Policy Debate", *Media International Australia*, No. 102, 2002, pp. 35-53.

[15] Frau-Megis, D., "'Cultural Exception', National Policies and Globalisation: Imperatives in Democratisation and Promotion of Contemporary Culture", *Quaderns del CAC*, No. 14, 2002.

[16] Only seventeen countries decided to partially open their audiovisual sectors to free trade, for details see Messerlin, P., Siwek, S., Cocq, E., *The Audiovisual Services Sector in the GATS Negotiations*, American Enterprise Institute for Public Policy Research, Washington, D.C., AEI Press, 2004.

The audiovisual sector was included on the list of "mandated sectors", to appear automatically on the agenda for a new Doha Round originally set to conclude by the end of 2005. As Ben Goldsmith points out

> fundamentally for the French, as for the Canadians and many other countries around the world, the capacity to make cultural policy which results in, what an economist – or an American trade negotiator – might describe as protectionist actions which unfairly distort a market and discriminate against non-national players is about the capacity to both perpetuate traditions and ensure media pluralism.[17]

For Ramón Torrentn "the request for particular treatment was obviously based on political arguments, i.e., the role of culture as a sector where strictly economic considerations should be subordinated to other political and social considerations".[18]

Supporting cultural traditions and media pluralism were of course an aim in itself, but Europe in the early 1990s had quite different reasons from the rest of the world *not* to agree to open its market entirely to foreign media services. In the 1993 Maastricht Treaty, EU member states agreed to make further progress in political cooperation. At the same time they worked on accession criteria for future members[19] which clearly defined the political identity of those already in the EU. In addition, they discussed the switch to their new currency, the Euro, another politico-economic symbol. Brussels embarked on what was called "A People's Europe". A European *demos* was needed to support the European project and that was envisaged as the product of action taken mainly in the media.[20] It took European trade negotiators a few years, while the GATS was struggling to reach a compromise in the early 1990s, to realise that there was a link between reaching European citizens through the media and allowing those media to be fully open to free trade. The last thing that Europe wanted at that time was for its audiovisual market to be dominated by American productions. And as

---

[17] Goldsmith, B., 2002, *op. cit.*, p. 43.

[18] Torrent, R., 2002, "The 'Cultural Exception' in the World Trade Organisation (WTO): the Basis of the Audiovisual Policy in Catalonia", *Quaderns del CAC*, No. 14, pp. 17-24.

[19] The EU Copenhagen Summit in 1993 established three criteria for aspiring states: introduction of democracy with the respect for human and minority rights, a functioning market economy and the transposition of European laws into their national legislation.

[20] Shore, C., *Building Europe; the Cultural Politics of European Integration*, London/New York, Routledge, 2000.

Frau-Megis argues, the challenge was to take "a stand as non-American whilst avoiding anti-Americanism".[21]

Culture Industries and European Identity

Although the Treaty of Rome of 1957 did not explicitly spell out the promotion of a European cultural or political identity, it would have been considered vital to promote an increased standard of living.[22] By 1974, the European Parliament was calling for the European Community (EC) to become an active partner on the cultural stage. Jean Monnet, the "Father of Europe", was believed to have once said "if we were to start the integration process again, we should start from culture".[23] Through culture, the Commission decided to create the "common European feeling" and by mid-1980s its actions entered the cultural arena, initially with no budget and no legal basis. Culture became a tool in achieving political aims. A number of policy initiatives were developed in several areas, particularly in education and training programs, and audio-visual policy.[24] By the mid-1980s, the Commission estimated that television would play both economic and cultural roles, firstly, by creating jobs and opening up production and advertising industry and, secondly, by fostering a European identity. The Commission's information policy, and subsequently, its audiovisual policy were officially designed to sustain and develop European self-awareness. The Green Paper on Television without Frontiers of 1984 spelled out clearly the link between European identity and integration that the Commission saw:

> Information is decisive, perhaps the most decisive, factor in European unification [...] European unification will only be achieved if Europeans want it. Europeans will only want it if there is such thing as European identity.

---

[21] Frau-Megis, D., 2002, *op. cit.* p. 6.

[22] A direct aim of the Treaty of Rome as expressed in Article 2.

[23] The attribution is uncertain. Richard Collins, a media scholar, has combed through all Monnet's speeches but has found no trace of the famous (presumably apocryphal) sentence.

[24] Through the 1980s the Commission implemented numerous initiatives such as the European Academy of Science, the Euro-lottery, school exchange programs and a "European dimension" was introduced into history lessons. The symbolic harmonization of European passports, driving licences and car number plates took place and a European anthem, flag and logo were created. The Commission introduced new events for celebration. The European weeks, the European culture months and the European years were dedicated to the promotion of certain themes: the European year of cinema, or the environment etc. The most important date introduced to the calendar was 9th of May, the anniversary of the Schuman Declaration, which officially celebrated "Europe's Day".

European identity will only develop if Europeans are adequately informed. At present, information via the mass media is controlled at national level.[25]

Television, particularly the pan-European channels, was envisaged as providing Europe-wide information and thereby bestowing European consciousness on the people. Although the Commission did not have any competences or budget in the area of culture at the time, its officials were determined to make culture and media the two key driving forces for integration. This strategy was made clear by Jacques Delors in his first speech as Commission president to the European Parliament in 1985:

> The culture industry will tomorrow be one of the biggest industries, a creator of wealth and jobs. Under the terms of the Treaty we do not have the resource to implement a cultural policy, but we are going to try to tackle it along economic lines [...] We have to build a powerful European culture industry that will enable us to be in control of both the medium and the content, maintaining our standards of civilization and encouraging the creative people amongst us.[26]

Dealing with culture on the basis of *economic* terms changed dramatically with the 1992 Maastricht Treaty, which substantially enlarged the EU sphere of governance. It introduced European citizenship[27] and new areas like culture, education, youth, consumer protection and public health were now under the jurisdiction of the EU. The phrase "unity in diversity" appeared on the EU agenda, suggesting that Europeanization must go together with respect for the regions, nations, peoples and their cultures. In its cultural provisions Maastricht stated that "the Community shall contribute to the flowering of the cultures of the member states while respecting their national and regional diversity and at the same time bringing the common cultural heritage to the fore".[28] The Commission now acknowledged that television and broadcasting were crucial tools in the creation of "Europeans".

---

[25] "Television without Frontiers: Green Paper on the Establishment of the Common Market for Broadcasting especially for Satellite and Cable", COM(84) final, Luxembourg, OOPEC, 1984, p. 2.

[26] In Collins, R., *Audiovisual and Broadcasting Policy in the European Community*, London, University of North Press, 1993, p. 14.

[27] EU citizenship established free movement and residence within the Community, rights to vote in EU Parliamentary elections and local elections in the country of residence, diplomatic protection abroad for all Europeans, non judicial means of redress (petitions to the EU Parliament and complaints to the EU Ombudsman). All the rights were not offered to non-EU nationals, and the citizens of EU member states had already enjoyed them on the basis of their national citizenship.

[28] Article 128, Treaty of Maastricht, 1992.

Not all media were perceived as playing an equal role in this process. The "Television without Frontiers" Directive of 1989, the major document in the field, specifically excluded radio from its ambit, while the print media were also excluded. Only television was seen as important to the process of European economic, cultural and political integration. It was regarded as a "more influential and less nationally encumbered medium than print".[29] With the launch of the Single European Market in 1986, breaking down the walls between national markets became the order of the day. The broadcasting sector was only one of many to face the same treatment. Deregulation and liberalization of protectionist national policies were necessary mechanisms in achieving a truly open European market. These steps envisaged the creation of a European public sphere as a step towards the eventual unification of the European people.

The legal framework for broadcasting, the Television without Frontiers Directive, provides support for European films and television programs by setting quota requirements for "European works" on television. According to Article 4, all broadcasters must reserve "where practicable and by appropriate means" a majority of air time for European output, excluding time devoted to news, sports, games, advertising, teletext services and teleshopping. "European works" refer to any audiovisual productions originating from EU member states or from countries that are parties to the European Convention on Transfrontier Television (Article 6), on condition that they are made, supervised or controlled by producers residing in the European Union. The concept of the "European works" has been extended by the revised in 1997 Directive to include co-productions with any countries outside Europe.[30]

Since the early 1990s, the European Union has also been supporting its member states in strengthening their audiovisual sectors and meeting the obligatory quota requirement. Through the MEDIA Programs,[31] the EU tries to stimulate and increase the competitive supply of European productions, to step up intra-European exchanges of films and programmes, promote cultural and linguistic diversity, and to increase European producers' share in the world markets.

---

[29] Williams, K., *European Media Studies*, London, Hodder Education, 2005, p. 13.

[30] Productions made under co-production treaties with EU member states are regarded as European works if co-producers from the EU have the majority stake in total production costs, and control the production.

[31] MEDIA Program (1991-1995) with a budget of 200 million euros (then ECU).
MEDIA II (1996-2000) with a budget of 310 million euros, divided into two strands: MEDIA II Development and Distribution and MEDIA II Training.
MEDIA Plus (2001-2005 extended to 2006) with 470 million euros.

From a market point of view, the primary aim of trans-national legislation for the television sector was to attract the capital necessary for the growth of a trans-European infrastructure.[32] The enlargement of broadcasting companies was to produce trans-national programming in order to make profit trans-nationally on an enlarged market. The supranational regulation was to ensure there were no disparities amongst member states.[33] The Television without Frontiers Directive sought to establish the free movement of television broadcasts across borders, principles of jurisdiction, media pluralism, advertising rules and limitations, protection of minors from harmful content, right of reply and regulation of content by the introduction of European quotas. Both the MEDIA programs and the Directive aimed to improve the circulation of European works.

From a cultural standpoint, trans-national television was to contribute to the development of a European identity,[34] quotas and financial aid were to "contribute to the flowering of the cultures of member states and artistic and literary creation, including in the audiovisual sector".[35]

In taking television into its jurisdiction, it appears that the EU believes that the media can have a decisive impact on audiences, and that, if used appropriately, this impact can result in increased integration. The aim of filling television schedules with European productions, long since achieved by most broadcasters across Europe,[36] would suggest that, in the future, the EU will let go and relax its rigid and controversial legislation. But in 2005, although satisfied with the performance of television across the member states, the EU refused to reduce its European quotas and, in fact, went a step further, extending the quotas from television alone to all audiovisual media services.[37] This change is potentially all the more significant because, as we have seen with cinema and television in the past, audiovisual services may come to eclipse television at some future date.

---

[32] "Strategy Options to Strengthen the European Programme Industry in the Context of Audiovisual Policy of the European Union" (Green Paper), COM(1994), 96 final.

[33] Wheeler, M., "Supranational Regulation Television and the European Union", *European Journal of Communication*, Vol. 19, No. 3, 2004, pp. 349-369.

[34] Bakir, V., "An Identity for Europe? The Role of the Media" in M.J. Wintle (ed.), *Culture and Identity in Europe*, Aldershot, Avebury, 1996, p. 177.

[35] Article 151 of the Maastricht Treaty on the European Union, 1992.

[36] "New Figures Show: Almost two thirds of EU television time is 'Made in Europe'", Commission, IP/08/1207, Brussels, 25 July 2008.

[37] "Proposal for a Directive of the European Parliament and of the Council amending Council Directive 89/552/EEC on the Coordination of certain provisions laid down by law, regulation or administrative action in member states concerning the pursuit of television broadcasting activities", COM(2005) 646 final, Brussels, 13 December 2005.

It is not the purpose of this chapter to establish whether or not a European identity exists. Our purpose is rather to highlight the role of culture, and media in particular, that the Commission sees in the identity-creating process. Since the inception of the European Communities, there has always been a question as to whether or under which circumstances a European identity might take shape. A political identity of the people of Europe has been, and still is, considered essential to underpin political unification.

Efforts to "engineering" Europeans through television which have been under way since the mid-1980s would be in danger if the EU removed its quotas and subsidies. It is these two mechanisms that have been the most controversial from the GATS-related, free-trade perspective. Before the Uruguay Round talks, the Commission explicitly stated:

> Cultural and linguistic identities [...] must be protected. [...] The Community is therefore approaching these negotiations with the firm intention of achieving international liberalization within the limits already achieved within the Community, i.e. by leaving intact cultural specificity of the sector and the Community measures dependent on this specificity.[38]

And again, while preparing for the next round of talks in Doha in 2000, the EU could not offer its audiovisual services for full liberalization. The double aim of economic, as well as cultural unification could not be separated for the purpose of signing an *economic* agreement. Lifting the quotas would mean, in the eyes of European policy makers, the demise of the European project.

Between Uruguay Round 1994 and Doha Round 2000

Although expected to establish rules for trade in services, the Uruguay negotiations, according to Divina Frau-Megis, had a broader meaning, "the debate on 'cultural exception' is one of the post-Cold War confrontations to have tested the alliance between Atlantic countries. And it is perhaps for this aspect it will be remembered. [...] It represents the first real conflagration between the idea of globalisation and that of Americanization".[39] The number of states not ready to open their markets spoke for itself. As Pierre Sauve argues, "the fact that only 13 out of 105 present at the close of the Uruguay Round (of which only 3 countries from the OECD zone), [...] – have agreed liberalizing measures for this sector, is a sign of its evident particularism".[40]

---

[38] "Communication from the Commission to the Council and Parliament on Audiovisual Policy", COM(90) 78 final, Brussels, 21 February 1990, p. 64.

[39] Frau-Megis, D., "Cultural Exception", *op. cit.*, p. 4.

[40] Sauve, P., "The WTO Doha Round: What's at Stake Culturally", *Quaderns del CAC*, No. 14, pp. 25-31.

For the following decade, both sides – "liberalisers" and "exemptionists" alike – continued to seek stronger arguments that could determine or copper-fasten the status of audiovisual products. Since the "abandoning" of the liberalization process in cultural sectors, it is the "exemptionists" who have largely benefited. Recent reviews in the European Union demonstrate a strong growth in domestic film productions, higher audiences, better dissemination of works and even higher audience preferences for national products.[41]

In Europe, film production has been on the rise since 1995, mainly due to the UK, France, Italy, Germany and Spain. Television programs made in Europe are also the majority of scheduled programming on European television. European works represent 2/3 of total qualifying transmission time, with the new EU members in 2004 also fulfilling their quotas.[42] Audiences tend to show a preference for local productions, which has led to an increase in market share.[43] As a result, American programs, although still significant in overall programming, are no longer scheduled in prime time as in the 1980s. Between 6 pm and midnight has come to be successfully dominated by national productions throughout Europe.[44] Advertisers, aware of audience preferences, demand their advertising spots to be scheduled around the most popular national programs.[45] Public aid continues to rise and boost the industry with an average 10% of annual growth since 1997. The only weak point on the European audiovisual scene is the circulation of output, both cinematographic and televisual. Films and television programmes produced in one country predominantly stay in that country, rarely crossing borders to enjoy success in the neighbouring market.[46] Works from central or eastern European countries rarely, if ever, appear on television in Western Europe.[47]

---

[41] *VII Progress Report on the Promotion of European Works*, 2006, also Press Release IP/06/1115, Brussels, 22 August 2006.

[42] "New Figures Show: Almost Two Thirds of EU Television Time is 'Made in Europe'", Commission, IP/08/1207, Brussels, 25 July 2008.

[43] Interviews with Boguslaw Chrabota, Programming Manager, Telewizja Polsat (Polish private broadcaster) and with Krzysztof Wojciechowski, Legal Office, Telewizja Polska S.A. (TVP), Polish Public Service Television, Warsaw, June 2006.

[44] Interview with Anna Harold, EU Commission, Media and Information Society Directorate General, Audiovisual Policy Unit, Brussels, July 2006.

[45] Interview with Boguslaw Chrabota, Programming Manager, Telewizja Polsat (Polish private broadcaster), Warsaw, June 2006.

[46] Interview with Anna Harold, EU Commission, Media and Information Society Directorate General, Audiovisual Policy Unit, Brussels, July 2006.

[47] Interviews with Karol Jakubowicz, National Broadcasting Council of Poland, Krzysztof Wojciechowski, Legal Office, Telewizja Polska S.A. (TVP), Polish Public

With arguments such as these at the ready, "exemptionists" steeled themselves for further debate and did not offer their audiovisual services for liberalization. The evidence of the late 1990s and early 2000s did much to legitimize the application of quotas and public, national and supranational aid to the sector. At the same time, it proved that treatment of the audiovisual industry based solely on economic grounds did not meet the cultural and political expectations of European elites or audiences. The decision of other WTO members not to schedule the sector for further liberalization also proved that other states considered it special.

Evaluation of the functioning of "cultural exception" is difficult in regard to overall market performance. It has been extremely successful in cinema and prime-time television programming, but those who expected to find "Europeanization" being promoted by intra-European circulation have been disappointed. Yet it has led to the development of new trends: a national preference for local programmes, and the rise of national cinema and television production. This, however, is inimical to the stated European aims of "creating" Europeans, as *national* production and growing *national* consciousness is what Europe has tried to overcome.

From Cultural Identity to Cultural Diversity

In the meantime, national identity, which has always been at the heart of the "exemptionist" debate, has drifted over the last decade from the notion of "cultural exemption" towards "cultural diversity".[48] "Cultural exemption", as a means of representation of one nation with its common values and beliefs, serves a nation as a whole. A nation here is understood as a unitary entity with no diversity within. "Cultural diversity" acknowledges the difference amongst individuals, with their particular values different from others within the same society. It gives nations the right to care for cultures within their borders which previously had been overlooked or marginalized (like those of the Spanish regions or of the UK's constituents) or worldwide with respect to their former colonies and people who have arrived from these colonies, people, who brought their languages, traditions, and beliefs. Diversity also, according to Frau-Megis, turns the main arguments against America "[...] it's no longer just France that is putting a spanner in the works

---

Service Television and Boguslaw Chrabota, Programming Manager, Telewizja Polsat (Polish private broadcaster), Warsaw, June 2006.

[48] "UNESCO and the Issue of Cultural Diversity, Review and Strategy 1946-2004", UNESCO, Paris, September 2004.

of the WTO but rather Hollywood which is blocking all other countries' expression of cultural diversity".[49]

Whither GATS?

The GATS applies, in principle, to all service sectors with two exceptions: Article I (3) excludes "services supplied in the exercise of governmental authority" which are supplied neither on a commercial basis nor in competition with other suppliers (e.g. social security schemes), and the Annex on Air Transport Services exempts measures affecting air traffic rights and services directly related to the exercise of such rights.

There are possible exemptions from countries' obligations. These are contained in country-specific lists. The Annex to the GATS, however, refers to them as *temporary*. Point 6 states: "In principle, these exemptions should not exceed a period of 10 years. In any case they shall be subject to negotiation in subsequent rounds of trade liberalisation". The list of MFN clause exemptions for the European Union as well as other countries excluding certain services expired in 2004. Before the Doha Round, one line of argument from the "exemptionists" camp concentrated on "services supplied on [a] non-commercial basis". Free-to-air television, it was claimed, as a public service for communities, nations and groups of interests is or should be supplied on a "non-consumer basis". But this argument is fundamentally undermined by the very name of the service itself. "Commercial television" is exactly what it says it is: commercial. A second exception from the GATS (Air Transport) was added to the Agreement on the request of the United States. This may give Europeans an option to insist on a *quid pro quo* measure, establishing another annex, which would meet *their* particular needs.

The WTO has shown little sign of placing the value of respect for cultural diversity on an equal footing with the right to make profits. It has demanded that countries provide a list of commitments in all sectors. Before the new Round, there were no talks about acknowledging the dual nature of the audiovisual sector, either in the preamble or in any of its annexes. Consultations on the possibility of taking culture, cinema and television out of the GATS completely and putting them into a new legally binding international instrument that would give states the right to support what is important to them without fear of sanction started in the late 1990s. By 2002, three drafts of a possible Convention on Cultural Diversity were circulating internationally. One, developed by a cultural industries sectoral advisory group appointed by the Canadian Minister of Foreign Affairs and International Trade, known as SAGIT,

---

[49] Frau-Megis, D., "Cultural Exception", *op. cit.*, p. 8.

the second, composed by the International Network for Cultural Diversity (INCD), a cultural NGO, and the third developed by the International Network on Cultural Policy (INCP), an association of over 50 Ministers of Culture.[50]

The main stage, however, for an international debate on the nature of audiovisual goods and services has recently become the United Nations Educational, Scientific and Cultural Organization (UNESCO). In the unanimously adopted 2001 Universal Declaration on Cultural Diversity, 188 Ministers of Culture referred to cultural goods and services as "vectors of identity, values and meaning" which "must not be treated as mere commodities or consumer goods" (Article 8). Cultural policies, according to Article 9:

> [...] must create conditions conducive to the production and dissemination of diversified cultural goods and services through cultural industries that have the means to assert themselves at the local and global level. It is for each State, with due regard to its international obligations, to define its cultural policy and to implement it through the means it considers fit, whether by operational support or appropriate regulations.

The EU supported the UNESCO Declaration on Cultural Diversity, explaining that "promotion and preservation of cultural diversity are among the founding principles of the European model".[51] They are enshrined in the Treaty on European Union (TEU),[52] the Charter of Fundamental Rights of the European Union,[53] and figure prominently in the Treaty establishing a Constitution for Europe.[54] In May 2005, however, the peoples of France and the Netherlands rejected the proposed Constitution. Originally expected to enter into force in January 2007, the Constitutional Treaty was revised into the Lisbon Treaty which is now ratified. One of its objectives under Article 3 is that "the Union shall respect its rich cultural and linguistic diversity, and shall ensure that Europe's cultural heritage is safeguarded and enhanced". This provision does not touch on the core of the French and Dutch voters' rejection of

---

[50] For details see Smeers, J., "A Convention on Cultural Diversity: From WTO to UNESCO" in *Media International Australia Incorporating Culture and Policy*, The University of Queensland, Australia, 2004.

[51] "Towards an International Instrument on Cultural Diversity", *Communication from the Commission*, COM (2003) 520 final.

[52] Article 151.1: "The Community shall contribute to the flowering of the cultures of the Member States, while respecting their national and regional diversity and at the same time bringing the common cultural heritage to the fore"; Article 151.4: "The Community shall take cultural aspects into account in its action under other provisions of this Treaty, in particular in order to respect and to promote the diversity of its cultures".

[53] Article 22: "The Union shall respect cultural, religious and linguistic diversity".

[54] Article 128.

the Constitutional Treaty. The subsequent rejection of the Lisbon Treaty by Irish citizens in 2008 did not touch upon its cultural provisions either.

Particularly "safeguarded" and "enhanced" will be the audiovisual sector, as while revising the Television without Frontiers Directive in 2005 the EU did not reduce the required amount of European output on television. On the contrary, all new accession member states had to adopt the entire Directive including quotas, and some of the "old" member states[55] have decided to follow the example of France with its highest (60%) requirement[56] of European production on television. The new 2007 Media Program received an increased budget.[57] This increased allocation has less to do with the increased number of EU member states and much more to do with demonstrating how serious the EU is about its cultural policies and cultural services. Another example of the EU's commitment to the sector is its signing of the UNESCO "Convention on the Protection and Promotion of the Diversity of Cultural Expressions".

Maintaining quotas, increasing financial support for the industry and obliging its twelve new members to adopt the same measures in their sectors does not suggest that the European Union is going to surrender its strategic interest in this sector. On the other hand, the United States will be equally reluctant to forego the US$8 billion earned annually from exports to the European market. The EU did not schedule audio-visual sectors on its latest list of commitments submitted in May 2005 to the WTO Secretariat. It seeks to maintain the exceptions to the MFN clause in the sphere of cultural policy, such as support for its members' co-production agreements and the preferential treatment (quotas) accorded to audiovisual productions originating in European countries (the EU). A recent study of cultural sectors throughout Europe proves that culture "drives economic and social development, as well as innovation and cohesion".[58] Cultural and creative sectors out-perform the rest of the

---

[55] In the interview with EFE news agency, Spanish Secretary of Culture, Carmen Chacón, announced that the Government is preparing serious measures to defend "cultural diversity from monopoly of the giant American audiovisual companies [...] the measures could use quotas [...]", 20 September 2004, www.audiovisualcat. net/forumbcn2004/eng/news/news_200904.htm, accessed 10 November 2006.

[56] According to Article 27 of the French Broadcasting Law No. 86-1067 of 30 September 1986, revised by Law No. 2000-719, all terrestrial broadcasters must broadcast, particularly during prime-time, a proportion of at least 60% of European audiovisual and cinematographic works. Cable and satellite channels have the same obligation, with regard to European cinematographic works (Article 33 of the French Broadcasting Law).

[57] Decision of the European Parliament and the Council concerning the implementation of a program of support for the European audiovisual sector (MEDIA 2007), COM(2004) 470 final.

[58] "Economy of Culture in Europe", *KEA European Affairs*, 2006.

economy in terms of employment and turnover. In 2003, they contrib-uted to the EU GDP more than other sectors. In addition, European integration is possible mainly due to cultural and creative sectors, which "forge a sense of belonging as well as spread democratic and social values".[59] Maybe the most important consideration is that culture indus-tries drive many other sectors of the European economy, in particular innovation and Information and Computer Technologies (ICTs). Other sectors are also much indebted to cultural industries, which act as good ambassadors for European tourism, cosmetics, cars, food and beverages.

Conclusion

The debate over the real status of audiovisual output has a very hard commercial edge. When the Doha Round collapsed in 2007, no final determination had been made on the vexed question of how to deal with the so-called "trade distorting practices" in the audiovisual sector. The sudden burst of national and European consciousness that informed the European Community position during the Uruguay Round has had a strong knock-on effect: more countries than ever are now lining up behind the EU position and seeking to avoid the liberalization of the sector. They are drawing encouragement from figures indicating rapid growth of audiovisual industries, production, talent, ideas and even viewers' preferences for local productions.

Development, which is the ultimate aim of liberalization, in the European case, seems to be better served under the strict content laws and financial support regime supported by the EU. It shows that regulat-ing and intervening in the sector limits neither the countries' perform-ances nor the people's choices. It encourages the self-development of nations and of their national industries and consciousness. What is more, nobody has proven that untrammelled free trade can better assist devel-opment or democracy. On the contrary, as more markets rise, mainly in Asia and South America, they build their economies in line with their own needs and rights. In so doing, they prove that "the emergence of the global economy does not imply the extension of western values and institutions to the rest of humankind".[60] The global financial crisis of 2008 has also questioned the unregulated operation of capitalism with little or no government intervention.

In this sense, Europe has fallen victim to its own actions from the past: from founder and facilitator of the rules for global trade, it now finds itself to be the rallying voice against them in the culture arena. The

---

[59] *Ibid.*

[60] Grey, J., *False Dawn. The Delusions of Global Capitalism*, London, Granta, 1998, p. 4.

free market in its most extreme form ceased to exist by the end of the First World War,[61] and it has been impossible to reinvent. Whatever its ability to maximize profits, the free market has consistently proven itself inadequate in meeting human needs such as the need for personal freedom, freedom of expression, culture and identity. For this reason, the media and cultural industries should not proceed to full liberalization. "Imagined communities" to use the phrase of Benedict Anderson,[62] be they local, national or supranational, cannot be imagined and thus cannot become communities if all the means through which to articulate their imagination are dominated by foreign and distant voices.

Although the search in the early years of this century for an alternative instrument to regulate trade in the audiovisual sector clearly showed that there was now a strong trend towards the cultural self-awareness of nations, it is still not clear how this decades'-long dispute will be solved. UNESCO's approach towards diversity is now visibly present in rhetoric on culture amongst and within numerous states, not only in Europe. Nearly all nations have aligned themselves with UNESCO values by signing the Convention on the Protection and Promotion of the Diversity of Cultural Expressions. Only five states, the US and a group of four close allies (Israel, Australia, Nicaragua and Panama) have not done so.

Thus, a predominance of nations wishes to protect and promote their identities. This is one and the same predominance of countries engaged in trade liberalization, a movement whose guiding values are diametrically opposed to protection and the "cosseting" of national media sectors. The problem remains one of hierarchy of values: whose principles override whose? It has not been established how the two organizations, the WTO and UNESCO, should go about respecting each other's priorities. This chapter has argued that Europe has far more important reasons to keep its cultural field out of the free trade arena than just the protection of the industry alone. European integration is expected to take place mainly through cultural and creative sectors, which can forge a sense of belonging and spread democratic and social values. To open the sector entirely to free trade might, as in the past, benefit Americans, letting down not only the European industry but also everything that Europe stands for in its "European dream".[63]

---

[61]   *Ibid.*, Grey, J., p. 5.

[62]   Anderson, B., *Imagined Communities: Reflections on the Origin and Spread of Nationalism*, New York, Verso, 1991.

[63]   The phrase is borrowed from Rifkin, J., *The European Dream: How Europe's Vision of the Future is Quietly Eclipsing the American Dream*, New York, Jeremy P. Tarcher/Penguin, 2004.

CHAPTER 8

Development Policy, Conflict Prevention and EU Visibility in Africa[1]

Patrick KIMUNGUYI

Introduction

The end of the Cold War provided the European Community/Union (EC/EU) with the opportunity to realise its ambition to become a key international actor.[2] In this period, the discourse regarding the EU's policy towards Africa developed in two strands.

The first strand was within the framework of EU development cooperation with African, Caribbean and Pacific states (ACP states)[3] and humanitarian assistance, which has dominated the agenda since the 1990s. The Lomé IV/bis Convention introduced political conditionality by incorporating clauses on human rights, democracy and good governance and the rule of law as an "essential" part of this cooperation.

In 2000, the Cotonou Partnership Agreement (CPA) introduced other major changes towards strengthening the political dimensions of the partnership. Further changes to the cooperation included the introduction of clauses dealing with a broad range of political issues that fall outside traditional development cooperation, such as peace and security,

---

[1]   This chapter is based on a paper entitled "The Security-Development Nexus in EU-ACP Relations", delivered at the *New Europe, New Governance, New Worlds?* conference hosted by the Monash European and EU Centre, Melbourne, Australia, 12-14 April 2007.

[2]   Hill, C. and Smith, M., "International Relations and the European Union: Themes and Issues" in C. Hill and M. Smith (eds.), *International Relations and the European Union*, Oxford, Oxford University Press, 2005; Cameron, F., "The EU as a Global Actor: Far from Pushing its Political Weight Around" in C. Rhodes (ed.), *The EU in the World Community*, Boulder, CO, Lynne Rienner, 1998, pp. 19-44; Bretherton, C. and Vogler, J., *The EU as a Global Actor*, London, Routledge, 1999.

[3]   The abbreviation "ACP" refers to African, Caribbean, and Pacific countries, which at present include 78 countries, including 48 of the 54 African states. The five Mediterranean states belong to the Euro-Mediterranean partnership (1995) and South Africa signed a specific Trade, Development and Cooperation Agreement (TDCA) with the EU in 2000. The agreement was formally adopted by the ACP group and the EC, as the EU had no legal personality yet.

the arms trade and migration. Human rights, good governance and the rule of law are now key elements of the relationship and violation by a country of associated provisions can lead to suspension of EU aid. Cotonou has extended the partnership to new actors, including civil society groups and the private sector. It also introduces a new WTO-compatible trade policy of regionally focused Economic Partnership Agreements (EPAs), intended to be effective from January 2008, as well as a more rationalised and performance-based aid management.[4]

The second strand of this discourse ran parallel to the EU's development cooperation. In the early 1990s European institutions were making efforts to establish ways of preventing conflicts in Africa.[5] Bretherton and Vogler note that, in this period, many actors lobbied strongly for the reinforcement of the EU's international position through the Common Foreign and Security Policy (CFSP),[6] which has since become an important instrument in this regard.

The predicate question is this: why should the EU focus on sub-Saharan Africa, especially in the area of conflict prevention and development cooperation? Gorm Olsen explains that "sub-Saharan Africa remained on the post-cold war foreign policy agenda of the EU simply because the region became one of the elements of the effort to develop 'Europe' into a significant international actor".[7] But there are also more compelling reasons for the EU's growing interest in the region.

Firstly, the geographical proximity of Africa and Europe has ensured a close, but not always harmonious, relationship between the two continents for centuries. Long before the systematic colonisation of Africa in the 19th century, there were significant relations between Europe and Africa. On the positive side, trade links and a history of exchange of cultural ideas and developments were forged. On the negative side events such as the slave trade contributed to showing the dark side of these relations. Colonialism not only imposed European dominance on the African continent, but it also strengthened ties between particular countries, especially through the use of common languages such as

---

[4] Kimunguyi, P., "From Lomé to Cotonou: An Assessment of the European Union's Trade Relations with African, Caribbean and Pacific Countries", *Journal of International Relations*, Vol. 1-2, No. 33, Warsaw University, Scholar Publishers, July 2006; ECPDM, *Innovations in the Cotonou Agreement (4)*, Cotonou Infokit, Maastricht, ECDPM, 2001.

[5] *Ibid.*

[6] See Bretherton, C. and Vogler J., *The European Union as a Global Actor*, London, Routledge, 1999.

[7] Olsen, G.R., "Challenges to Traditional Policy Options, Opportunities for New Choices: The Africa Policy of the EU", *The Round Table*, Vol. 93, No. 375, July 2004, pp. 425-436.

English and French. A number of European countries, notably France, the United Kingdom (UK), Portugal and Belgium, for example, have maintained close relations with their former colonies.[8]

Secondly, Europe has also kept very close economic links with Africa. In fact, trade and investment with Europe have remained of particular importance to Africa and the EU is the main trading partner for almost all African countries.[9] Africa also receives most of its foreign investment from Europe. Leading investors are France, the Netherlands, Belgium and the UK. Inflows from these countries represented more than half of the inflows of foreign direct investment (FDI) to the continent in 2005.[10] Such economic links trigger the direct interest of governments and businesses in Europe in promoting sustainable development. The rationale behind this is that investment in infrastructure and governance initiatives, for example, are helpful in creating a favourable environment for investment.

Thirdly, it is not only economic interests that underlie European involvement in Africa, but the growing awareness in Europe that Europe's security interests are very closely linked to those of its neighbours. The EU's European Security Strategy (ESS) expresses this awareness by stating that Europe now faces threats which are diverse, hidden and unpredictable, such as terrorism, regional conflicts, state failure and organised crime, and that they are located in the world's poorest and poorly governed regions.[11]

For Europe, the increase in the numbers of migrants from Africa is a significant challenge. Africa's population is growing rapidly and there are plenty of economic incentives for workers to seek employment – whether legally or illegally – in the developed world. The sharing of languages and the geographical proximity of Africa to Europe obviously encourage this trend. This also includes the movements of refugees in conflict-torn countries. Thus, although relations between the EU and Africa have been predominantly economic and oriented towards devel-

---

8 *Ibid.*

9 Kimunguyi, P., "The European Union and Developing Countries: The Challenges of Trade Liberalisation in the Cotonou Process", refereed article delivered at *The 3rd Conference of European Union and Asia Pacific Association of European Studies*, hosted by Keio University in Tokyo, Japan, 8-10 December, 2005, http://www.soc. nii.ac.jp/eusa-japan/download/eusa_ap/chapter_PatrickKimunguyi. pdf; See also http://ec.europa.eu/trade/issues/bilateral/regions/acp/index_en.htm, accessed 4 April 2007.

10 United Nations, *World Investment Report 2006*, Overview.

11 Council of the European Union, A Secure Europe in a Better World: European Security Strategy, Brussels, 12 December 2003.

opment and humanitarian agendas, they have also been shifting to encompass the promotion of security, stability and democracy.

In examining the role of the EU in preventing conflict in Africa, this chapter argues that the EU's involvement in conflict prevention and resolution in Africa is driven by the dual aims of making the EU more visible as a major international actor and of enhancing its presence on the continent. To this end, the EU has been re-inventing development cooperation, and instruments for humanitarian assistance since the 1990s. It has also been creating instruments for crisis management in the framework of the CFSP. By so doing, the EU has placed itself in a better position to exercise its influence on conflict prevention on the continent. This chapter reflects firstly on the post-Cold War discourse on the EU policy towards Africa. It then focuses on the EU's development cooperation policy and how it has been re-invented into a conflict prevention instrument. It also examines the EU's humanitarian assistance with specific regard to the establishment of the European Community Humanitarian Aid Office (ECHO) as an instrument for responding to humanitarian crises. Part Four of this chapter examines the EU's policy on conflict prevention in Africa within the CFSP framework. Finally, the conclusion identifies challenges ahead for further EU involvement in Africa in the area of conflict prevention.

The EU and Development Cooperation

Development cooperation is one of the main features of the EU's relations with sub-Saharan Africa. The development cooperation and the perceived strategic economic and security interests of the EU in sub-Saharan Africa enable the EU to be comparatively well placed, in relation to other external actors operating in Africa,[12] and to have a profound impact on the prevention of conflicts. Three reasons justify this claim.

Firstly, the EU is the largest international donor of development aid to Africa. According to the Development Assistance Committee of the Organization of Economic Cooperation and Development (DAC/OECD), the EU and its member states provided approximately 64% of the world's aid flows in 2004.[13] Together with its member states, the EU provides about 67% of DAC aid in the form of official development assistance (ODA) for the sub-Saharan region.[14] This aid is set to increase

---

[12] This not only includes international actors such as the United States, but also EU member states themselves.

[13] Organization for Economic Cooperation and Development (OECD), *Development Co-operation Report 2005*, Paris, 2006, p. 158.

[14] European Commission, The Reform of the Management of the European Community's External Assistance: An Overview, Report, October 2002, p. 2.

as the EU and its member states have committed themselves to meeting the UN's target of 0.7% of combined gross national income (GNI) by 2015, which other non-EU states are less likely to achieve. At least half of any new financial resources to be found over the next decade have been promised to Africa.[15]

Secondly, with its renewable and contractual agreements with the ACP countries, the EU is well placed, especially in sub-Saharan Africa, to get involved and have an effect on cooperation issues at national, sub-regional and regional levels. This includes tackling the challenges posed by conflicts in Africa. The EU and ACP states have launched a joint institutional framework,[16] which provides the EU with the space (at political diplomatic and developmental levels) to leverage patterns and influence communication, not only between the two groups, but also with other international actors in sub-Saharan Africa.

Thirdly, the position of the EU in Africa can be viewed from a psychological perspective. As Sébastien Loisel notes, unlike its member states, the EU "is not stigmatised by a colonial past and it has repeatedly tried to distance itself from the colonial history of many of its member states". As a whole, he notes, the EU has "a relatively positive image among social and national elites in Africa".[17]

Furthermore, it emphasises the need to pay attention to the role of ethnic, national, and regional identity groups in many African conflicts. This is illustrated clearly in the Development Council's observation in 1998 that aid "should be designed and implemented in a way that it helps to address the root causes of conflict in a targeted manner [...] through supporting measures towards balancing political, social, economic and cultural opportunities among the groups with varying identities in recipient countries".[18] Aid should also provide sound mechanisms that could foster peaceful conciliation of group interests in conflict

---

[15] Council of the European Union, "Resolution of General Affairs and External Relations Council [8817/05]", Brussels, 24 May 2005.

[16] These joint institutions are respectively: the ACP-EU Council of Ministers; the ACP-EU Joint Parliamentary Assembly; the ACP-EU Committee of Ambassadors; the Centre for the Development of Enterprise and the Technical Centre for Agricultural and Rural Development.

[17] Loisel, S., "The European Union and African Border Conflicts: Assessing the Impact of Development Cooperation", *Working papers Series in EU Border Conflicts Studies*, No. 8, Centre d'études et de recherches internationales, Paris, Institut d'études politiques de Paris, July 2004, p. 10.

[18] The Council of the European Union, "The Role of Development Cooperation in Strengthening Peace-building, Conflict Prevention and Resolution", *Conclusions adopted by the Development Council*, 30 November 1998.

situations.[19] Thus, an approach for including these groups in development projects, as well as in peace negotiation processes, could be an indirect form of political recognition with profound effects on conflict.

Political Conditionality

This chapter concentrates on a significant feature of development cooperation: the emphasis on political dimensions that within the EU-ACP relationship can have profound influence on conflict prevention in Africa. Notably, the Cotonou Partnership Agreement has strongly politicised EU-ACP relations.[20] It is now structured around three pillars, namely preferential trade relations, development aid through European Development Funds and a permanent political dialogue. It is necessary to illustrate the gradual introduction (in the Lomé Convention) of political conditionality in the EU-ACP relationship in order to demonstrate how it gives the EU profound influence over the recipient states.

The EU-ACP development cooperation has been constructed historically on a contractual basis, beginning from the first Lomé Convention (1975).[21] Through this contractual approach, the EU allocates a given amount of funds to the European Development Fund based on a 5-year rolling programme. In the beginning, the first Lomé Convention identified the importance of respect of the sovereignty and self-determination of partners, which practically prevented the EU from using its aid as "carrot" or "stick" in its relations with ACP countries.[22]

Indeed, EU development cooperation policy towards ACP countries has been steadily politicised since the mid-1980s, when references to political norms were introduced, which were later to become legally

---

[19] See Organization for Economic Cooperation and Development, *DAC Guidelines: Helping Prevent Violent Conflict*, Paris, OECD, 2001, http://www.oecd.org/dataoecd/15/54/1886146.pdf, accessed 13 August 2009.

[20] Kimunguyi, P., "Changing Paradigms or Symbolic Rhetoric? Perspectives on the European Union's Development policy", conference chapter prepared for the *29th Annual Conference of African Studies Association of Australasia and the Pacific*, Macquarie University, Sydney, 20-22 September 2006. See also Loisel, S., "The Politicisation of the EU-ACP Relationship after the Cold War", article delivered at the *33rd ACES Annual and 8th Research Conference*, Newcastle, 2-4 September 2003.

[21] *De facto* relations between the EU/EC and Africa stretch as far back as the Treaty of Rome (1957). They were followed by the Yaoundé Conventions (1963-1975) that were signed shortly after the independence of former French colonies, plus Madagascar and established an "association" between the EEC and the former French colonies and Madagascar. The Lomé Convention (1975), signed after the accession of Britain to the EEC, abandoned the term and adopted "co-operation" between EEC and ACP countries.

[22] The First Convention of Lomé, 28 February 1975, Article 2.

binding.[23] According to Carl, the ACP states themselves initiated this process when they asked for a reference to the respect of human rights as a common "belief" in the third Lomé Convention of 1985. In so doing, African states sought to stigmatise the UK and the Netherlands, which continued to maintain economic relations with the South African apartheid regime. However, the EC insisted on the inclusion of this statement in an annex rather than in the main body of the Convention.[24]

Towards the end of the 1980s, circumstances changed and it was the EC/EU's member states that now exerted pressure to include human rights, democracy and rule of law clauses in the body of the Lomé IV Convention.[25] Later, in 1995, the revised Lomé IV Convention declared these values "essential" to what the Convention was seeking to achieve. It further developed the possibility to suspend EU development aid, but it introduced a consultation procedure determining circumstances of aid suspension.[26]

Lomé's successor, the Cotonou Partnership Agreement (2000) fills this gap by establishing a formal procedure for aid suspension in the event of gross abuse of human rights.[27] It has also, unlike Lomé, intro-duced mechanisms for potential aid reduction, through a new rolling programme and potential adjustment of Country Strategy Chapters (CSP), especially in relation to the so-called "conflict-fuelling" regimes. Furthermore, Cotonou has also made the mid-term reviews of develop-ment cooperation already envisaged in Lomé IV/bis more systematic. This in turn allows for a certain level of aid and resource redistribution, with the aim of rewarding countries which perform well while limiting or denying poor performers access to unused funds.[28]

Hence, it can be argued that in the EU-ACP relationship develop-ment cooperation is an important diplomatic tool for the EU in its negotiations with ACP countries, which, as Reiterer observes, gives the EU powerful political leverage and influence over its developing coun-try partners.[29] This power can be noted in aid sanctioning scenarios. As

---

[23] *Ibid.*

[24] Carl, G., "Return to Colonialism? The New Orientation of European Development Assistance" in M. Lister (ed.), *New Perspectives on European Union Development Cooperation*, Boulder/Oxford, West View Press, 1999, p. 116.

[25] *Ibid.*

[26] Revised Fourth EU-ACP Convention of Lomé, 4 November 1995, Article 366.

[27] Cotonou Partnership Agreement, Article 96.

[28] Kimunguyi, P., "AID: A Critical Review of the Dialogue on 'Poorly Performing Countries'", *Journal of International Relations*, No. 31:1-2, University of Warsaw, Scholar Publishers, 2005, pp. 155-172.

[29] Reiterer, M., "Inter-regionalism: A New Diplomatic Tool, European Experience in East Asia", article delivered at the *3rd Conference of European Union and Asia*

Loisel remarks, in such scenarios, from a procedural perspective, the consultation process is theoretically reciprocal, which could account for the few occurrences of aid suspension. But the EU retains in practice much of the deciding power. In explaining the mixed results in aid suspension as a tool on the part of the EU, Loisel and Karin Arts explain that the results could be seen as

> consequences of diverging interests among EU member states. Even though the mere possibility of aid suspension might act as an inhibiting factor, many African leaders seem to rely on their privileged relations with particular EU member states and on the consequent divisions in the Council to block effectively most sanctions[30]

which hinders the impact that political conditionality could otherwise have. This explanation may be a valid one for African leaders such as the late Mobutu Sésé Seko and Eyadéma of Togo.

The case of Togo under General Gnassingbé Eyadéma, is an interesting one as it illustrates the way the EU used the political conditionality tool when it suspended aid to Togo in 1993 and resumed it only in 2005. At the time, Togo was experiencing a very strong "democratic deficit" in the aftermath of elections, which had been biased and characterised by large scale fraudulence of national resources, political assassinations and arbitrary arrests. A number of EU member states also followed the EU's example and sanctioned Togo on a bilateral basis. France did not endorse sanctions to Togo because it had a strong alliance with the Togolese regime.[31] For the rest of the 1990s, the domestic situation in Togo did not significantly change. However, in 2002, General Eyadéma changed the constitution to allow him to run for presidency for another term.[32] He was re-elected to presidency in June 2003, following his modification of the Constitution to the extent of disqualifying his opponents. In an attempt to recast itself, General Eyadéma's regime embarked on leading a number of initiatives within the Economic Community of West African States' (ECOWAS) structure that aimed at

---

Pacific Association of European Studies, hosted by Keio University, Tokyo, Japan, December 8-10, 2005, wwwsoc.nii.ac.jp/eusajapan/download/eusa_ap/chapter_MichaelReiterer.pdf, accessed 24 May 2007.

[30] Loisel, S., "The Politicisation of the EU-ACP Relationship after the Cold War", chapter prepared for the 33rd ACES Annual and 8th Research Conference, Newcastle, 2-4 September 2003; Arts, K., "Development Co-operation and Human Rights: Turbulent Times for EU Policy" in M. Lister (ed.), *New Perspectives on European Union Development Cooperation*, Westview Press, 1999, pp. 7-28.

[31] *Ibid.*

[32] See *Humanitarian News and Analysis, In-depth: Togo Elections*, http://www.irinnews.org/InDepthMain.aspx?InDepthId=27&ReportId=69840, accessed 14 August 2009.

resolving conflict in the Côte d'Ivoire. Other initiatives included inviting ACP ambassadors in Lomé to meet opposition leaders and human rights association representatives. In 2003, the European Council began engaging in formal political dialogue with Togo, to reinforce democracy and the rule of law, which moved the Togolese government towards a policy for making democracy "real" in the country. In February 2005, General Eyadéma died and his son Faure Gnassingbé was sworn in as President. However, international pressure forced him to step down 20 days after assuming the presidency and in April 2005, elections were held. Faure Gnassingbé won, vowing to concentrate on the promotion of development, the common good, peace and national unity in the country. Only in December 2005, did Togo receive the first EU aid since 1993. In 2006, the Benelux countries (Belgium, Netherlands, and Luxemburg) decided to resume cooperation with Togo. In June 2007, the EU and Togo concluded an agreement on the funding of the support program for the 2007 electoral process in Togo aimed at securing a favourable environment for the conduct of the general elections, reinforcing the capacity of civil society organizations in the domain of electoral observation, as well as strengthening the surveillance of media utilisation. The Parliamentary elections took place on 14 October 2007.[33]

On the account of these events, in Togo, a number of analyses on political conditionality as an element of EU aid have been conducted. For example, analyses for the period after Lomé IV/bis (1995) revealed that a small number of aid sanctions were adopted. For example, one study illustrates the way such measures were restricted to human rights abuses as has been the case in Sudan or Libya in the 1990s; or to cases of striking disruption of fragile democratic processes, for example the *coups d'état* in Comoros, Ivory Coast, Niger and Togo. In other instances, cooperation was only streamlined to encompass cases of civil and internal conflicts, such as Rwanda, Burundi and Somalia.[34] Richard Young, for example, points to the example of Nigeria, which was sanctioned only after the elimination[35] of Ogoni activists in

---

[33] The EU sent over 80 election observers and the EU specifically set up a grant of 13.6 million euros from the European Development Fund to the United Nations Trust Fund. See European Commission, "Togo: all calm as parliamentary elections are held on 14 October 2007", http://europa.eu/rapid/pressReleasesAction.do?reference=IP/07/1502&format=HTML&aged=0&language=EN&guiLanguage=en, accessed 11 October 2008.

[34] Kimunguyi, P., "The Security-Development Nexus in EU-ACP Relations", paper delivered at the *New Europe, New Governance, New Worlds?* conference, Monash European and EU Centre, Melbourne, Australia, 12-14 April 2007.

[35] McLuckie, C. and McPhail, A. (eds.), *Ken Saro-Wiwa: Writer and Political Activist*, Boulder, CO, Lynne Rienner Publishers, 2000, p. 129.

1995.[36] Indeed, aid suspension, as Young notes, has characteristically occurred too late after tensions, security and civil strife strategies have reached alarming levels.[37] This was also the case in Zaïre (present-day Democratic Republic of Congo, DRC), Zambia, Kenya and Zimbabwe.

From a local perspective, political conditionality can be used against neighbouring states supporting the rebel movements – provided that there is sufficient political will and a regional approach to development cooperation. The difference between France and the UK on Rwanda is a good illustration of the diverging interests of states and political conditionality, which can also be directed at neighbouring countries. Since 1997, the UK began to fully support the Rwandan regime under Paul Kagame.[38] This new regime perceived France as an enemy for having supported the former extremist Hutu regime, which was largely responsible for the 1994 genocide. Notably, according to Loisel, although France had strong reservations about the democratic nature of Rwanda and withheld part of its bilateral aid, the UK provided the Rwandan government with a large package of direct budgetary support.[39] However, circumstances changed when the British and the French operated jointly in Ituri, DRC during the 2003-Operation *Artemis*.[40] The two saw their interests head towards convergence following the success of the *Artemis* mission. At this time, the EU adopted a common position in relation to interfering regional parties, especially Uganda and Rwanda. This was mainly in order to stop them from supporting their respective militias in the DRC. Aldo Ajello, the EU Special Representative in the Great Lakes region and High Representative for CFSP, partially used informal political conditionality, notably during the EU High Representative's visit to Kampala, Uganda and Kigali, Rwanda, in July 2003.[41] For Albert Mathias and Thomas Diez, such "covert 'carrots' and 'sticks' probably helped to stop the Rwandan-backed DRC-Goma offensive in Northern Kivu at the beginning of July, which was potentially threatening the stability in Ituri and about which the EU Operational Headquarters in Paris had asked the Political and Security Committee (COPS) for

---

[36] Young, R., "European Union Democracy Promotion Policies: Ten Years On", *European Foreign Affairs Review 6*, 2001, p. 356.

[37] *Ibid.*

[38] Loisel, S., *op. cit.*, 2003.

[39] *Ibid.*

[40] International Security Information Service, Europe, "Operation Artemis: Mission Improbable?", *European Security Review*, No. 18, July 2003, http://www.isiseurope.org/ftp/download/operation%20artemis,%20mission%20improbable%20-%20esr%2018.pdf, accessed 26 May 2007.

[41] *Ibid.*

diplomatic action".[42] This example shows that conditionality can also be useful, in influencing regional dimensions of conflict management in Africa.[43]

Although the EU agreed to a significant increase in aid towards Africa in 2005, there has also been a striking shift in the flows of aid, motivated in part by the necessity to address patterns of conflict in Africa.[44] There is clearly a high political priority in allocating aid for conflict prevention and crisis management. In the specific case of the DCR and Sudan, apart from being a major concern for the EU's Security and Defence Policy, these two countries have been in chronic conflict (Sudan) or in a post-conflict condition, and it is here that aid can be one of the most crucial stabilising instruments (as in the Togolese case). This rise in aid flows to crisis-torn countries also reflects the EU's commitment to the Millennium Development Goals (MDGs).[45] Consequently, as typical examples of the most marginalised countries in

---

[42] COPS is the French acronym for *Comité politique et de sécurité*, which means Political and Security Committee. See http://europa.eu/scadplus/glossary/political_security_committee_fr.htm, accessed 11 October 2008; and Mathias, A. and Diez, T., "The European Union and the Transformation of Conflicts: Theory and the Impact of Integration", paper presented at the *CESA/SA Convention*, South Africa, Cape Town University, 2-6 June 2006.

[43] On aid, the EU member states pledged to increase their ODA at the UN Millennium Summit in September 2000. The aim of this promise was mainly to secure resources for reaching the Millenium Development Goals (MDGs), one of which is to halve the number of people living in extreme poverty by 2015. Later on, the EU declared its full commitment and dedication to the MDGs on several occasions. For example, at the EU's Barcelona summit in March 2002, EU member states reached agreement on allocating at least 0.33% of their individual GNI for ODA by 2006. The goal was later revised upwards as the EU countries agreed to reach 0.51% of individual GNI in development aid by 2010 and 0.7% by 2015. In the context of this chapter, it is important to observe that a decision was reached that about 50% of the increase in aid should be directed to Africa. See Council of the European Union, *Presidency Conclusions: Brussels European Council 16 and 17 June*, Brussels, 15 July 2005, http://www.consilium.europa.eu/ueDocs/cms_Data/docs/pressData/en/ec/85349.pdf, accessed 16 June 2007.

[44] Between 2000 and early 2006, some aid recipient countries experienced increases in the amount of aid, but others experienced a reduction in EU aid. For example, EU aid to the Côte d'Ivoire was reduced by more than 70%. While aid to Kenya dropped between 2001 and 2003, the country witnessed very high increases of aid flows in the years 2004 and 2005. Between 2001 and 2005, the DRC saw an increase in EU aid of about 500%; Mozambique about 200%; and EU aid to Sudan increased up to about 1000%, Organization for Economic Cooperation and Development, *Development Co-operation Report 2005*, Paris, 2006.

[45] For example, at the UN Summit on Millennium Development Goals, the EU's Commissioner for Development noted, "the European Union has geared its development policy firmly towards poverty reduction. We share the vision of the UN's Millennium Declaration: a world free from want", http://www.jpn.cec.int/PHPprintPage.php, accessed 4 June 2007.

Africa, the DRC and Sudan top the list of the EU's aid recipients, based on the levels of poverty and impoverished circumstances of their populations. Lastly, in addition to these two motives, EU assistance and policy towards Africa is a reflection of the necessity to develop a coherent and efficient CFSP with an aim to increasing the role of the EU internationally.

The EU and Humanitarian Aid

This part of the chapter examines the degree to which EU humanitarian assistance is a significant and relevant tool that supports the EU's objective of establishing an effective foreign and security policy in order to affirm its position as a key international player, especially in Africa.[46] Joanna Przetakiewicz notes that following the frustration of the EU's incapability to effectively deliver humanitarian assistance during the crisis based on the war to liberate Kuwait in 1991, a decision was reached to establish ECHO in 1992.[47] But there were also underlying interests for the EU to have an institution in the humanitarian area. The failure in Kuwait and the EU's politically motivated desire to have its own humanitarian institution aimed at "fulfilling a third motive, which had nothing to do with the sufferings of the victims in the numerous emergency situations [...] It was to give the European Community much more international visibility in an area that is very visible in the media".[48] It is worth noting that from 1995 to 1999, ECHO attracted global attention through its large range of interventions from the former Yugoslav Republic to the Rwandan refugee camps and storm-devastated countries in the Caribbean.[49]

It is a common view that humanitarian aid is driven by selfless, moral and ethical motivations. The establishment of ECHO could be understood as a means through which the EU could re-organise its

---

[46] Holland, M., *The European Union and the Third World*, Hampshire, Palgrave, 2002, p. 100; Olsen, R., "Between Development Policy and Foreign Policy Ambitions: The European Union Strategy for Africa", chapter prepared for the *EUSA 10th Biennial International Conference*, Montreal, 17-19 May 2007, p. 14.

[47] Przetakiewicz, J., "The European Community Humanitarian Office: A Political Tool?", *Collegium – Journal of College of Europe*, No. 12, October 1998, pp. 42-45.

[48] Haglund, A., "The EU and Humanitarian Assistance" in Cosgrove-Sacks, C. and Santos, C., *Europe, Diplomacy and Development*, New York, Palgrave, 2001, pp. 154-155; Olsen, G.R., "Effective Foreign Policy without Sovereignty: The European Union's Policy towards Africa", paper presented at *The 6th Pan-European Conference on International Relations*, Turin, 12-15 September 2007, p. 13.

[49] Emma Bonino, cited in Haglund, A., "The EU and Humanitarian Assistance" in Cosgrove-Sacks, C. and Santos, C., *Europe, Diplomacy and Development*, New York, Palgrave, 2001, p. 156.

humanitarian assistance.[50] Its importance in the EU's external policy is also reflected in the extensive financial resources allocated to humanitarian assistance by ECHO and EU member states on a bilateral basis; the EU and its member states being the largest provider of humanitarian aid. For example, according to ECHO, EU commitments in the 1990s accounted for 53-54% of the global humanitarian assistance on average and ECHO's separate contributions accounted for around one-third of this amount, placing it among the top global donors of humanitarian aid.[51]

ECHO statistics show that a striking 37% of all humanitarian assistance from the EU was allocated to Africa in the period between 2000 and 2006.[52] These statistics indicate an on-going commitment by the EU to providing humanitarian aid. This can be interpreted in part as an ECHO strategy to realise the EU's humanitarian aid policy of directing assistance to crisis-torn regions, in which other donors were hesitant to intervene because of the lack of media attention, such as the crisis in West Sahara.[53] However, the EU in the early 1990s, as Daniela Dalia notes, "lacked a real foreign policy, so it needed a body to carry its flag overseas. It was a paradox that the EU was one of the main financial contributors in responding to humanitarian crises, yet no one was aware of its role since NGOs or UN agencies executed the operations".[54] Olsen and Carol Cosgrove-Sacks share the common view that this pattern of aid allocation to Africa shows that the EU is making efforts towards pursuing a coherent and consistent foreign policy.[55]

Overall, in the period since the 1990s, the EU has increasingly integrated humanitarian assistance into its foreign policy. Humanitarian assistance is being channelled to areas of political importance to the EU where it can provide Europe with "visibility" as an international actor. In addition, Africa is a centre of focus for the EU because of the many emergency and post-emergency crises in the region, such as in the Great

---

[50] *Ibid.*

[51] European Community Humanitarian Office, *Caught in the Storm. Annual Review, 1998*, Luxemburg, ECHO, p. 29.

[52] European Commission, *Key Figures of ECHO Humanitarian Assistance*, http://ec.europa.eu/echo/statistics/echo_en.htm, accessed 24 June 2007.

[53] Olsen, G.R., "Effective Foreign Policy without Sovereignty: The European Union's Policy towards Africa", paper presented at *The 6th Pan-European Conference on International Relations*, Turin, 12-15 September 2007, p. 15.

[54] Dalia, D., "The European Union's Humanitarian Aid and Cooperation with Partners: The Framework Partnership Agreements" in C. Cosgrove-Sacks and C. Santos, *Europe, Diplomacy and Development*, New York, Palgrave, 2001, p. 171.

[55] *Ibid.*

Lakes region, the DRC, the Central African Republic, Rwanda, Burundi, Chad and more recently the Horn of Africa.[56]

Conflict Prevention in the CFSP

Conflict Prevention

This part of the chapter examines the concept of conflict prevention and how it can be understood in the context of the European Union. The European Commission defines conflict prevention as "actions undertaken over the *short term* to reduce manifest tensions and/or to prevent the outbreak or recurrence of violent conflict".[57] However, this definition contradicts the April 2001 European Commission Communication on Conflict Prevention in which conflict prevention is distinguished, not only as the projection of long-term stability, but also as a quick and short-term reaction to emerging conflicts (i.e. crisis management). In the Communication, long-term conflict prevention seems to imply a spectrum of actions, such as supporting regional integration, building trade links, supporting democracy, the rule of law, civil society, gender equality in development policy and so forth, while the short-term actions encompass early warning systems, rapid reaction mechanisms, and the use of special representatives.[58]

It is important to note that both the European Commission and the European Council identify this differentiation between long- and short-term measures.[59] This definition has been further developed in EU documentation to mean (a) preventing a conflict from escalating into a violent confrontation; (b) preventing a conflict from spilling over to other areas; and (c) preventing the resurgence of violence in a post conflict situation. For example, the 2001 Gothenburg Programme states that "successful conflict prevention relies on preparedness to take action before a situation deteriorates into violence".[60] However, a more com-

---

[56]   Cosgrove-Sacks, C., "The EU as an International Actor" in C. Cosgrove-Sacks and C. Santos in *Europe, Diplomacy and Development*, New York, Palgrave, 2001, pp. 3-28; Olsen, G.R., "Effective Foreign Policy without Sovereignty: The European Union's Policy towards Africa", paper presented at *The 6th Pan-European Conference on International Relations*, Turin, 12-15 September 2007.

[57]   This definition can found on the European Commission's site at: http://www.europa. eu.int/comm/development/prevention/definition.htm, accessed March 2007.

[58]   European Council, EU Programme for the Prevention of Violent Conflicts, Gothenburg, 15-16 June 2001.

[59]   Report presented to the Nice European Council by the Secretary General/High Representative and the Commission on "Improving the Coherence and Effectiveness of European Union Action in the Field of Conflict Prevention", Press Release 14088/00, Brussels, November 2000.

[60]   European Council, 2001, *op. cit.*

prehensive definition is given by the European Peace Liaison Office (EPLO), which states that

> conflict prevention refers to long-term activities to reduce structural tensions or prevent the outbreak, escalation or recurrence of violence. Conflict prevention denotes the full range of activities oriented to this aim, such as, early warning, crisis management, peace-keeping, peace-building, conflict management, conflict resolution and conflict transformation.[61]

Beyond the EU's definition of conflict prevention, it is important to distinguish between conflict prevention and the overall dimension of the EU's foreign policy objectives, such as development aid, humanitarian assistance, democracy support and human rights promotion. Elisabeth Johansson warns that confusion can be compounded by the integrated approach adopted by the EU in matters of treating the root causes of conflict. In this context, the Commission states that "development policy and other co-operation programs provide, without doubt, the most powerful instruments at the Community's disposal for treating the root causes of conflict".[62] These root causes have been identified (for example, in the ESS) to be: mal-governance, government illegitimacy, repression of minorities, proliferation of arms, economic degradation, migration, lack of full civil society participation or regional instability.[63]

However, a significant question emerges in academic literature as to whether or not the EU has conceptually combined normal peaceful relations between countries into a broad, umbrella concept of conflict prevention. Michael Lund argues that there could be a

> misleading tendency to equate conflict prevention with one or other of the broad ideals of the ascendant liberal internationalist agenda, such as market-oriented economic reform, democracy, human rights, rule of law, arms control and open trade. [...] promoting these global themes does not necessarily prevent a violent conflict.[64]

This notion was also reflected in the International Crisis Group's Report (ICG). While evaluating the EU's involvement in conflict prevention, the ICG asserted that

> the EU does not evaluate appropriately the impact of its conflict prevention policies against their purposes. In fact, the EU seems to rely on the assump-

---

[61] See International Alert, *EU Conflict Prevention, Management and Resolution in Africa*, Rome, July 2003 and The European Peace-building Liaison Office, 2001, http://www.eplo.org, accessed 21 June 2007.

[62] *Ibid.*

[63] European Council, A Secure Europe in a Better World, European Security Strategy adopted by the European Council, 13 December 2003.

[64] Lund, M., "Preventing Violent Conflicts: Progress and Shortfall" in P. Cross (ed.), *Contributing to Preventive Action*, Baden-Baden, CPN Yearbook, 1998.

tion that development cooperation and support for democratisation and conduct of elections *ipso facto* support long-term or structural conflict prevention.[65]

The ICG pointed out that although they do, the effect is not uniform across the countries with which the EU has been involved.

For Esther Barbé and Johansson, although the EU's development cooperation, aid and support for democracy, human and minority rights may contribute positively to conflict prevention, it is necessary to assess their effects and they should not be "used blindly as a 'cure-all formula'".[66] This view is shared by Karin Arts and Anna Dickson who warn that purely technical assistance may indeed lead to a perpetuation, or even aggravation, of many problems one had originally sought to resolve.[67]

The CFSP and Africa

The EU and Africa's Security Problems in the Post-Cold War Era

In the period after the Cold War, security problems in Africa became a special concern of the EU, mainly because of the growth in the number of violent conflicts.[68] The need to focus on conflicts and conflict prevention in Africa was specifically recognised by the European Commission as early as 1993, when it introduced the first initiative on "Peace-building, conflict prevention and resolution in Africa".[69]

Along with focusing on development aid, parallel to conflict prevention, the EU aimed to enhance the African capacity to manage conflict. This manifested itself in a number of initiatives that sought to develop closer relations between the EU and the Organization of African Unity (OAU). From the beginning, the notion reflected in the debate with the OAU was that conflict prevention and conflict resolution were primarily the responsibility of Africans themselves. Therefore, the EU's summit in Essen in December 1994 called for "an intensive political dialogue between the EU and OAU in particular regarding conflict prevention in

---

[65] International Crisis Group, *Katanga: Congo's Forgotten Crisis*, Report No. 103, 9 January 2006.

[66] *Ibid.*

[67] Arts, K. and Dickson, A. (eds.), *EU Development Cooperation: from Model to Symbol*, Manchester, Manchester University Press, 2004.

[68] Pinheiro, J. de D., *Peace-Building and Conflict Prevention in Africa*, European Commission, Directorate General for Development, Brussels, 1999.

[69] Landgraf, M., "Peace-building and Conflict Prevention in Africa: A View from the European Commission" in U. Engel and A. Mehler, *Gewaltsame Konflikte und ihre Prävention in Afrika*, Hamburg, Institut für Afrika-Kunde, 1998, p. 103.

Africa".[70] In December 1995, the EU Summit in Madrid officially made the security problems of Africa a public concern of Europe.[71] Furthermore, parallel to the Madrid declaration, this is the time when the Western European Union (WEU) began to recognise the need for national forces to be made available for preventive operations in Africa and mainly for support and reinforcement actions.[72]

In March 1996, the European Commission released a "communication" on conflict and conflict prevention in Africa, emphasising that the use of development aid and related instruments (Petersberg Tasks[73]) were considered to be important to the European Union. In June 1997, a "common position" was reached, which clearly stressed that conflict prevention was a priority of the EU. It made reference to the need for implementation of the defence implications of EU actions within the initiative on conflict prevention by the WEU. Shortly after this, the Council of Development Ministers reached agreement on a resolution that clearly indicated that conflict prevention was now a main concern of the European Community.[74]

At the Anglo-French summit in December 1998 in St. Malo, important decisions were reached, which showed that the two former colonial powers recognised the need to end their competition over influence in Africa.[75] After this, Africa became a potential element in the EU's pursuit of a CFSP, as it provided a handy platform for high-profile

---

[70] *Ibid.*, p. 105.

[71] European Council, *Madrid Summit 1995*, Madrid, 15-16 December 1995.

[72] Lenzi, G., "WEU's role in sub-Saharan Africa" in W. Khüne *et al.*, *WEU's Role in Crisis Management and Conflict Resolution in Sub-Saharan Africa*, Paris, Institute for Security Studies of WEU, 1995, p. 45.

[73] The Petersberg Tasks were constructed at a Western European Union Council meeting in Petersberg, Germany in 1992. They defined the type and scope of military tasks the WEU can undertake. These tasks are classified as humanitarian and rescue tasks, peacekeeping, and crisis management, including the deployment of combat troops in peacemaking. The Petersberg Tasks were later adopted as EU policy in the Treaty of Amsterdam in 1997 and provide the framework for the European Security and Defense Policy.

[74] See European Commission, "Conflict Prevention and Resolution in Africa", *Common Position and Council Conclusions adopted by the General Affairs Council on 2 June 1997* and European Commission, "The Role of Development Cooperation in Strengthening Peace-building, Conflict prevention and Resolution", *Conclusions adopted by the Development Council on 30 November 1998*, http://www.ec.europa.eu/development/policies/legislation/confprevleg_en.cfm, accessed 22 June 2007.

[75] Foreign and Commonwealth Office, "St. Malo: Britain and France Working Together in Africa", archived content at http://collections.europarchive.org/tna/20080205132101/www.fco.gov.uk/servlet/Front%3Fpagename=OpenMarket/Xcelerate/ShowPage&c=Page&cid=1017756004455, accessed 26 June 2007.

cooperation between Europe's largest military powers at that time.[76] This argument was also very much in line with the thinking about Africa within the WEU framework. For instance, Guido Lenzi noted that sub-Saharan Africa was important because the region is an area for Petersberg missions and it can also contribute to "a global affirmation of the European Security and Defence Identity".[77]

Cotonou Partnership Agreement (2000)

The CPA which focused on peace-building, conflict prevention and resolution policies provided a framework against which policy statements and initiatives were adopted and stressed the importance of development policy as a crucial instrument for addressing the "root" causes of conflict.[78] The instruments were expected to be part of the EU's integrated approach, which was complementary to other direct and indirect EU tools for conflict prevention. In May 2001, the Council of the European Union adopted a Common Position Concerning Conflict Prevention, Management and Resolution in Africa, which in its preamble recalled the Cotonou Agreement. A month later, following a proposal by the EU's CFSP High Representative, the European Council meeting in Gothenburg adopted the EU Programme for the Prevention of Violent Conflicts.[79] In the same year, the Rapid Reaction Mechanism (RRM) was launched.[80]

---

[76] See Olsen, G. R., "Changing European concerns: security and complex political emergencies instead of development" in K. Arts and A. Dickson, *EU Development Cooperation: Model or Symbol*, Manchester, Manchester University Press, 2004, pp. 80-100.

[77] Lenzi, G., "WEU's Role in Sub-Saharan Africa", *op. cit.*, pp. 64 and 63. In December 1999, the Helsinki European Council established a common European Headline Goal (HG) to develop European military capabilities by 2003, which would be able to deploy within 60 days, and to sustain for at least one year operationally capable forces of up to 60,000 troops called the Rapid Reaction Forces (RRFs). This HG included agreement on developing collective capability goals in the fields of command and control, intelligence and strategic transport, to enable the EU to carry out the full range of the "Petersberg" tasks, Duke, S., *The EU and Crisis Management: Development and Prospects*, Maastricht, European Institute of Public Administration, 2002.

[78] Article 11 stresses that "in situations of violent conflict, the Parties shall take all suitable action to prevent an intensification of violence [...] The Parties shall ensure the creation of the necessary links between emergency measures, rehabilitation and development co-operation", *Cotonou Partnership Agreement*, 23 June 2000.

[79] European Council, EU Programme for the Prevention of Violent Conflicts, *op. cit.*

[80] The RRM is a Community-funded mechanism designed to allow the EC to respond rapidly and flexibly to the needs of countries faced with natural disasters or conflict. In crisis situations, it functions as a bridge to the EC's non-crisis assistance programmes that support short-term initiatives, with the aim of safeguarding or re-establishing favourable working conditions. The RRM is designed to avoid any

Artemis Operation (June 2003)

In the context of Africa's crises, the RRM and RRF (Rapid Reaction Force) concepts were first tested in the Great Lakes region, particularly in the DRC, when in June 2003, the EU deployed a French-led military operation to Bunia, capital of Ituri. The operation code-named *Artemis*, deployed 14,000 personnel with the aim of contributing to the stabilisation of security conditions, improving the humanitarian situation, and protecting refugees. It was a temporary mission lasting three months before handing over to the United Nations Organization Mission in the Democratic Republic (UN MONUC) in September 2003.[81] In the context of the CFSP, *Artemis* was significant in that it was the first "autonomous" (independent of NATO) EU military mission under the European Security and Defence Policy (ESDP), deployed outside of Europe. It also proved how European member states could join forces and instruments in order to prevent a crisis from escalating into violence; lastly, it led to new ways of conceptualising and responding to crises, which spearheaded a number of significant developments regarding the EU's approach to conflict prevention.

EU's Approach to Conflict Prevention in the post-Artemis Period

The first of these developments concerns the new battle group concept, which is regarded as an important part of the implementation of the defence aspects of the 2003 European Security Strategy and also as an integral part of the new Headline Goal 2010 (a continuation of the 1999 Helsinki Headline Goal). The idea of developing such a concept was initially floated at a bilateral Franco-British summit in Le Touquet on 4 February 2003 and was made more explicit in the 24 November 2003 meeting in London, when the two powers recognised the need to build upon the precedent of *Artemis* and establish "credible 'Battle Group' sized forces" so as to strengthen the EU's rapid reaction capability, which would support the United Nations' operations.[82] Soon

---

activities that could overlap with humanitarian assistance handled by ECHO. Since 2001, the RRM has been used to respond to regional or country-level programmes around the world including election support, tsunami-affected countries, and assistance. Furthermore, a number of RRM projects have been implemented in conflict prevention and peace-building. As a transitional relief measure, RRM usually follows EC humanitarian aid and/or the civil protection mechanism. For details, see Nowak, A. (ed.), "Civilian Crisis Management: the EU Way", *Chaillot Paper*, No. 90, June 2006, p. 51.

[81] Faria, F., "Crisis Management in Sub-Saharan Africa: The Role of the European Union", *European Union Institute of Security Studies*, Occasional Chapter, Paris, 2004.

[82] Lindstrom, G., (2007), "Enter the EU Battlegroups", *Chaillot Paper*, No. 97, Institute for Security Studies, Paris, p. 14; The Quille, G., *The EU Battle Groups*, Directorate

afterwards, the EU published the Council's Joint Action on 27 April 2006, "on the European Union military operation in support of the United Nations Organization Mission in the Democratic Republic of the Congo (MONUC) during the election process" in the presidential and parliamentary election process of July 2006. This mission implied the return of EU forces to the DRC for the first time since Operation *Artemis*. This was undertaken at the request of the UN Secretary General on 27 December 2005. The EU force (EUFOR RD Congo) was launched and it was stationed in the capital, Kinshasa, mainly as a "deterrent force" in order to prevent or (if necessary) contain acts of armed violence in the capital. The electoral process – the first to have been launched since the country became the DRC on 17 May 1997 – was successful. Joseph Kabila was reinstated as president. A very significant outcome of this mission was that it allowed the first ever democratic elections since independence in the 1960s to proceed without incident.[83]

Another significant issue, on the part of the EU, is that the post-*Artemis* period was marked by a shift in strategy from a top-heavy, 60,000-strong RRF to smaller units. In November 2004, the EU Defence Ministers stated at the Military Capabilities Commitment Conference their intention to establish 13 "battle groups". Rather than pursue the strong RRF, each battle group could number 1,500 men and could be deployable rapidly for crisis management around the world. These groups were established in 2005 and they reached full operational capability (FOC) in January 2007. In response to a crisis, or to an urgent request by the UN, the EU should be able to undertake two battle group-sized operations for a period of up to 120 days simultaneously. Forces should be on the ground no later than 10 days after the EU decision to launch the operation.[84] The first two battle groups were formed by Germany and the Netherlands/Finland while France and Belgium provided the second. In 2008, the countries forming the EU battle groups were Sweden and Spain for the first half of the year and Germany and the UK for the second half of the year. In addition to this, a Civilian Cell is being developed, which will assist in coordinating civilian operations and have responsibility for generating the capacity to plan and run autonomous EU military operations.[85]

General for External Policies of the European Union, DGExPo/B/PolDep/Note/2006_145, Brussels, 12 September 2006.

[83] Gutiérrez, I., *European Union Operations in the Democratic Republic of Congo (DRC) – Reply to the annual report of the Council*, Document A/1954, Brussels 20 December, 2006, http://www.assembly-weu.org/en/documents/sessions_ordinaires/rpt/2006/1954.php#P115_9294, accessed 20 June 2007.

[84] *Ibid.*

[85] Bayne, S., Gourlay, C., and Ojanen, H., "Developing International Capacities for Crisis Management and Crisis response in Africa" in *Finnish Institute of*

As a result of the experiences of *Artemis*, and other EU Missions (for example, in Afghanistan, and the former Yugoslav Republic of Macedonia) as well as the impact of the 11 September 2001 terrorist attacks in the US, the wider security dialogue shifted. This is so because it began getting more involved in the debates especially in the areas of the EU's external and defence policy. In fact, this led to further implementation of the EU's concept of security and the adoption of the European Security Strategy in December 2003.[86] Apart from terrorism, the proliferation of weapons of mass destruction, state failure, and organised crime, the ESS highlights regional conflicts within the EU neighbourhood and the world as areas of concern. This is because they impact on "European interests directly or indirectly and can lead to extremism, terrorism and state failure".[87] Furthermore, the ESS strongly insists that security is a precondition for development. In the understanding of the European Centre for Development Policy Management (ECPDM), the vision of the ESS is

> broad and comprehensive and does not confine itself to traditional notions of "hard" security. The Strategy also acknowledges the influence and interplay of different areas of EU external policies. In doing so, it recognises the value of the work that has been done for years by the development side in supporting measures to promote good governance and conflict prevention [...].[88]

This also demonstrates the need to re-model coherence, coordination, and consistency within the EU's external policies in dealing, particularly, with developing countries and in the context of this analysis, Africa is central to this debate.

Launch of the EU-Africa Dialogue in June 2003

In addition, in the continuous search for complementarity between the CFSP and development cooperation, the European Commission relaunched the EU-Africa Dialogue in June 2003.[89] This was meant to

---

International Affairs & the Centre for International Cooperation and Security, Chapter 2, Helsinki, 2006, p. 14.

[86] *Ibid.*; ECDPM, 2006, p. 26; Olsen, G.R., "The Post-September 2001 Security Agenda: Have the European Union's Policies on Africa been Affected" in G. Bonno (ed.), *The Impact of 9/11 on European Foreign and Security Policy*, Brussels, VUB Press, 2006, pp. 162-164.

[87] See European Council, European Security Strategy (ESS) – A Secure Europe in a Better World, December 2003.

[88] *Ibid.*

[89] European Commission, *Communication from the Commission to the Council: The EU-Africa Dialogue*, COM(2003) 316 final, Brussels, 23 March 2003, not published in the *Official Journal*.

provide impetus to what was agreed upon at the first EU-Africa Summit in April 2000 in Cairo, which focused on making efforts towards building a strategic partnership with Africa.[90]

From a global perspective, the focus on peace, stability and security by the ESS, not only highlights the recent awareness in international discourse that these conditions are crucial for the promotion of development, but it also highlights Europe's desire to adapt its external policies to the changing global security environment in the post-9/11 era. In this sense, re-thinking and re-designing the EU's policy towards developing countries has become a necessity.

Therefore, the 2003 Communication on the EU-Africa dialogue proposed the strengthening of institutional links to help Africa deal with the political problems and development-related issues it faces.[91] December 2003 saw some of the effects of this when the EU Council adopted the decision on the financing of an African Peace Facility (APF) from European Development Fund resources. This move was in response to a request made at the African Union summit and was intended to support African institutions and peacekeeping measures. The APF was meant to ensure cooperation between the African Union (AU), regional organizations in Africa,[92] the EU and the United Nations.

More notably, in response to the situation in Sudan, the EU and its member states have been providing a wide range of support to the AU's efforts to help stabilise the situation in Darfur since January 2004 after the launch of the APF.[93] This support has included financial, personnel

---

[90] A Plan of Action was adopted that focuses on economic issues, particularly regional economic cooperation and integration in Africa; integrating Africa into the world economy; deepening the link between trade and development at international level in order to ensure that trade liberalisation contributes to poverty reduction; respect for, and protection of, human rights, democratic principles and institutions, the rule of law and good governance; peace-building and conflict prevention, management and resolution in Africa; and development measures to combat poverty (in the areas of education, health and food security, for example). New areas of cooperation include the situation in Sudan and the Great Lakes and the fight against terrorism.

[91] European Commission, Communication from the Commission to the Council: The EU-Africa dialogue, *op. cit.*

[92] Apart from sub-regional organizations, these institutions include the African Union created in March 2001 to replace the Organization of African Unity (OAU). The AU provides a framework for, and strengthens, political and economic regional cooperation and integration between African countries. Also, the New Partnership for Africa's Development (NEPAD) was developed by African states with a commitment on the part of Africans to co-operate towards eradicating poverty and promoting sustainable development and growth.

[93] The EU has committed a total of EUR 242 million from the African Peace Facility in support of AMIS since June 2004. European Union – Fact Sheet, *EU Support to the African Union Mission in Darfur* – AMIS II/06, May 2007, http://www.

and political support to the Abuja talks process and the Ceasefire Commission. It also includes support to the AU Mission in the Darfur region of Sudan (AMIS) through the provision of equipment and assets, planning and technical assistance, military observers, training of African troops and civilian police officers and strategic transportation (EU civilian-military supporting action, which was also coordinated under the auspices of NATO under the Berlin-Plus Agreements). In the same period, EU member states have provided coordinated strategic airlifts for well over 2,000 African Union personnel, which continued until 2007. Since July 2005, the EU has had a Special Representative (EUSR) for Sudan. The EUSR, Mr Torben Brylle, who was appointed in May 2007, ensures coordination and coherence of the EU's contributions to AMIS with the assistance of roughly 200 EU military and police advisers based in Addis Ababa, Ethiopia.[94]

Apart from the APF, the EU-AU dialogue has also been intensified and so far a number of notable results have been achieved. The EU, reporting on its partnership with Africa, says that "in 2005 it undertook to increase public development aid by EUR 20 billion per year by 2010, [...] of which over half *will be earmarked for Africa*".[95] A new Strategy for Africa (SA) was also adopted in October 2005 to further support the continent's efforts to achieve the United Nations' Millennium Development Goals. In the first instance, the SA proposes forging a strategic security and development partnership between the EU and Africa. It focuses on key requirements for sustainable development such as peace and security, good and effective governance, trade, interconnectivity, social cohesion and environmental sustainability. New initiatives have also been launched, most notably, in July 2006, a governance initiative and a Euro-African Partnership for Infrastructure. Under the Governance Initiative, the EU will, for instance, provide support for reforms triggered by the African Peer Review Mechanism (APRM) of the AU, a unique tool for peer review and peer learning in good democratic governance by and for Africans. And in the context of the Partnership for Infrastructure, the EU will support programmes that facilitate interconnectivity at continental level to promote regional trade, integration, stability and development.[96]

---

consilium.europa.eu/uedocs/cmsUpload/070507-factsheet6-AMIS_II.pdf, accessed 20 June 2007.

[94] Cazalles, C., "The EU as an International Organisation: the case of Darfur", Paris, Centre of Strategic Analysis, 2007, p. 22.

[95] European Commission, "EU-Africa Partnership", *Activities of the European Union: Summaries of Legislation*, last updated 17 August 2007, http://europa.eu/scadplus/ leg/en/lvb/r12106.htm, accessed 26 May 2007.

[96] *Ibid.*

Furthermore, two years after the adoption of the Strategy for Africa, the EU and Africa re-defined their partnership through the adoption of a Joint EU-Africa Strategy at the second EU-Africa Summit in Lisbon in December 2007. According to the European Commission, the Joint EU-Africa Strategy outlines a long-term shared vision of the future of EU-Africa relations in a globalised world and the Lisbon Summit further reinvents the EU-Africa partnership.[97] For example, the Joint Strategy aims to strengthen the EU-Africa political dialogue so as to bring the EU-Africa partnership: (1) beyond development cooperation by opening up the EU-Africa dialogue to issues of joint political concern and interest; (2) beyond Africa by moving away from a focus on African affairs only and openly addressing European and global issues of concern and to act accordingly in the relevant forums to make globalisation work for all; (3) beyond fragmentation in supporting Africa's aspirations to find regional and continental responses to some of the most important challenges; (4) beyond institutions in ensuring a better participation of African and European citizens, as part of an overall strategy to strengthen civil society on both continents. Further joint EU-Africa policy initiatives that would also be discussed on this occasion include a Partnership on Energy, Climate Change; Migration, Mobility and Employment; Democratic Governance and EU-Africa political and institutional architecture.[98]

Conclusion

This chapter has identified some of the factors making Africa a centre of concern for the EU, especially in the area of development cooperation and humanitarian assistance. The first one regards the historical links based on the colonial legacy that has developed into the postcolonial period, which are a basis of the EU-ACP development cooperation. The second one regards the strong economic links between the two groups through trade and investment. The EU is the main trading partner with many African countries, and the main ODA donor for most countries in Africa.

The third factor concerns the EU's ambition to become a major international actor. To this end, it has developed its CSFP/ESDP instruments (military and civilian) for crisis management. Conflict prevention, and especially the EU's focus on Africa, would also help it in realising this ambition. In this regard, the EU has re-invented development coop-

---

[97] European Commission, Commission Adopts a Communication on the Future Joint EU-Africa Strategy, IP/07/947, Brussels, 27 June 2007.

[98] European Commission (2008), "The Africa-EU strategic partnerships", *Geographical Partnerships: EU-Africa Relations*, http://ec.europa.eu/development/geographical/regionscountries/euafrica_en.cfm, accessed 12 November 2008.

eration into a civilian instrument that could help in preventing conflict, for example through political conditionality, democracy building, and political dialogue, which was sealed through the Joint EU-Africa Strategy in Lisbon 2007. It has also developed its instruments of humanitarian response to crises, especially through ECHO. The EU has declared its commitment to working with multilateral institutions, such as supporting the AU and UN peace keeping operations in Sudan and the Great Lakes (DRC), as well as the commitment to the MDGs.

Lastly, by focusing on Africa, the EU would, in fact, be targeting the security threats it faces. The ESS identified these as terrorism, illegal migration, refugees, human trafficking, illicit trade in arms and drugs and state failure, which are located in the world's poorest regions.[99] It is no surprise that given these perceived security threats and its proximity to Africa, the EU has given strong priority to development cooperation and conflict prevention in the region.

---

[99] European Council, A Secure Europe in a Better World: European Security Strategy, Brussels, 12 December 2003.

CHAPTER 9

Renegotiating Roles
in the Transatlantic Partnership
EU Role Claims Transforming the West[1]

Franz OSWALD

Introduction

A renegotiation of the roles in the transatlantic partnership has been under way since the end of the Cold War. The transformation of the West has been less obvious than the implosion of the East, the other side in the Cold War. Yet, as Christoph Bertram argued as early as 1995, in spite of "the measured pace of developments in Western Europe", the West "would be in for a massive redefinition".[2] The integration of a Europe no longer divided by the Iron Curtain is transforming the West. Role conceptions about oneself and role expectations regarding the other were shaped in the formative years of the transatlantic relationship, in the first decade after the Second World War. The security environment of the time ensured that a military alliance was the centre piece of the relationship, and the imbalance in the relative power of the United States and post-war Europe made for an asymmetrical relationship. Over several decades these roles became entrenched in habits and institutions. Although European integration created a powerful economic actor, the transatlantic role allocation remained stable as long as the Cold War security environment lasted. Only with the end of the Cold War did the EU begin to claim a role in foreign and security policy. This role claim has the potential of transforming the West into a "twin-pillar" partnership.[3]

Three connected claims are made in this chapter. First, the sociological role concept can be usefully applied to transatlantic relations. The

---

[1] An earlier version of this text has been published in the *Asia-Pacific Journal of EU Studies*, Vol. 5, No. 2, 2007.

[2] Bertram, C., *Europe in the Balance: Securing the Peace Won in the Cold War*, Washington, D.C., Carnegie Endowment for International Peace, 1995, p. 40.

[3] See Oswald, F., *Europe and the United States: The Emerging Security Partnership*, Westport, CT, Praeger Security International, 2006.

transatlantic partners have role conceptions about themselves and role expectations regarding the other. Renegotiating roles by making role claims and by rejecting or accepting them is part of the change in transatlantic relations, besides shifts in relative economic and military power. That role theory helps to understand the EU's role in international relations is argued by Lisbeth Aggestam, Ole Elgström and Michael Smith.[4] Role conceptions (about one's own role) and role expectations (about other states' roles) explain foreign policy, supplementing the realist emphasis on military and economic power as determinants of international relations. Such role conceptions are relatively stable but they are also subject to renegotiation. Changing role conceptions can lead to new role claims, and if these are accepted by others, new role allocations can be agreed upon. Renegotiating roles can be considered soft balancing through symbolic action.

A constructivist interest in intersubjectively constituted roles need not be incompatible with taking into account relative power. Thus, to discuss balancing behaviour or balancing effects does not imply abstention from constructivist themes. Instead, a combined analysis of roles and relative power is suggested by Naomi Bailin Wish's "national-attribute/national-role conception model", in analogy to a "motivation-capabilities model" in psychology.[5]

Second, the renegotiation of transatlantic roles can be linked with the realist discussions about counterbalancing in the post-1991 unipolar international system. After the implosion of the Soviet Union, structural realists had suggested that unipolarity contained the seeds of its own undoing because other powers would necessarily engage in counterbalancing US primacy.[6] In the one and a half decades since the end of the Cold War, hard balancing has not taken place, neither "externally" through the formation of alliances nor "internally" through armament efforts of competitors.[7] But recently the debate has shifted to the question of whether great powers could be engaged in soft balancing to counter US primacy. Unlike hard balancing, soft balancing aims to

[4]   Aggestam, L., "Role Theory and European Foreign Policy: A Framework of Analysis" in Elgström, O. and Smith, M. (eds.), *The European Union's Roles in International Politics: Concepts and Analysis*, London/New York, Routledge, 2006, pp. 11-29; Elgström, O. and Smith, M. "Introduction" in *Ibid.*, pp. 5-7.

[5]   Wish, N., "National Attributes as Sources of National Role Conceptions: A Capability-Motivation Model" in S.G. Walker (ed.), *Role Theory and Foreign Policy Analysis*, Durham, Duke University Press, 1987, p. 97.

[6]   E.g.: Waltz, K., "The Emerging Structure of International Politics", *International Security*, Vol. 18, No. 2, Fall 1993, pp. 44-79.

[7]   On internal and external balancing, see Lieber, K. and Alexander, G., "Waiting for Balancing: Why the World is Not Pushing Back", *International Security*, Vol. 30, No. 1, Summer 2005, pp. 109-39.

change the balance of non-military power factors such as diplomatic influence, relative economic power, cultural prestige and the allocation of roles in the international system.

Four articles in the same issue of the journal *International Security* asked whether the power and the policy choices of the United States have resulted in counterbalancing by other states. Two of these articles claimed other great powers were engaged in "soft balancing" against US supremacy, noticeably so in response to the unilateralism of the Bush administration since 2001.[8] Thazka Varkey Paul argued that "second-tier major powers [...] are concerned about the increasing unilateralism of the United States" and have "begun to engage in 'soft balancing'".[9] The other two articles opposed this view and claimed there was neither hard nor soft balancing, nor had any been provoked by recent US unilateralism.[10]

The present chapter differs from both sides of this argument and contends that there has indeed been soft balancing and that it started before 2001. The most successful soft balancer of US supremacy, the EU, has pursued economic integration for several decades to form a unitary economic actor of global relevance, and it has, since 1991, claimed and acquired a security role. This version of counterbalancing while maintaining positive transatlantic relations could be called soft balancing between friends.

Changes in the relative power of the transatlantic partners since the late 1940s and the current renegotiation of roles combine to create a mixture of intentional and unintentional balancing. Since the initial role allocation in the Atlantic alliance, economic recovery and European integration have had *de facto* balancing effects, albeit as collateral effects of the pursuit of economic growth and regional stability or as the intended effect of a Gaullist vision of Europe as an autonomous power. The narrow concept of soft balancing employed by Stephen Brooks and William Wohlforth tends to exclude all actions not explicitly undertaken with the intention to change the balance of power.[11] Unfortunately this approach is insensitive to the balancing side effects of the pursuit of

---

[8]   Pape, R., "Soft Balancing against the United States", *International Security*, Vol. 30, No. 1, Summer 2005, pp. 7-45; Paul, T.V., "Soft Balancing in the Age of US Primacy, *International Security*, Vol. 30, No. 1, Summer 2005, pp. 46-71.

[9]   Paul, T.V, "Soft Balancing in the Age of U.S. Primacy", *op. cit.*, p. 47.

[10]   Brooks, S.G: and Wohlforth, W.C., "Hard Times for Soft Balancing", *op. cit.*, *International Security*, Vol. 30, No. 1, Summer 2005, pp. 72-108; Lieber, K. and Alexander, G., "Waiting for Balancing: Why the World is Not Pushing Back", *op. cit.*, pp. 109-39.

[11]   Brooks, S.G and Wohlforth, W.C., "Hard Times for Soft Balancing", *op. cit.*, pp. 74 and 106.

other objectives such as economic growth, regional stability or cooperative crisis management. Yet, the effects of unintended *de facto* balancing
are relevant in conjunction with explicitly stated intentions. The EU's
European Security Strategy of 2003, for example, aims to bring about
"an international order based on effective multilateralism",[12] that is, to
counterbalance the unilateralism practised by the transatlantic partner.

Efforts by Russia and China to counter US supremacy attracted most
attention because, according to Brooks and Wohlforth, "in some respects, Russia's strategic partnership with India and especially China
represent the strongest case of soft balancing".[13] On the other hand, the
EU's *de facto* soft balancing remained almost unnoticed, either because
the EU was perceived as part of a unitary West or because soft balancing between friends was inherently less conspicuous than hard balancing
between adversaries. One exception to this tendency among US analysts
was Samuel B. Huntington's acknowledgement of long-term anti-
hegemonic balancing through European integration.[14] Similarly, it is
argued here that European integration constituted *de facto* soft balancing
over several decades, and, more recently, intentional soft balancing
through the claim for an autonomous EU security role.

Arguing that there was no soft balancing, Brooks and Wohlforth ad-
mit "that other states can take actions that end up constraining the
United States". These actions should not be regarded as balancing
because "these constraint actions […] are not an outgrowth of balance of
power dynamics". Instead, "alternative explanations" should be considered such as "economic interest, regional security concerns, policy
disputes, and domestic political incentives".[15] However, their narrow
definition of soft balancing is overly restrictive. Such alternative explanations merely show that soft balancing is not taking place in a pure,
unadulterated form. Instead, it is driven by a combination of economic
interests, security concerns, domestic motives, and, occasionally, the
explicit desire to counterbalance.

Anti-hegemonic counterbalancing is also bound to encounter a problem of collective action. Lesser powers would have to bring together a

---

[12] European Council, A Secure Europe in a Better World: European Security Strategy,
Brussels, December 12, 2003.

[13] Brooks, S.G. and Wohlforth, W.C., "Hard Times for Soft Balancing", *op. cit.*, p. 83.

[14] "Undoubtedly the single most important move toward an anti-hegemonic coalition,
however, antedates the end of the Cold War: the formation of the European Union
and the creation of a common European currency. […] Clearly the euro could pose an
important challenge to the hegemony of the dollar in global finance" (Huntington, S.,
"The Lonely Superpower", *Foreign Affairs*, Vol. 70, No. 2 March/April 1999, p. 45).

[15] Brooks, S.G. and Wohlforth, W.C., "Hard Times for Soft Balancing", *op. cit.*,
pp. 106 and 74.

coalition in spite of the temptations of "band-wagoning". It may be more attractive to remain a follower of the hegemon than to risk sanctions or the failure of a weak balancing coalition. Moreover, the motivation to balance against a benign hegemon, ally and protector cannot have the same urgency as countering an obvious threat. This does not, however, preclude successful counterbalancing. Instead, it only requires that balancing be conducted as soft balancing, restrained by the need to maintain overall cooperation. The problem of collective action can be minimised by a low-risk method of renegotiating roles by symbolic action and small practical steps. The Maastricht Treaty stated the intention to have a Common Foreign and Security Policy (CFSP). With this symbolic action EU members took the initiative to change their own role conception and to renegotiate roles in the transatlantic relationship.

Third, although the EU's claim for a security role has been resisted by the United States, it can be interpreted as compatible with US interests. David P. Calleo distinguished three approaches of US foreign policy to Europe immediately after the Second World War. A universalist approach was pursued by President Franklin D. Roosevelt and Secretary of State Cordell Hull, aiming to relegate Europe to the sidelines in a world order guided by US hegemony. This was replaced in 1946-1947 by the Marshall Plan vision. As Paul Hoffman, the Marshall Plan's first administrator, observed "the idea is to get Europe on its feet and off our backs".[16] Economic recovery was to be followed by European responsibility for security and a retreat of US troops from Europe. Yet by 1949 the "NATO First" approach prevailed, with the conclusion of the NATO Treaty, followed two years later by the upgrading of NATO into an integrated military command structure with a large, permanent US troop presence in Europe, in response to the Korean War.

For several decades, "NATO First" appeared to be the only conceivable US approach to Europe. However, it is contended here that European integration has achieved exactly what the Marshall Plan envisaged, albeit with considerable delay, and EU responsibility for European security has become feasible.

Renegotiating Roles in the Transatlantic Alliance

Role Allocation of 1949 Based on Second World War Effect

The roles of European NATO members were defined in the late 1940s. They were junior allies, accepting and welcoming US leadership and enjoying US protection. This role allocation reflects the security

---

[16] Foot, P., "America and the Origins of the Atlantic Alliance: A Reappraisal" in J. Smith (ed.), *The Origins of NATO*, Exeter, University of Exeter Press, 1990, p. 83.

environment of 1949 and the relative economic and military power of the transatlantic partners at that time. A temporary peak of comparative economic and military power had enabled the United States to shape alliance relations within the West. The roles institutionalised in the 1940s have become entrenched habits.

The transient nature of the 1940s peak of relative US power was noted, for example, by Henry Kissinger. He acknowledged, in the 1960s, that US supremacy had to decline somewhat since the "temporary loss of Europe's ability to play an effective international role" could not be expected to last.[17] Indeed, in the six decades since the Second World War the distribution of military and economic power has changed fundamentally. In the transatlantic relationship, the relative economic weight of the partners is very even today compared to the 1940s. Yet, for its first thirty years, such economic rebalancing had little impact on the allocation of roles regarding European security. As long as the confrontation with the Soviet Union lasted, Western Europe remained a group of junior US allies, irrespective of its increasing economic weight.

Yet, continued shifts of relative economic power can hardly fail to affect security relations. Introducing the Euro in 1999 was another instance of economic balancing with implications for security roles. It was "the single most important event in European and transatlantic politics since the demise of the Soviet Union".[18] Since then the euro has grown into a second world currency, constituting over 20% of the currency reserves held by reserve banks. While this was still clearly less than the equivalent figure held in US Dollars (over 60%), it was much more than the 4% held in Deutsche Marks before 1999. "A bipolar currency regime dominated by Europe and the United States" was expected by Fred C. Bergsten to "replace the dollar-centred system".[19] While the euro is a long way from replacing the US dollar as the world currency of choice, its success has had implications for the EU's security role: "To put it bluntly, a Europe whose money is challenging the dollar around the world will be unlikely to remain comfortable as a U.S. military protectorate".[20]

---

[17] Kissinger, H., *The Troubled Partnership: A Re-appraisal of the Atlantic Alliance*, Garden City/New York, Anchor Books, 1966, p. 6.

[18] Calleo, D., "The Strategic Implications of the Euro", *Survival*, Vol. 41, No. 1, Spring 1999, p. 5.

[19] Bergsten, F.C., "The Dollar and the Euro", *Foreign Affairs*, Vol. 76, No. 4, July/August 1997, p. 83.

[20] Calleo, D., "Imperial America and its Republican Constitution" in Gardner, H. and Stefanova, R. (eds.), *The New Transatlantic Agenda: Facing the Challenges of Global Governance*, Aldershot, Ashgate, 2001, p. 9.

Failure of EC Role Claims in the "Year of Europe" 1973

The EU's determination to claim a security role has come a long way since its failed role claims by the EC in the 1970s. When Kissinger on behalf of the Nixon administration, declared 1973 the Year of Europe, he envisaged minor role adjustments in the transatlantic alliance. By 1973, the Second World War effect had worn off to some extent, European economies had recovered, and the European Economic Community (EEC) of Six had grown into the European Community (EC) of Nine. The US, on the other hand, had lost some of the enormous economic supremacy of the 1940s resulting in the 1971 devaluation of the US dollar. Nevertheless, the transatlantic role allocation of the late 1940s was to be confirmed in "a joint declaration that restated the differentiated roles that had been valid up to that point (the global role of the United States, the regional role of the Western European states) [...]".[21]

On the European side, there was some desire to have a greater role in a more balanced relationship acknowledged by the United States. The EC presented a "draft agreement" that "contained what amounted to a declaration of the political equality of the EC, and was an attempt to have this recognised by the American government. [...], the very first phrase expressed quite unmistakably that there should be a 'new bilateralism between Western Europe and the United States'".[22] However, after objections by Washington, the EC abandoned its role claims. Instead, the Atlantic Declaration of June 1974 confirmed the existing transatlantic role allocation. Europe's security dependence ensured that US hegemony continued. Although the transatlantic balance of economic power had shifted between 1949 and 1974, US role expectations prevailed over the EC's own role conception.

Escalating EU Role Claims since 1991

The role claims implied in the EU's CFSP in the 1990s were clearly much stronger than any EC ambitions in the 1970s but still rather limited. When the EU included foreign and security policy in the Maastricht Treaty, beyond the customary economic role, it did not have the capability to implement them. Yet, just putting a claim for an extended role on paper was a significant action. It signalled that there was consensus to modify the EU's role conception and to challenge the role expectations embodied in NATO. A parallel role claim was pursued through the adoption by the Western European Union (WEU) of the Petersberg

---

[21] Link, W., "Historical Continuity and Discontinuity in Transatlantic Relations: Consequences for the Future" in Kahler, M. and Link, W., *Europe and America: A Return to History*, New York, Council on Foreign Relations Press, 1996, p. 80.
[22] *Ibid.*

Tasks in 1992. The WEU's role claim went no further than limited crisis management capabilities for low-level security tasks, leaving the high-end task of collective defence to NATO. In 1997 these WEU tasks were incorporated into the EU's Amsterdam Treaty, thus widening the EU's role conception.

The crises in Bosnia and Kosovo showed that the EU's role claim was not substantiated by corresponding capabilities. The EU's failure led Atlanticists to conclude that US leadership was still indispensable. Europeanists, on the other hand, noted the reluctance of US involvement and the lack of consultation with allies during the interventions. Atlanticists felt they had to make an effort to keep the United States interested in Europe by upgrading the capabilities of NATO-Europe. Europeanists also intended to strengthen capabilities but with the purpose of enabling autonomous European crisis management. Two contrasting motives could lead to the same practical conclusion.

In their St. Malo agreement of 1998, Britain and France asked EU members to develop European military capabilities. France expected this to lead to EU security autonomy whereas Britain hoped greater capabilities would enhance Europe's contribution to NATO. Guided by this Anglo-French initiative, the EU agreed on its European Security and Defence Policy (ESDP) at the Cologne summit in June 1999. The "Headline Goal" to establish a 60,000 man European Rapid Reaction Force (RRF) was adopted in Helsinki (December 1999) and declared achieved at the Laeken summit (December 2001), although the RRF was no more than an administrative aggregate of earmarked national units.

EU claims for a security role escalated from the CFSP of 1991 to the ESDP of 1999. The adoption of the European Security Strategy (ESS) in 2003 further consolidated these role claims and signalled sufficient consensus for a limited but substantial security role. A more extensive role claim was made in the proposed European Constitution which included a collective security guarantee by the EU. Although the Treaty establishing a Constitution for Europe was rejected by voters in France and the Netherlands and not ratified in another five EU countries, it had been signed in October 2004 by senior political figures from the then 25 EU member states and ratified by 18 countries. This indicated a certain level of acceptance of a security role among EU elites.

In contrast to 1973, when the EC abandoned its role claims quickly and accepted Washington's role prescription that the EC was merely a regional actor, the post-1991 EU insisted on its own role conception: "The European Union is a global actor, ready to share in the responsibility for global security. With the adoption by the European Council in December 2003 of the European Security Strategy (ESS), it affirmed the role it wants to play in the world, supporting an international order based on effective multilateralism within the UN".[23]

Giving Substance to Role Claims: Beyond Importing Security

The likely outcome of soft balancing is not to make the EU a challenger to US global military supremacy, but to enable EU members to assume responsibility for European security. Since the Second World War, Western and Eastern Europe had both been heavy importers of security. NATO-Europe relied on US nuclear guarantees and accepted US leadership in the alliance. However, with the end of the Soviet Union in 1991 the need to import security declined in spite of fears of a residual Russian threat or a revival of German hegemonic ambitions. Security dependence was, admittedly, evident in the 1990s during the crises in Bosnia and Kosovo, where the United States demonstrated that it was still "the indispensable nation". However, reliance on the United States declined further as the EU assumed greater responsibility for stability in southeast Europe.

Europe was no longer an importer of security to the same extent as during the Cold War. The EU has become a stabiliser of its own enlarged territory. The EU has even become, to a limited extent, an exporter of security beyond its own boundaries. The ESS outlined the range of security tasks to be undertaken by EU forces. "By focusing on global challenges", the ESS "transcends traditional geographic and conceptual limitations of European strategic thinking". It also moved away from the Cold War preoccupation with territorial defence "by identifying terrorism, the proliferation of weapons of mass destruction (WMD), regional conflicts, state failure and organised crime as key threats", and extended "the zone of security in the EU's neighbourhood by supporting 'a ring of well-governed countries'". Here the EU claimed a wider regional area of responsibility, including "the Balkans, Eastern Europe, Southern Caucasus, Mediterranean, and Middle East".[24] Global concerns, on the other hand, were to be addressed in transatlantic cooperation since "acting together, the European Union and the United States can be a formidable force for good in the world".[25]

These role claims were given substance in the development of a European Defence Industrial and Technological Base (EDITB) through

---

[23] Council of European Union, "Headline Goal 2010", doc. 6309/6/04/REV 6, Brussels, 17 May 2004, cited in Lindstrom, G., "Enter the EU Battlegroups", *Chaillot Paper*, No. 97, Paris, Institute for Security Studies – EU, February 2007.

[24] Becher, K., "Has Been, Wannabe, or Leader: Europe's Role in the World after the 2003 European Security Strategy", *European Security*, Vol. 13, No. 4, 2004, p. 350.

[25] European Council, "A Secure Europe in a Better World: European Security Strategy", Brussels, December 2003, Chapter III.

the cross-national consolidation of European defence industries. This resulted in BAE Systems, EADS (European Aeronautic Defence and Space Company), Thales and Finmeccanica becoming four of the ten biggest defence contractors globally, holding fourth, seventh, eight and ninth position, respectively. They were still clearly smaller than the three biggest US firms resulting from mergers encouraged by the Clinton administration. Lockheed Martin, Boeing and Raytheon were the biggest defence contractors, with another three US firms in the top ten (Northrop Grumman (fifth), General Dynamics (sixth), and Honeywell (tenth)).[26]

Compared to the United States', everyone else's defence budget was small. Nevertheless, the aggregate sum of EU members' defence spending of about $200 billion in 2003 exceeded the defence budgets of China ($56 billion), Japan ($43 billion), and Russia ($65 billion). Even taken separately, defence spending of the leading EU powers (UK, France and Germany: $43 billion, $46 billion, and $35 billion, respectively) was of a similar order of magnitude as that of China, Japan, and Russia.[27]

EU efforts to develop an integrated European Defence Equipment Market (EDEM), and to coordinate planning through a European Defence Agency (EDA) constituted *de facto* soft balancing, although the stated objectives were economic competitiveness, technological autonomy, and strategic autonomy, rather than explicit and intentional counterbalancing of US primacy. Keir A. Lieber and Gerard Alexander suggested that there was no significant "internal" hard balancing because "the United States' nearest rivals were not ramping up defence spending to counter U.S. power".[28] However, this ignored that the EU's effort to rationalise its aggregate defence spending of $200 billion could achieve *de facto* soft balancing and reduce security dependency even without increasing defence budgets.

To enhance its role as crisis manager, the EU has acquired a unique set of civilian and military instruments of crisis management including pre-crisis prevention and post-crisis stabilisation. The EU summit at Feira in June 2000 decided to develop "four aspects of civilian crisis management: police, rule of law, civil administration and civil protection". For this purpose, EU members would "provide up to 5,000 police

---

[26]   Vlachos-Dengler, K., *Off track? The Future of the European Defense Industry*, Santa Monica, RAND Corporation, 2004, p. 5.

[27]   International Institute for Strategic Studies, *The Military Balance, 2004-2005*, London, Oxford University Press/IISS, 2004, pp. 353-54.

[28]   Lieber, K. and Alexander, G., "Waiting for Balancing: Why the World is Not Pushing Back", *op. cit.*, p. 109.

officers for international missions by 2003, with 1,000 available at 30 days' notice".[29]

The EU's claim for a security role has been substantiated further when the EU conducted its first military and police missions in the Balkans and in Africa. The European Union Police Mission in Bosnia-Herzegovina, launched on 1 January 2003 to replace the UN's International Police Task Force, was the EU's first civilian crisis management operation under the ESDP. The first military operation of the EU was the *Concordia* mission in Macedonia, launched on 31 March 2003, replacing NATO's Operation Allied Harmony. *Concordia* was followed by an EU police mission called *Proxima*, launched on 15 December 2003 and involving 200 police officers. The EU's first military operation outside Europe was the *Artemis* mission under a UN mandate (Security Council Resolution 1484, 30 May 2003). Launched on 12 June 2003 and ending on 1 September 2003, *Artemis* intended to stabilise security in the Ituri region of the Democratic Republic of Congo. In spite of the small number of personnel involved (circa 1000 in the European Union Police Mission (EUPM); circa 350 in *Concordia*; circa 1800 in *Artemis*), these missions demonstrated the will and capability to act as EU and to fulfil most of the Petersberg Tasks set out in 1992.[30]

The decision of April 2004 to establish a dozen so-called "battle groups" of 1,500 soldiers each promised to be of more practical relevance for crisis management than the 1999 Headline Goal to form a 60,000-man RRF. Besides battle groups composed only of British or French troops, several multinational battle groups were planned. Non-EU Norway was to participate in a Nordic battle group, together with EU members Denmark, Finland, and Sweden.[31]

The involvement of US forces in the Bosnian and Kosovo crises in the 1990s had been taken by Atlanticists as proof that US military capabilities and its "role as *primus inter pares*" were still indispensable for European stability, "for the same reasons that required American engagement when NATO was founded half a century ago".[32] This was underlined by the unwillingness of EU powers to take on responsibility for post-conflict stabilisation unless US troops remained present on the ground. Berlin, London, and Paris insisted "that their troops will stay in

---

[29] Hagmann, H.C., "European Crisis Management and Defence", *Adelphi Paper*, No. 353, Oxford/New York, Oxford University Press, 2002, p. 25.

[30] Lynch, D. and Missiroli, A., "ESDP Operations", *Briefing Paper*, Paris, ISS-EU, 2005, pp. 1-4.

[31] Zecchini, L., "L'UE se dote d'une nouvelle force militaire rapide", *Le Monde*, 23 novembre 2004; Lindstrom, G., *Enter the EU Battlegroups*, *op. cit.*

[32] Pond, E., *The Rebirth of Europe*, Washington, D.C., Brookings Institution Press, 2002, p. 204.

Bosnia only as long as US forces remain".[33] However, this reluctance to act without the US has since been replaced by growing EU responsibilities, for example, when in 2004 the EU took on "its first big military mission on December 2nd, replacing NATO in charge of the 7,000-man Bosnia task force".[34] Although "most of the troops" remained "the same, merely switching from NATO to EU insignia", the changeover was politically significant.[35] A decade after the Bosnian civil war ended in the Dayton agreement and half a decade after the Kosovo war, EU military and police missions were guaranteeing stability while Stability and Association Agreements held out the prospect of economic development and eventual EU membership for the Western Balkans.[36]

The EU's array of civilian and military instruments of crisis management remained rather modest compared to the military might of the US. It was also small compared to the national military capabilities of larger EU member states. Nevertheless, together with economic and diplomatic instruments it enabled the EU to extend the European security community to the Balkans and to contribute to UN crisis management in Africa.

US Ambiguity towards EU Role Claims

Throughout the 1990s the Bush and Clinton administrations responded negatively to EU claims of security autonomy. European ambitions should not undermine NATO's pre-eminent role as security provider. Yet, there was also US interest in cost-cutting and devolution of responsibilities. The Bush administration had welcomed a European Security and Defence Identity (ESDI) within NATO, that is, a small degree of relative autonomy. However, Secretary of State James Baker also made it clear "that one of our key goals must be to ensure that NATO remains the principal venue for our consultations and the forum for agreements on all security and defence commitments of its members".[37]

The Clinton administration's reluctance to get involved in European crises not threatening vital US interests was visible in the Yugoslav

---

[33] Daalder, I.H., "Bosnia after SFOR: Options for Continued US Engagement", *Survival*, Vol. 39, No. 4, 1997-98, p. 9.

[34] Evans-Pritchard, A., "EU to Field Quick-reaction Battle Groups", *Washington Times*, 22 November 2004.

[35] *Ibid.*

[36] Triantaphyllou, D., "The Balkans between Stabilisation and Membership" in J. Batt *et al.*, "Partners and Neighbours: A CFSP for a Wider Europe", *Chaillot Paper*, No. 64, Paris, ISS-EU, September 2003, pp. 60-76.

[37] Friedman, T., "NATO Tries to Ease Military Concerns in Eastern Europe", *New York Times*, 7 June 1991, p. A8.

crises of the 1990s. Although US military capabilities were decisive in the end, the United States was initially reluctant to intervene or to get involved in warfare on the ground, preferring instead the use of air power. US interest in devolution became obvious when NATO's 1994 summit agreed that the ESDI could become operational through the WEU, acting as NATO-approved Combined Joint Task Forces (CJTF). The CJTF concept retained ultimate US/NATO responsibility but it made US involvement in European crises optional, in contrast to the obligatory involvement during the Cold War. Washington was willing to delegate crisis management in Europe to the WEU, acting with NATO approval but without US participation.

Subsequently, NATO concluded the Berlin Agreement of 1996 with the WEU, whereas a security role for the EU was still unwelcome. This, however, changed within a few years. In 1999 the WEU was absorbed by the EU, and in 2002 the Berlin Plus Agreement was signed. This was no longer a deal between NATO and the WEU but between NATO and the EU, indicating that NATO and the United States had accepted the EU's claimed security role.

US efforts at counter-counterbalancing continued under President George W. Bush. When the leaders of France, Germany, Belgium, and Luxembourg, at their mini-summit on 29 April 2003, suggested "the establishment of an EU operational planning staff in the Brussels suburb of Tervuren",[38] this was strongly rejected by the United States and the UK because this EU planning staff could have evolved into military headquarters independent of NATO. Later France, Germany, and the UK agreed on the compromise of setting up a much smaller planning cell for EU military missions. Although this planning cell "of perhaps a few dozen people" was not much of a threat to NATO's centrality, it still drew a negative response from US Defence Secretary Donald Rumsfeld and caused US officials to "worry the move could lead to [...] competition with NATO, and open the door to a further erosion of the alliance's importance".[39]

The United States also expressed its misgivings about the EU's *Galileo* global positioning system without, however, being able to stop this step towards technological and operational autonomy. One of the US counter-measures was the inclusion of as many European partners as possible in the gigantic Joint Strike Fighter (JSF) project. In order to prevent the formation of a defence-industrial "Fortress Europe", the JSF

---

[38] Grant, C., "EU Defence Takes a Step Forward", *Briefing Note*, Centre for European Reform, London, December 2003, p. 2.

[39] Graham, B., "Rumsfeld criticises EU Defense Plan", *Washington Post*, 3 December 2003, p. A18.

project served as a "Trojan horse".[40] Last, but not least, when France, Germany, and Russia undertook diplomatic counterbalancing of US intentions to use military force against Iraq without prior UN approval, the United States mobilised Atlanticist support among European governments in the "Letter of Eight" and the "Letter of Ten" of early 2003.

US actions have continued to bolster the "NATO First" approach but, on the other hand, NATO's centrality has been weakened. Indicators of this are US troop withdrawals from Europe, the relegation of NATO to backfilling tasks during the 2001 intervention in Afghanistan, and the discontinuation of the "Quad".[41] When German Chancellor Gerhard Schröder in early 2005 deplored that NATO was no longer the place for strategic discussion, he was, in Robert Hunter's words, "not saying that NATO *should not* be 'the primary venue where transatlantic partners discuss and coordinate strategies' but that it no longer played that role. NATO was no longer this primary venue because the United States had 'in recent years chosen not to use NATO in this way'".[42]

Acceptance of ESDP by Old and New Atlanticists

US resistance to an EU security role was supported within the EU by Atlanticists fearing that EU role claims would drive the United States out of Europe. Yet, the reduction of the US military presence in Europe as well as the reorientation towards East Asia and the Middle East in the Bush administration's *Quadrennial Defense Review* of 2001 made Atlanticist reliance on US protection less convincing. West European Atlanticists began to accept some EU responsibility for European security, as long as the EU extended its role without any overt anti-NATO or anti-US rhetoric.

On the other hand, new EU members in central and eastern Europe adopted strong Atlanticist positions. Poland, in particular, expected much from joining NATO in 1999 and regarded very close links with the United States as essential guarantees of security and sovereignty. For Poland, US hegemony was an insurance against Germany and Russia whereas without a balancing US presence the EU could easily fall under

---

[40] Kapstein, E., "Capturing Fortress Europe: International Collaboration and the Joint Strike Fighter", *Survival*, Vol. 46, No. 3, Autumn 2004, p. 138.

[41] The informal directory composed of the United States, Britain, France and Germany that guides NATO meetings.

[42] Hunter, R., "NATO and the European Union: Inevitable Partners" in S. Serfaty (ed.), *Visions of the Atlantic Alliance. The United States, the European Union, and NATO*, Center for Strategic and International Studies, Washington, D.C., CSIS Press, 2005, p. 66. Hunter's emphasis.

the hegemony of the "Franco-German monster".[43] Nevertheless, even in Poland the tide was turning against initial enthusiastic Atlanticism. "In Iraq Polish Atlanticism reached its apex and now needs to be rethought and adjusted. [...] The Atlanticism of the CEE states may have begun to erode as a consequence of their costly and largely unrewarded involvement in Iraq" although they "will certainly support the continuation of the US's involvement in European security".[44]

Poland opposed French-German initiatives because "ESDP must not challenge the US presence and role on the continent and must be kept within a NATO framework". Polish leaders "believed that the Atlantic Alliance's ultimate strength rested on its collective defence commitment" and "wanted to join a NATO in which the leading role of the US would never be questioned".[45] Yet, Polish fears that NATO was becoming an "organisation for collective security at the expense of its central defence mission" were coming true in spite of Polish efforts to prove "that it was a staunch ally of the US and its leadership role in the alliance".[46]

Some acceptance of an EU security role was also emerging in central-eastern Europe: "Poland – and this is a sea-change in the attitude – clearly recognises that in the course of time, the EU will become the equal partner of NATO. Important is, however, that it will be a natural process driven by common-sense since any political haste or institutional competition may result in undermining NATO as well as the ESDP".[47]

As European security became less central to US strategy, it became "not unlikely that those Europeans who continue to advocate strong transatlantic bonds – the British and the CEE states – are in fact fighting a losing battle. [...] In other words, whatever view prevails in the EU, transatlantic relations may be weakening anyway".[48] Even Polish Eurosceptics, afraid that the EU might develop into an anti-American "poten-

---

[43] Sedivy, J. and Zaborowski, M., "Old Europe, New Europe and Transatlantic Relations", *European Security*, Vol. 13, No. 3, 2004, pp. 206 and 209.

[44] Longhurst, K. and Zaborowski, M., "The Future of European Security", *European Security*, Vol. 13, No. 4, 2004, p. 385.

[45] Osica, O., "Poland: A New European Atlanticist at a Crossroads?", *European Security*, Vol. 13, No. 4, 2004, pp. 309 and 312.

[46] *Ibid.*, p. 311.

[47] Osica, O., "A Secure Poland in a Better Union? The ESS as Seen from Warsaw's Perspective" in M. Overhaus *et al.* (eds.), "The European Security Strategy: Paper Tiger or Catalyst for Joint Action. Part II", *German Foreign Policy in Dialogue*, Vol. 5, No. 14, October 14, 2004, p. 14.

[48] Longhurst, K. and Zaborowski, M., "The Future of European Security", *op. cit.*, p. 389.

tially hostile bloc", wondered about the reliability of the transatlantic link: "Much of central and eastern Europe senses that the United States is steadily withdrawing from the region, [...] CEE countries perceive the US diplomatic and business presence as shallow and shrinking compared with the growing western European role".[49]

Conclusions: Role Claims and Soft Balancing

European integration has resulted, over several decades, in *de facto* soft balancing of US economic power. On the military chessboard, European security dependency has declined substantially compared to the Cold War period, and the EU has successfully claimed a limited security role. Soft balancing between friends is inherently limited in its objectives and methods, but it can nevertheless be effective. In the post-1991 security environment, the EU can initiate a renegotiation of roles without incurring great risks.

It could perhaps be argued that the post-1991 EU claim for a security role did not constitute balancing because the EU was merely filling a void left behind by a partial US withdrawal. However, there were also visible role conflicts indicating that soft European counterbalancing and US counter-counterbalancing were taking place. Washington repeatedly asserted its leadership role and opposed steps towards EU security autonomy. On the other hand, the EU filled the void when US troops withdrew from the Balkans but there were also Franco-German attempts to expand the EU's security role faster than Washington considered acceptable. Soft balancing between friends involves role conflicts but these are never driven to breaking point.

Soft balancing did not start in 2001 in response to US unilateralism. European integration has, *de facto* or intentionally, constituted soft balancing for half a century, and the claim for a security role was made as early as 1991, at the Maastricht conference. Balancing will remain soft and transatlantic cooperation indispensable, not least because of massive economic interdependence. Nevertheless, transatlantic security cooperation cannot retain its Cold War format.

The renegotiation of roles in the transatlantic alliance is taking much longer than the sudden redefinition of the roles of Warsaw Pact members with the collapse of the Soviet Union. The western alliance is being

---

[49] See the "bifurcation scenario" in H. Mouritzen, "Prospects for Europe" in H. Mouritzen and A. Wivel (eds.), *The Geopolitics of Euro-Atlantic Integration*, London/ New York, Routledge, 2005, p. 210: "The poles are constituted by an 'inner' Europe and an 'outer', Atlantic Europe. [...] The UK and presumably Poland will function as European leaders for the Atlanticists and together with the US form the pole base. Correspondingly, France and Germany will lead inner Europe".

transformed not by sudden disintegration but by gradual renegotiation of entrenched role conceptions and role expectations. The problem of collective action experienced by the European side of the transatlantic partnership can be overcome. Economic coalition forming has prepared the EU's collective claim for a security role.

Soft balancing among friends includes challenges to the rather benign hegemony of the United States through limited role claims without destroying the entire partnership. The EU's role claims escalated in 1991 compared to the Cold War period, and went even further with the ESDP of 1999. The acceptance of such role claims has grown, in contrast to the absolute taboo still evident in the 1970s and 1980s.

After decades shaped by the "NATO First" approach, it is time to revisit the Marshall Plan vision. Instead of insisting on the roles of 1949, the United States could welcome a more symmetrical relationship. The Marshall Plan implied economic recovery and integration followed by European responsibility for security. This vision was unrealistic in the 1940s but six decades later the prerequisites are in place. In line with the Marshall Plan vision, Washington should welcome an integrated Europe taking responsibility for its own security. This redefinition of the West is leading from the Cold War constellation of "two Europes and one West" to "one Europe and two Wests".[50]

---

[50] Moïsi, D., "Reinventing the West", *Foreign Affairs*, Vol. 82, No. 6, November/December 2003, p. 67.

CHAPTER 10

Arm-in-Arm? The European Security and Defence Policy and the EU Armaments Industry

Dr. Rémy DAVISON

Introduction

The promulgation of the European Security and Defence Policy (ESDP) in 1999 was the culmination of over forty years of incremental EU defence integration, which had its origins in the abortive European Defence Community (EDC) of 1952. In the wake of crises in eastern and southern Europe, such as Bosnia-Herzegovina (1993) and Albania (1996), EU member states sought to develop a European security identity, and a military capability, distinct from that of NATO. This culminated in the adoption of the ESDP at the Potsdam European Council in 1999.

The foundations of ESDP found their first expression in the Anglo-French *entente cordiale* at St. Malo in 1998. At St. Malo, UK Prime Minister Tony Blair and French President Jacques Chirac outlined a vision for collective EU security which included the capability to act where NATO did not. In summary, ESDP would operate, effectively, as an *extension* of NATO, not as a replacement. Moreover, Blair was not conceding a great deal; in 1998, there were no EU armed forces and no EU-specific military assets. Consequently, the EU was forced to rely upon the common assets of the Western European Union (WEU), and ultimately integrated the WEU into ESDP. Indeed, viewed critically, one might argue that *Concordia* and *Artemis*[1] – limited actions, made possible only by NATO assets – were merely "proof-of-concept" illustrations that ESDP was, in fact, "operational". The EU has also struggled with the development of its own combat forces; its Rapid Reaction Force (RRF), a 60,000-strong force which was expected to be opera-

---

[1] Operation *Concordia* is the EU security mission to the former Yugoslav Republic of Macedonia that took over from NATO in March 2003 and is still in place. Operation *Artemis* was the EU military mission to the Democratic Republic of the Congo in June 2003.

tional by 2003, is well behind schedule. Political, budgetary and logistical constraints are likely to delay full RRF operability until 2009-10.

Despite the rupture in Franco-British relations in 2002-03 during the prelude to the Iraq war, Blair and Chirac nevertheless achieved a consensus on the establishment of a European Defence Agency (EDA), which became operational in 2004. However, British and French perspectives on defence procurement were at significant variance. French defence policy makers see the EDA as the key to developing a single European market in defence procurement. This stance accords with a similar programme through which industry sectors were cartelised as a consequence of French government initiatives, or under the rubric of the EU. Examples of this range from the European Atomic Energy Community (Euratom) and the European Coal and Steel Community (ECSC) to HD-MAC,[2] Airbus Industrie and Concorde. As Hayward notes,[3] the Franco-German preference is for "Eurochampions" to replace "national champions", which can compete head-to-head with US and Japanese firms across a range of industry sectors.[4] Military exports have helped subsidise the EU's high-technology research and development (R&D) programme, such as the European Strategic Programme for Research and development in Information Technology (ESPRIT), the Joint European Torus (JET), and Research and development in Advanced Communications technology for Europe (RACE). The EDA framework also accords with Rhenish capitalists' predilection for central-planning agencies, rather than market-driven initiatives.[5] Ultimately, French governments view a strong EU defence sector, exemplified by the transnational Airbus consortium, as one of the keys to Europe's growth, employment, high-tech investment, technology spin-offs and industrial competitiveness. Moreover, as one EU official has noted, France is

---

[2] A European digital television standard proposed in 1986, which, after meagre success, was abandoned in 1993 in favour of the global Digital Video Broadcasting (DVB).

[3] Hayward, J. (ed.), *Industrial Enterprise and European Integration: From National to International Champions in Western Europe*, Oxford, Oxford University Press, 1995.

[4] EU Commission President Delors (1985-1994) also encouraged EU firms to cartelise, although he was largely unsuccessful. See Grant, C., *Delors: Inside the House that Jacques Built*, London, Nicholas Brearley, 1994, pp. 153-7; Ross, G. "Sidling into Industrial Policy: Inside the European Commission", *French Politics and Society*, Vol. 11, No. 1, 1993, pp. 20-43.

[5] Davison, R., "An Ever Closer Union? Rethinking European Peripheries" in P.B. Murray and L.T. Holmes, (eds.), *Europe: Rethinking the Boundaries*, Ashgate, Aldershot, 1998, pp. 63-92; Davison, R.., "Intervention or Regulation? Australian and European Policies on Competition", *Law in Context*, Vol. 20, No. 1, 2002, pp. 63-95.

likely to press for a "buy Europe" programme in defence procurement, in order to diminish the EU's level of dependence upon US imports.[6]

British defence planners take a different view. They believe that encouraging armaments cooperation will take time, and that leasing, rather than buying equipment, will be necessary. This materiel will be sourced from both EU and US firms, as the EU defence industry currently has serious weaknesses. In summary, British policy makers argue that if Europe wants rapid reaction forces, it will need to source its defence materiel from a number of different markets, rather than merely fostering the "buy Europe" programme advocated by the EDA.

The first section of this chapter provides an overview of the development of the ESDP. Part two canvasses the development of a collaborative European defence procurement industry since the mid-1990s. EU defence contractors have pooled some of their resources and formed a number of consortia, but national markets remain fragmented and cross-border collaboration, although significantly stronger than a decade ago, is still restricted largely to joint ventures between the three major arms-exporting states: Britain, France and Germany.

This chapter discusses the problems and challenges faced by the EU and its defence industries in the context of a single market in defence procurement. The EU defence sector faces a preponderant US arms industry, which accounted for 31% of global military exports in 2007.[7] The EU faces myriad challenges: small defence budgets; a widening capability gap between Europe and the US; problems relating to asset interoperability; increasing demand for peacekeeping and rule of law operations, both within Europe and out-of-area and, finally, a fractured and still largely nationally-oriented defence procurement market.

The Petersberg Declaration

The "Petersberg Tasks" were incorporated into the Maastricht Treaty in 1992. The Petersberg Declaration stated that the objectives of the EU's security policy were to be accomplished by the WEU.[8] The Petersberg Tasks included humanitarian and rescue tasks; peace keeping and management tasks; and peace making.

By co-opting the WEU as its defence arm for the broad range of Petersberg Tasks, the EU was confronted with the Albanian crisis in 1996. At this stage, the WEU still had no operational forces available. Conse-

---

[6] Interview conducted by author, Brussels, 29 June 2005.

[7] Stockholm International Peace Research Institute (SIPRI), *SIPRI Yearbook 2008*, Stockholm, SIPRI, 2008, chapter 7.

[8] The WEU's functions were absorbed into the EU under the rubric of the European Security and Defence Identity (ESDI) and, later, the ESDP.

quently, NATO made some of its own assets available to the WEU. Joint NATO-WEU operations, labelled Combined Joint Task Forces (CJTFs) permitted the WEU to utilize NATO assets for EU-led missions. In order to confront the Albanian crisis, Italy led a "coalition of the willing", acting under a UN Security Council mandate, to restore peace in Albania. In 1999, the EU absorbed the WEU and undertook the Petersberg Tasks under its own framework.

The European Security and Defence Policy

The concept of an ESDP emerged from the seminal 1998 Franco-British summit between Blair and Chirac at St. Malo, which represented a profound shift in the strained Franco-British relationship of the Thatcher/Major and Mitterrand eras. St. Malo appeared to mark a new era in Franco-British cooperation on defence issues which reactivated the long-dormant concept of an integrated EU defence force. The summit envisaged ESDP *within* NATO, rather than a discrete collective security organization. The St. Malo declaration argued that the EU must be ready and able to respond to international crises; capable of autonomous action; back up its actions with credible military force.

The St. Malo declaration was supported at the 1999 Cologne European Council; subsequently, the 1999 Helsinki European Council announced plans to develop a Rapid Reaction Force.

The British position is that European security institutions should co-exist with, not displace, NATO. Thus, St. Malo satisfied both British and French strategic objectives. For the French, St. Malo meant that European security and a rapid reaction force would be operationalised and controlled within the institutional framework of the EU (the European Council, General Affairs Council and Defence Ministers' Council). For Tony Blair, it meant that the UK could participate in the development of ESDP without jeopardizing the special status of the NATO alliance. Indeed, given its lack of autonomous operational capabilities and of a mutual defence clause, ESDP is merely a "pillar" within NATO.

The Rapid Reaction Force

The RRF is an integral part of the ESDP, but ESDP capabilities have been severely limited by a lack of force availability, logistics support and military assets. Consequently, ESDP operations have been forced to rely upon NATO assets under the CJTF agreements. These arrangements were formalized under the "Berlin Plus" agreements of 2002.

Under the Helsinki Headline Goals, the RRF was to assume the following form: a force strength of 50,000-60,000; capable of undertaking the full range of Petersberg Tasks; EU member states would provide the requisite troops, equipment and other resources.

However, by 2002, sufficient resources for ESDP were still not in place, leading to the "Berlin Plus" agreements (2002). "Berlin Plus" allows the EU to utilize NATO resources to carry out operations.

The RRF was scheduled to become operational in 2004. However, it was postponed until 2007, and is now only likely to become functional in 2009-2010. Consequently, until the RRF gains sufficient capabilities, EU missions will continue to be carried out under the auspices of the Berlin Plus EU-NATO CJTFs. Under this agreement, the first major EU takeover of an operation took place in December 2004 – Operation *Althea* – which conducts peacekeeping operations in Bosnia-Herzegovina. Other missions have included Georgia (rule-of-law); Macedonia (police); and Congo (peace-keeping).

The objective of the ESDP is to act in situations where NATO is not willing or able to do so. Operationally, the RRF should be able to deploy its 60,000-strong force within sixty days. Although the add-up of EU forces totals 2.5 million (significantly larger than US regular forces, not including strategic reserves), it has been conceded that only 55,000 EU troops are readily deployable without overstretching force commitments. A key problem is that the RRF will not be a standing army; thus, it will rely upon force availability and equipment according to the task at hand. Due to the RRF's lack of progress, EU defence ministers in 2004 initially opted to form 13 battle groups, each comprising 1,500 troops, deployable within 15 days. Allowing for rotations, this gives a total force of 156,000 combat troops. Fifteen battle groups were operational by 2008,[9] and another three scheduled for 2010. However, while the battle groups can be deployed within tight timeframes, NATO Secretary-General Jaap de Hoop Scheffer and EU defence ministers may be optimistic about the speed with which the RRF can deploy: during the 2003 Iraq war, for example, the UK took seventy days to deploy 45,000 troops.[10] Moreover, former NATO Secretary-General, George Robertson, asserts that only 3% of NATO member forces are equipped to operate in combat situations in out-of-area operations. The US and UK possess the most capable troops for these types of operations, but both countries are stretched militarily, given the sizeable forces they

---

[9] The Nordic battle group includes EU neutrals and non-EU members. It comprises Estonia, Finland, Ireland, Norway and Sweden. There is also an Italian-Romanian-*Turkish* battle group.

[10] Economist Intelligence Unit, "Europe's not-so-rapid reaction force", *EIU Newswire*, 23 May 2003.

currently have stationed in Iraq.[11] France also has significant out-of-area operational capabilities, evidenced by its role in the Afghanistan conflict, but it also has over 10,500 troops deployed in Africa and no long-range air transport capability.[12]

By comparison, NATO-assigned forces are markedly superior. By 2006, NATO had its own 21,000-strong rapid reaction forces, which are capable of deploying air, sea and land forces within five days, and in a maximum of thirty. The air service of the NATO Response Force (NRF) is capable of flying up to 200 sorties per day, and the combined forces are self-sustaining anywhere in the world for up to one month. Nevertheless, the NRF itself is not without its own problems. Issues such as airlifting, communications and logistics still need to be addressed more thoroughly, while parliamentary approval for the use of troops in combat operations could delay deployments in times of crisis.[13] However CFSP/ESDP initiatives – such as peace-enforcement missions in Bosnia-Herzegovina, Operation *Concordia*[14] (former Yugoslav Republic of Macedonia) and Operation *Artemis* (Democratic Republic of Congo) – all obtained parliamentary consent *post hoc*, in some cases, well after British, French and Italian representatives on the General Affairs Council had granted approval for the commencement of operations.[15]

EU Military Spending

The EU's total defence spending is approximately $312 billion (all amounts quoted are in US dollars), less than half the US's $711 billion in defence expenditures,[16] and a third of the amount the US spends on a

---

[11]   Wall, R. and Taverna, M., "Rapid, Global Response: NATO Begins Two-year Process to Build 21,000-strong Quick-Reaction Force", *Aviation Week and Space Technology*, Vol. 159, No. 16, 2003, p. 58.

[12]   12,000 troops, according to A. Hansen. The French government does not reveal how many troops it maintains in Africa. There is also mounting evidence that French governments utilize EU troops to defray the costs of France's military commitments in Africa. See Hansen, A., "The French Military in Africa", New York, Council on Foreign Relations, 2008; "The Glory Days are Passing", *The Economist*, 13 December 2006; Davison, R., *Foreign Policies of the Great and Emerging Powers*, Upper Saddle River, N.J, Prentice Hall, 2008, chapter 7.

[13]   Wall, R. and Taverna, M., "Rapid, Global Response", *op. cit.*, p. 56.

[14]   Operation *Concordia* was the EU's first security mission, with EU personnel replacing NATO forces in 2003.

[15]   *Concordia* obtained Italian parliamentary agreement three months after the Italian government had agreed to its mandate. See Bono, G., "National Parliaments and EU External Military Operations: Is there any Parliamentary Control?", *European Security*, Vol. 14, No. 2, 2005, pp. 203-29.

[16]   EU figure in US dollars at February 2008 exchange rates. US figure based upon Pentagon request for fiscal 2009. See Centre for Arms Control, "The FY 2009 Pentagon Spending Request – Global Military Spending", 22 February 2008,

per capita basis.[17] The EU figure is somewhat misleading as the US dollar's sharp decline, and the euro's commensurate rise since after 9/11 suggests the EU's military spending is rather more impressive than it actually is (see Table 1). The reality is that US defence spending dwarfs Europe's; for example, the US's $80 billion increase in its defence budget in 2002 was greater than the total French and British defence budgets combined. In R&D, the US spent $40 billion in 2001, versus France, Germany and the UK's combined total of $7 billion.[18] The EU defence procurement market also has structural inefficiencies, due to its fragmented customer base, while the US's scale efficiencies derive partly from the fact that its defence market is 2.3 times larger than the EU's.

Although EU defence expenditures are the world's second-largest, this does not buy Europe the world's second-best military machine. A key problem is that EU defence budgets and industries are emphatically "national" in their orientation. As a consequence of these exceedingly small domestic markets, combined with cost constraints and technological gaps, EU countries are compelled to import or acquire over 50% of their defence materiel, either from US firms directly, or via US subsidiaries operating within Europe or third countries.

The EU Armaments Industry

A series of mergers and acquisitions has led to the emergence of a number of new transnational European defence corporations. These include the Franco-German-Spanish European Aeronautic Defence and Space Company (EADS), British-based BAE Systems, French-based Thales, and MBDA, a missile manufacturer owned by French, German, British and Italian interests.[19] EADS, BAE Systems and Thales, the largest EU defence contractors, view intra-EU defence collaboration as an opportunity to bolster both EU and global armaments sales. Conversely, Washington views this development as a broad attempt to challenge the US in both armaments technology and worldwide market share. The proposed lifting of the EU-China arms embargo merely

---

http://www.armscontrolcenter.org/policy/securityspending/articles/fy09_dod_request_global/, accessed 28 February 2008.

[17] Keohane, D., "Europe's new defence agency", *Policy Brief*, Centre for European Reform, June 2004.

[18] $US75 billion was devoted to military R&D in fiscal year 2006. See Meeks, R., "President's FY 2006 Budget Requests Level R&D Funding", *NSF Infobrief*, October 2005; Keohane, D., "The EU and armaments cooperation", *Working Paper*, London, Centre for European Reform, December 2002, p. 7.

[19] *Ibid.*

consolidated this view.[20] Critics of the EDA argue that the EU needs to guarantee interoperability with NATO and US equipment, focusing domestically upon counter-terrorism and other policing measures, rather than striking out on its own in competition with the US in the defence procurement market.[21] However, EU defence industries are high-value exporters and the sector has a turnover of €70 billion, exports of $36.1 billion (2003-07)[22] and employs 770,000 people.[23] Consequently, it is important to recognise that the defence industry is integral to the EU's strategic trade policy.

Britain is the world's fifth-largest arms exporter,[24] with sales of $19.2 billion, exports of $6.7 billion in 2000, accounting for the direct employment of 155,000 workers.[25] The UK's share of the global armaments market for 2003-07 was 4%, well behind the US's 31%. France, too, has long been a leading arms exporter. Between 1981 and 1985, France sold $5.1 billion in high-performance armaments to Iraq, comprising 40% of France's total arms exports.[26] By 2000, even taking into account the bad conversion rate with the euro, the industry was far smaller, with $2.6 billion in exports. Export sales rose to more than $5.75 billion in 2002 and $5.6 billion in 2003, but fell to $4.47 billion (7.4% of the world market) in 2004, the worst result since 1996. It would not be stretching the point to argue that much of the impetus for the EDA and the integration of the EU's defence industries emerged as a consequence of France's diminishing share of the global arms export

---

[20] Davison, R., "China in the Asia-Pacific" in M. Connors, R. Davison and J. Dosch, *The New Global Politics of the Asia-Pacific*, New York, Routledge Curzon, 2004, p. 65; Davison, R., *Foreign Policies of the Great and Emerging Powers, op. cit.*, p. 95.

[21] North, R., "The End of Independence: the Implications of the "Future Rapid Effects System" for an Independent UK Defence Policy", *The Bruges Group*, News Article, 2003, http://www.brugesgroup.com/news.live?article=227&keyword=1, accessed 25 November 2004; Sangiovanni, M.E., "Why a Common Security and Defence Policy is bad for Europe", *Survival*, Vol. 45, No. 3, 2003, pp. 193-206.

[22] SIPRI, *SIPRI Yearbook 2008, op. cit.*, Appendices 7A and 7B.

[23] Commission of the European Communities, "Creating a Single Market for EU Defence Industry: Commission Opens Consultation", *Press Release*, Brussels, 3 April 2006, http://europa.eu/rapid/pressReleasesAction.do?reference=IP/06/419& format=HTML&aged=0&language=EN&guiLanguage=en, accessed 4 June 2006.

[24] The UK was the world's largest arms exporter in 2007. See "Britain is the World's Biggest Arms Exporter", *The Times*, 18 June 2008.

[25] "SIPRI Military Expenditure and Arms Production Project", Stockholm International Peace Research Institute, June 2003.

[26] Chapin, H.M. (ed.), *Iraq: A Country Study*, Washington, D.C., Library of Congress, 1988.

market. Approximately 33% of sales go to European countries,[27] making France the world's fourth-largest arms supplier. It is also the largest arms exporter to the Third World. German arms exports ranked third globally for 2003-07, with 10% of the world market; it is also the third-largest supplier of small arms. Italy was the world's eighth-largest arms supplier in 2003-07, but it is second only to the US in small arms sales, many of which are re-exported to global trouble spots, leading to widespread accusations of excessive laxity in the EU's arms control regime.[28]

Consequently, the European Council established a common control regime for dual-use exports in 1994. However, there is a serious lack of oversight of arms export controls amongst the EU's largest arms vendors. For example, there was no parliamentary oversight of arms export licensing in France until 2000, when a report on France's 123 client countries was delivered to the National Assembly.[29] In Britain, there have been significant lapses of governance, such as no direct ministerial oversight of the issuance of end-user certificates, as the 1992 Matrix Churchill trial demonstrated. Moreover, a number of senior EU and national leaders have been associated with serious arms scandals. Former NATO Secretary-General Willy Claes was forced to resign over a commission concerning the sale of Italian helicopters to Belgium. Helmut Kohl was implicated in a financial scandal relating to armoured vehicle sales to Saudi Arabia. François Mitterrand's son was connected with bribery in an arms deal with Taiwan, while EADS sold arms to apartheid South Africa with significant kickbacks offered to South African officials by Daimler-Benz, a major shareholder in EADS.[30] Clearly, the lack of transparency of EU military deals, together with fierce international competition and the lucrative nature of arms contracts, provide incentives for individuals and firms to engage in dubious practices, both within the EU and with third countries. However, in 2000, a Council Decision established a Community regime for export controls on dual-use goods, thus removing authority over export licensing from the jurisdiction of member states.[31]

---

[27] "Paris still Third in Arms Exports Abroad", United Press International, *UPI Perspectives*, 2 February 2003.

[28] For 2003-07 figures see SIPRI, *SIPRI Yearbook 2008, op. cit.*

[29] Centre de Documentation et de Recherche sur la Paix et les Conflits, *La Lettre de l'Observatoire des transferts d'armements, Quarterly Review*, No. 21, March 2000.

[30] Broek, M., "Export Credit Agencies and arms trade", paper delivered at the *Third NGOs Strategy Session on ECA Reform*, hosted by Bioforum, Indonesian Environmental Group, in Indonesia 2-7 May 2000.

[31] "Council Decision Repealing Decision 94/942/CFSP on the Joint Action Concerning the Control of Exports of Dual-use Goods", *Official Journal of the European Union*, Vol. 43, 30 June 2000.

The European Defence Agency

In 1991, the Maastricht Treaty established the European Armaments Agency (EAA), a rudimentary collaborative armaments procurement programme, comprising ten member states.[32] In order to develop an integrated market for defence procurement, the EU formed the European Defence Agency in 2004.[33] Established with a staff of 80 and a $25 million budget, the EDA's brief is extensive:[34] developing defence capabilities in the field of crisis management; promoting and enhancing European armaments cooperation; contributing to identifying and, if necessary, implementing policies and measures aimed at strengthening the European defence industrial and technological base; promoting, in liaison with the Community's research activities where appropriate, research aimed at fulfilling future defence and security capabilities requirements and thereby strengthening Europe's industrial potential in this domain.[35]

The EDA works in the field of defence capabilities development, research, acquisition and armaments. It is not concerned with the territorial defence of Europe; that remains within NATO's purview. The EDA's key responsibilities are functional: encouraging EU cross-border military R&D; joint ventures; armaments industries; and developing the military-industrial base. The objective is to promote coherence, rather than fragmentation, in EU defence procurement. Currently, defence ministries in Britain, France, Germany and Italy largely source materiel from their own national armaments industries, although over 50% of EU arms imports originate from the US. The aim of EDA is to pool existing EU defence budgets. However, there is reluctance on the part of EU governments to engage in a significant increase in defence outlays.[36] A 2001 RAND Corporation study noted presciently that the requisite capital costs associated with ESDP/RRF could not be met by 2003, and that without either new outlays or substantial reallocations of military

---

[32] Belgium, France, Germany, Greece, Italy, Luxembourg, The Netherlands, Portugal, Spain, and the UK.

[33] Denmark negotiated an opt-out on EU defence-related issues, and is not a member of the EDA.

[34] Articles 296-298 (*ex*-Art. 223 EEC) of the Treaty of Amsterdam provide the legal basis for the EDA. The EDA is one of only three agencies specifically mentioned in the Lisbon Treaty (Articles 42, 45 and Protocol 10). See *Official Journal of the European Union*, Vol. 51, 9 May 2008.

[35] Western European Union, "The European Defence Agency – Reply to the Annual Report of the Council", Document A/1856, 3 June 2004.

[36] Dyson, T., "German Military Reform 1998-2004: Leadership and the Triumph of Domestic Constraint over International Opportunity", *European Security*, Vol. 14, No. 3, 2005, pp. 361-386.

investments, the cost of meeting the ESDP targets (including deployment of the 60,000-strong RRF) could not be met until 2010.[37] A 2005 European Council report by the British presidency noted that, of sixty-four key areas associated with the implementation of the European Capabilities Action Plan (ECAP), only ten issue areas were deemed "improved" or problems "solved" between 2003 and 2005. The majority of issues remained "approximately the same", indicating no progress in readiness or, in some cases, shortfalls.[38] In addition, the EDA has faced considerable obstacles to both its budget and its programmes. In April 2007, the EU failed to reach agreement over a triennial EDA budget, with France and Britain clashing over R&D and product duplication. Britain also decided to stay out of the EDA's first major research project, a three-year plan to develop force protection technologies.

There is a market for approximately 20,000 tanks and armoured vehicles in the EU. However, there has been only one cooperative venture: the forerunner to the British battlefield vehicle, FRES (Future Rapid Effect System), which is a German-Dutch copy of an American design, known as MRAV (Multi-Role Armoured Vehicle). It was the product of a quadrilateral partnership funded by the UK, France, Germany and the Netherlands, necessitated by the expense associated with producing such a vehicle. France extricated itself from the project and developed its own vehicle, the VBCI (Véhicule blindé de combat d'infanterie). As North notes, the trilateral consortium ultimately produced the Boxer, but its weight ruled it out of contention for airborne deployment, converting it into yet another burden to long-range capabilities.[39] There were also considerable logistical problems arising during Operations *Concordia* and *Artemis* due largely to a lack of a strategic transport capability, a situation even the Airbus A400M is unlikely to alleviate fully due to its relatively short range.[40]

EU-US Defence Procurement: between Collaboration and Competition

The high level of import dependence in the defence sector exhibited by the EU demonstrates the potential size of the defence procurement market that would be available to EU firms, if they were able to compete

---

[37] Wolf, C. and Zycher, B., *European Military Prospects, Economic Constraints, and the Rapid Reaction Force*, Santa Monica, Rand, 2001, p. xv.

[38] Council of the European Union, *Capability Improvement Chart I*, Brussels, Office for Official Publications, 2005.

[39] North, R., "The End of Independence", *op. cit.*

[40] Giegerich, B. and Wallace, W., "Not such a Soft Power: the External Deployment of European Forces", *Survival*, Vol. 46, No. 2, 2004, pp. 174-5.

effectively with US corporations.[41] Since the formation of the EDA, EU firms have positioned themselves aggressively in the US market, having made a number of significant strategic acquisitions within the US armaments industry. The level of EU penetration of the US defence sector has risen appreciably in recent years. Joint ventures have become important vehicles for EU defence industries' expansion, as successive US administrations have sought to reduce costs, increase efficiency and technology sharing, as well as gradually liberalising the defence procurement market. For example, EADS is one of the 10 largest US Department of Homeland Security contractors and a key partner in Northrop Grumman's KC-30 Tanker for the USAF.[42]

However, some European countries have opted to engage in major American programmes, to the detriment of investment in EU defence projects, such as the Eurofighter. The UK, Italy, the Netherlands and Denmark, as well as NATO partners Norway and Turkey, have committed significant funds to Lockheed's development of the F35 Joint Strike Fighter (JSF).[43] Britain is a full Collaborative Partner on JSF, with $2 billion invested in development, while the Netherlands, Denmark and Norway are Associate Partners. Italy is an Informed Partner. Moreover, US competition has also deprived EU firms of major contracts; for example, in 2003, Poland opted to purchase US F16 aircraft, rather than French Mirages or Swedish Gripens.[44]

The 2004 Commission Green Paper on defence procurement and the EDA have arguably already made their presence felt. The British MoD switched from American to German suppliers for all of their army trucks, eschewing several billion pounds worth of purchases from the US.[45] Following St. Malo, critics of the Blair government, such as

---

[41] Naturally, some high-technology imports would still need to be sourced from the US.

[42] The Airbus A330 provides the platform for the KC-30.

[43] The JSF contracts were finalised in 2001 and the JSF Partners announced in January 2003. Notably, most of these Partner countries committed forces to the US-led coalition against Iraq. However, JSF Partners' firms are not guaranteed contracts, even though most Partner countries will purchase the F35.

[44] The four largest EU CEE economies – the Visegrad states – account for only 5% of total EU defence spending. The Visegrad states have received substantial US military aid and arms contracts. The US foreign direct investment position in the Visegrad armaments sector, as well as the value of leasing agreements, are also considerably higher than those of the EU. "This imbalance will give US companies at least indirectly preferred access in particular to the Polish defence market and limit the possibilities of industrial partnerships with West European producers", quoted from Schmidt, B. (ed.), "EU Enlargement and Armaments: Defence Industries and Markets of the Visegrad Countries", European Union Institute for Security Studies, *Occasional Paper*, No. 54, September, 2004, p. 5.

[45] North, R., "The End of Independence", *op. cit.*

Richard North, pointed to London's "secret" reorientation of defence policy to favour purchasing from EU firms. For example, North cites the MBDA Meteor project, which utilizes a French missile design, as evidence of this, although BAE remains a major shareholder in the firm.[46] Nevertheless, it is true that Britain's rejection of the competing US Raytheon missile system points to a reduced emphasis upon NATO-RRF force interoperability.

However, this overlooks several aspects of the Anglo-American defence relationship, which is multifaceted, long-established and entirely different from any commercial-military linkages Britain has with its EU partners. First, Britain is heavily dependent upon the US for its submarine-based nuclear deterrent, which commenced in the late 1950s with Polaris missiles. Despite significant public and parliamentary opposition, Blair renewed the contract to purchase Trident missiles in December 2006, comprising a significant £20 billion commitment over 20 years. Second, the US grants some privileges to the British government and UK firms engaged in defence-related trade and R&D. In 2000, President Clinton agreed to an International Trade in Arms Regulation (ITAR) waiver for Britain, paving the way for significant UK foreign direct investment in US defence industries, as well as joint ventures.[47] However, the Anglo-American "special relationship" in defence procurement was jeopardised in 2004 by Congress's rejection of the ITAR waiver. British firms, such as BAE, have made significant inroads into the US defence market (see Table 2), as well as engaging in the joint development of cutting-edge military technologies. Due to reductions in Pentagon red tape, British firms face vastly reduced security clearance hurdles to participate in Pentagon contracts in comparison with their NATO and EU partners.[48] Thus, the complex level of interdependence between US-UK defence contractors, as well as the close defence procurement and intelligence relationship between the two states, effectively militates against large-scale British participation in an integrated EU defence industry. Third, interoperability – between NATO and EU

---

[46] *Ibid.*

[47] International Traffic in Arms Regulations waiver. The complex defence certification process for UK firms has been halved, from forty-four to twenty-two days. However, the lack of an ITAR waiver placed deeper Anglo-American joint defence industry collaboration in doubt, with then-Defence Minister Geoffrey Hoon threatening then-Defence Secretary Donald Rumsfeld that Congressional opposition to the waiver could lose US firms billions of dollars in UK weapons purchases. See North, R., "Defence integration – by stealth?", The Bruges Group, 2004, http://www.brugesgroup.com/news.live?article=246&keyword=1, accessed 5 December 2004.

[48] A further attempt at inserting an ITAR waiver into US legislation was made by the Bush Administration in the 2005 Defence Authorization Act. However, both houses of Congress indicated they would reject the bill unless the waiver was removed.

forces – virtually dictates standardisation. However, industry sector-specific policies, and EU commercial considerations, rather than efficiency, have resulted in rival product developments, such as the Airbus A400M long-range transport. Airbus Industrie's civil and military programmes have required significant national and EU subsidies to compete with firms like Boeing and Lockheed, further exacerbating US-EU trade tensions. Certainly, the A400M has received a hundred and ninety-two firm orders,[49] although cutbacks in German military spending reduced Germany's order from seventy-three to sixty.[50] Non-EU external orders have also been important, including those from Turkey, South Africa and Malaysia.[51] However, in 2007, the A400M lost a competitive tender for Canada's purchase of tactical airlifters, with contracts going to Lockheed and Boeing. Consequently, the A400M's primary customers remain EU member states, with the two largest EADS Airbus partners, France and Germany, accounting for more than half the current orders, while Britain (which, through BAE Systems, had a 20% share in Airbus until 2006)[52] will take 13% of A400M orders.

Nevertheless, US congressional action has, perhaps unwittingly, driven the British government towards closer collaboration with its EDA partners. The refusal of Congress to permit even modest amendments to US rules – such as sharing non-classified technologies – is likely to deter British firms from collaboration with US defence contractors due to costly and time-consuming bureaucratic certification processes. In part, UK firms are penalised due to EDA collaboration; US congressional conservatives cited the possibility that US technologies would filter through from British defence contractors or "front" companies to EU firms. Consequently, it is not surprising that critics of EU defence industry collaboration view deeper European defence integration as a threat to the Anglo-American alliance.[53]

The single European market in defence procurement has also faced obstacles due to competition from former Soviet states. Airbus Mili-

---

[49] Airbus Military, "First complete wing set delivered to A400M Final Assembly Line", Press Release, 11 April 2007, http://www.airbusmilitary.com/press.html, accessed 23 May 2007.

[50] Germany's parliament originally consented to the purchase of only forty Airbus A400Ms, while the government ordered seventy-three, again raising the question of transparency and parliament scrutiny in relation to the German government's defence procurement plans. See Mawdsley, J., "Arms, Agencies and Accountability: the Case of OCCAR", *European Security*, Vol. 12, No. 3, 2003, pp. 95-111.

[51] Chile cancelled its order for three A400Ms in 2007.

[52] BAE disposed of its Airbus shares in October 2006, with the stock acquired by EADS.

[53] North, R., "The End of Independence", *op. cit.*; North, R., "Defence Integration – by Stealth?", *op. cit.*

tary's problems have been exacerbated by an unwillingness of central and eastern European states to commit to A400M orders, with several countries preferring to employ Russian- or Ukrainian-owned Antonov C124 Condors for airlift capabilities (which were also used in various EU military operations under leasing arrangements). Indeed, competition between EADS' Airbus division and Antonov has contributed to the souring of EU-Ukraine relations,[54] leading to delays in negotiations concerning possible Ukrainian membership of the EU. In addition, the EU has maintained severe restrictions upon the Ukraine's access to the EU market. Meanwhile, NATO continues to use American-made C-17 transports, while fourteen NATO member and Partner countries also utilize C-17s.[55] In June 2007, NATO members agreed to establish a NATO Airlift Management Organization (NAMO) and the NATO Airlift Management Agency (NAMA) to acquire and support the C-17s. Although these agencies do not specifically exclude competing aircraft, these agreements clearly privilege Boeing at the expense of Airbus.

Vociferous critics of ESDP, such as the Bruges Group analysts, view Europe's new emphasis upon collaborative military programmes that are entirely discrete from NATO as a direct challenge to US national security.[56] As North argues, the monopolization of GPS navigation and satellite guidance systems by the US has placed its rivals at a significant strategic disadvantage as they cannot access the system without American consent. This has major implications for both offensive and defensive weapons systems, particularly early-warning systems.

However, the EU *Galileo* project, which was deployed in 2008 and scheduled to be operational by 2013, could represent a profound shift in the military balance, primarily because China is a major player in the EU consortium. The PRC has invested €230 million in *Galileo*, which is a 30-satellite programme. North estimates that China could acquire satellite guidance systems for air-to-ground ordnance for a mere $18,000, which would make the PRC entirely independent from the US. The loophole which makes *Galileo*'s infrastructure available to third countries relates to the notion that, under EU rules, satellite systems are

---

[54] As a result of the collapse of the USSR, the company became Ukrainian but many of its former assets are owned by other ex-Soviet republics, mainly Russia.

[55] The UK has purchased six Boeing Globemaster III airlifters, with eighteen NATO member and Partner countries signing letters of intent. Nevertheless, the heavy airlift market will remain a three-way competition between Boeing, Airbus and Antonov. See NATO, "Strategic airlift capability", 10 October 2008, http://www.nato.int/issues/strategic-lift-air-sac/index.html, accessed 12 October 2008.

[56] For a discussion of US-China security issues, as they relate to EU arms exports, see Grimmett, R. and Papademetriou, T., "European Union's Arms Control Regime and Arms Exports to China: Background and Legal Analysis", Washington, D.C., Congressional Research Service, Library of Congress, 1 March 2005.

"dual use", despite the longstanding EU embargo on arms and military-related exports to the PRC which has been in place since 1989.[57] Given that China is also developing laser systems capable of destroying space satellites, North concludes that this could not only render US guidance systems inoperable, but that China would also retain its own, separate use of *Galileo*, which will be entirely autonomous of the US GPS system.

Conclusions

"Europe needs larger defence budgets, not institutions and alphabet soup", Clinton's Defence Secretary, William Cohen, noted in 2000.[58] The implications of Cohen's point were clear: there should be only one collective security institution in Europe and its name was NATO. There was no point, Cohen argued, having "duplicative or redundant planning and operational planning institutions".[59] Madeline Albright was even more explicit articulating her "Three D's": "No duplication. No decoupling. No discrimination"[60] but there has been little in the way of "constructive duplication" to reduce EU reliance upon NATO assets.[61] The questions US administrations ask about European defence are salient: why does Europe need two collective security institutions? Why does Europe need two separate armed forces? Why does Europe need two military budgets? Why does it need both a Secretary-General of NATO and a "Monsieur PESC"?[62]

Mainstream security thinking amongst European policy elites remains centred around the concepts of soft power, deterrence and containment. Consequently, EU governments have sought to develop the capability to act in in-area and out-of-area crises (such as Albania, Yugoslavia and Congo) in instances where NATO is unwilling to act. The EU has met the Helsinki Headline Goals commitments in terms of

---

[57] For details on how the embargo is circumvented see Papot, T., "A 'Symbolic Instrument': the EU's Arms Embargo against China", *Current Affairs*, 25 January 2005. For figures, see Bauer, S. and Bromley, M., "The European Union Code of Conduct on Arms Exports: Improving the Annual Report", *SIPRI*, Policy Paper, No. 8, 2004, http://www.sipri.org/contents/armstrad/PP8, accessed 19 January 2005.

[58] Davison, R., "French Security after 9/11: Franco-American Discord" in P. Shearman and M. Sussex (eds.), *European Security after 9/11*, Ashgate, Aldershot, 2004, p. 72.

[59] US Department of Defence, "Secretary Cohen's Press Conference at NATO Headquarters, Brussels, Belgium, 5 December 2000, http://www.defenselink.mil/transcripts/transcript.aspx?transcriptid=1871, accessed 7 June 2004.

[60] Albright, M., "The Right Balance Will Secure NATO's Future", *Financial Times*, 7 December 1998.

[61] Schake, K., "Constructive Duplication: Reducing EU Reliance on US Military Assets", Centre for European Policy Reform, *Working Paper*, January 2002.

[62] Javier Solana has occupied both positions, but not concurrently.

the availability of troops, but it still falls far short in its ability to field those troops. There is still considerable progress to be made before the EU can field forces comprising up to 100,000 combat-ready troops, deployable within seven to thirty days, as well as a hundred warships and four-hundred combat aircraft.

In raw terms, the EU possesses the latent power to become a serious strategic competitor to the US, but this is an extremely unlikely scenario. Moreover, there is no genuinely "European" view on the purpose of ESDP; more accurately, EU common security and defence policies represent an amalgam of interests, but these interests also conflict in a range of issue areas. France, Germany and the UK have largely driven the EU defence and security agenda, while other actors, such as Italy and Spain, have played peripheral decision-making roles, while Denmark secured an opt-out on EU common defence provisions. EU neutrals – such as Austria, Finland and Ireland – have virtually no influence upon either ESDP or NATO issues.

The single market in defence procurement has experienced similar difficulties to previous attempts to develop "Eurochampions" in other industry sectors. First, the main consumers of EU cartelised defence industry products will be EU member governments, rather than third-countries, as the Airbus A400M project demonstrates. Second, the US retains a distinct competitive advantage in the global arms export market, due to scale economies and its large domestic market, which is highly integrated and efficient, as distinct from the largely fragmented EU market. National budgets, constrained by pressing domestic demands, as well as EMU strictures, also mean that there are quantitative limitations upon the expansion of an EU market for defence materiel. Third, UK defence corporations and the British government remain heavily dependent upon US firms for contracts and joint ventures, as well as their maritime nuclear defence capabilities. In the medium term, this is unlikely to change. Fourth, the US's technological edge means that projects, such as the JSF, force EU firms to cooperate in US-led consortia, at the expense of EU-based joint ventures. Consequently, it appears likely that most EU governments will remain reliant upon the US as a major source of military materiel for the foreseeable future, despite some progress in developing a more competitive, collaborative EU defence industry. The EU defence procurement market remains far from integrated, and there is currently little prospect of the "denationalisation" of European defence industries.

Table 1. Countries with the largest military expenditures, 2005[a]

	GDP ($US billion)[b]	Defence spending ($US billion)[b]	Defence spending (PPP; $US billion)[b]	Defence spending (% of GDP)
USA	12.416	478.2	478.2	3.98
Russia	763.7	21	64.4	4.3
China[d,e]	2.235	41[d]	188.4	4.1
Japan	4.534	42.1	34.9	1.0
France	2.127	46.2	45.4	2.6[c]
UK	2.199	48.3	42.3	2.4
Germany	2.795	33.2	32.7	1.5[c]
Italy	1.600	27.2	30.1	1.9[c]
Spain	937.6	9.9	n.a.	1.2
EU-25	**13.503**	**186.3**	**n.a**	**1.9**
India	805.7	20.4	105.8	2.5
Saudi Arabia	310.2	25.2	35	8.5[f]
Israel[d]	123.44	9.6	n.a.	9.1[c]
Iran	379.09[g]	4	23.8	3.8[c]
Brazil	493	9	24.3	1.39

[a] At 2003 prices and exchange rates.

[b] 2004 figure.

[c] 2003 figure.

[d] China and Israel do not release data on defence spending. Figures for Israeli military expenditures do not include US military aid.

[e] The CIA estimate for China's defence spending for 2005 was $US81.5 billion. See *World Factbook* (2006).

[f] 2006 figure.

[g] Estimate (approximate).

Source: Information from SIPRI, *SIPRI Yearbook 2006*, Stockholm, SIPRI, appendix 8A, table 8A.1 and table 8A.3; International Institute for Strategic Studies, *The Military Balance 2003/2004, 2004/2005*.

Table 2. Selected EU defence acquisitions
and contracts with US firms

US firm	Acquiring firm/contract winner	Country of origin
Racal Instruments	EADS	France/Germany
Boeing	EADS[a]	France/Germany
United Defense Industries	BAES	UK
Marconi[b]	BAES	UK
Tracor	BAES	UK
Lockheed Martin Control Systems	BAES	UK
Mevatec	BAES	UK
Boeing Commercial Electronics	BAES	UK
Alphatec	BAES	UK
DigitalNet Holdings	BAES	UK
Augusta Westland Helicopters	Finmeccanica	Italy
Colt	Beretta[c]	Italy

[a] Gained $US 25 billion contact from USAF for fuel tank replacements.

[b] Merger.

[c] Sidearms replaced in the US Army by Berettas.

PART III

THE EU IN THE ASIA PACIFIC REGION

CHAPTER 11

ESDP and the EU's External Governance

Implications for the Asia Pacific Region

Saponti BAROOWA

Introduction

European aspirations for security integration and greater defence autonomy are not merely post-St. Malo (1998) or post-Helsinki (1999) phenomena but can be traced to the years immediately following the end of the Second World War, and notably the Treaty of Dunkirk (1947) and the Treaty of Brussels (1948). But the emergence of the Cold War and its attendant complexities, together with Europe's problematic internal security dynamics, followed by the establishment of the Atlantic Alliance, rendered any exclusive and common European security discourse ineffective. This was exemplified by the failure of the European Defence Community (EDC) in the early 1950s. Despite repeated calls to the Europeans to play a greater role in sharing the security burden within the Alliance, and despite certain specific instances of common European attempts at security cooperation, management of security issues largely remained the preserve of the United States and of a US-led NATO. Four decades later, the fall of the Berlin Wall in 1989 signalled the end of the Cold War and a historic new opportunity for the Europeans to take greater responsibility and rally together for the cause of greater European autonomy. But the old division of Europe and the erstwhile Soviet threat gave way to new cleavages and the appearance of threatening historical forces that few would have imagined to have resided in Europe.

In the wake of the tumultuous events of the 1990s, the Atlantic Alliance neither lost relevance nor disintegrated, as had been predicted by many analysts in the immediate aftermath of the disintegration of the former Soviet Union. It reinvented itself and took upon itself collective security responsibilities in addition to its traditional territorial defence competencies. The Europeans, therefore, once again failed to seize the opportunity and found themselves, for want of a common strategy amongst other shortcomings, incapable of controlling or stopping on their own the horrors unleashed in the Balkans and the cataclysmic events that followed in their wake. Thus, the new security challenges facing Europe, and the realisation of Europe's inadequacies and lack of political will, gave the immediate impetus to the processes that shaped policy throughout the rest of 1990s. They were to ultimately lead to St. Malo and Helsinki. An underlying motivation was to enable EU foreign policy and its diplomacy to carry the weight necessary to fulfil its growing aspirations of becoming a truly global actor, commensurate with the EU's global economic profile.

This is, however, not to suggest any tendency towards global power projection. It reflects, rather, the EU's desire and willingness to play a more prominent role when it comes to sharing the responsibilities for global security governance. This can be furthered only by developing the capacities and capabilities, both military and civilian, for effective crisis management in the EU's immediate neighbourhood as well as in regions further afield. The European Security Defence Policy (ESDP) missions in the Democratic Republic of Congo in 2003 and in Aceh, Indonesia, in 2005 suggest a willingness on the part of the EU and its ESDP to "go global" in an effort to incrementally assume the role of a strategic actor on the world stage. The EU's adoption of its Security Strategy in 2003 has also provided a political framework for the future development of ESDP and its present operational direction is informed in part by the broad objectives outlined in the document. This chapter seeks to critically examine the role of ESDP as an instrument of the EU's external governance and its implications for the Asia Pacific. Additionally, an attempt is made to identify the challenges and opportunities for ESDP in crisis management in the Asia Pacific.

From the Balkans to Aceh:
ESDP as an Instrument of EU External Governance

From its initiation at the 1998 Franco-British Summit at St. Malo, and its formalisation and institutionalisation at the Cologne and Helsinki Councils in 1999 to its 2005 monitoring mission in Aceh, Indonesia, the EU's ESDP has made significant progress. In fact, the fast institutional growth of the ESDP is seen as "remarkable in a system where institutional change often proceeds at a glacial pace".[1] Of course, one must bear in mind that ESDP operations have started on a small scale and are of limited duration, and many of ESDP procedures are still relatively untested.[2] Nevertheless, its acquisition of operational capability in 2003

---

[1]   Bretherton, C. and Vogler, J., *The European Union as a Global Actor*, Routledge, London and New York, 2006, p. 198.

[2]   Missiroli, A., "ESDP – How it Works" in N. Gnesotto (ed.), *EU Security and Defence Policy: The First Five Years*, Paris, EU Institute for Security Studies, 2004, p. 66.

marked a significant shift from the general nature of the development of CFSP which has "often proceeded on the basis of rhetorical declarations followed by hesitant and inadequate implementation".[3]

In 2003, apart from its first-ever civilian crisis management operation, the EU Police Mission in Bosnia Herzegovina (EUPM), and its first-ever military crisis management operation, *Concordia*, in the former Yugoslav Republic of Macedonia, the EU, also for the first time, extended its ESDP operations beyond Europe by undertaking a peacekeeping mission in the Democratic Republic of Congo. This EU military deployment outside Europe was in response to UN Secretary General Kofi Annan's call for immediate intervention in Ituri, a region of instability in the Democratic Republic of Congo (DRC). The military intervention involved 1,800 troops under French command and was known as Operation *Artemis*. The force was also assembled in a very short period of time and involved all EU member states in the decision-making process. All previous operations involved "a lengthy period of advance planning and [had] not really tested crisis decision-making capability".[4] Operation *Artemis* was therefore "an undeniable success from the military point of view".[5] It marked another first in that it was a fully autonomous EU crisis management operation without any recourse to NATO assets. Apart from the military dimension, the Congo operation was significant in that the EU adopted a three-pronged strategy as regards the civilian aspects of the intervention. This included the disarming, demobilisation and reintegration of armed groups, the preparation of a socio-economic rehabilitation programme and the granting of an immediate aid package. The operation was accordingly the first concrete step towards implementing the EU's new security doctrine, "by taking a much longer-term view on crisis management and conflict prevention".[6] A similar approach was also adopted in the case of Macedonia where Operation *Concordia* was to be followed by a police mission on the model of what has been achieved in Bosnia. Most significantly, the EU's successful Congo operation signalled the fact that the ESDP had now changed its scale. It was no longer merely a "tool of crisis-management in the Balkans", but "[had] become a necessary device to enhance Europe's role in the world".[7] This changed scale also

---

3   Giegerich, B. and Wallace, W., "Not Such a Soft Power: The External Deployment of European Forces", *Survival*, Vol. 46, No. 2, Summer 2004, p. 164.

4   Bretherton, C. and Vogler, J., *The European Union as a Global Actor, op. cit.*, p. 202.

5   Yves-Haine, J., "ESDP: an Overview", *European Union Institute for Security Studies*, www.iss-eu.org.

6   *Ibid.*

7   *Ibid.*

suggests that in future the ESDP operations are unlikely to be limited to the "theatre of necessity in the Balkans" but also extend to the "theatre of choice" in other parts of the world, thereby enabling the EU to become a more responsible global player.[8] Significantly, in July 2005, the EU was engaged in another operation beyond its immediate neighbourhood, in Aceh, Indonesia. The Aceh Monitoring Mission (AMM) was given a robust mandate that included "monitoring demobilisation, decommissioning of arms, the withdrawal of government forces, the reintegration of former combatants and the launch of a new political process".[9]

The European Security Strategy and ESDP's External Dimension

The year 2003, despite the crisis over Iraq, marked the adoption by the EU of a common security strategy. In fact, one positive outcome of the Iraq crisis was that it forced the Europeans into a common strategic thinking, and therefore to "take their strategic relationship with the rest of the world more seriously".[10] The European Security Strategy (ESS) document was first presented in the Thessaloniki Council in June 2003, and a revised text was finally adopted at the European Council in Brussels in December 2003. The document also set in motion a dynamic that the EU badly needed in order to become a more effective security order. This dynamic "features a 'top-down' approach to security requirements: i.e. proceeding from a definition of basic interests and goals, to the identification of threats and risks, to the formulation of a set of coordinated policies and thus a security strategy for the EU".[11] Entitled, *A Secure Europe in a Better World: European Security Strategy*, the document, according to EU leaders, would enable Europe to "share in the responsibility for global security and in building a better world".[12]

---

[8]   Yves-Haine, J., "An Historical Perspective" in N. Gnesotto (ed.), *ESDP: The First Five Years*, Paris, EU Institute for Security Studies, 2004, p. 53.

[9]   Braud, P.A. and Grevi, G. "The EU Mission in Aceh: Implementing Peace", *Occasional Paper 61*, Paris, EU Institute for Security Studies, 2004, December 2005, p. 3.

[10] Gnessoto, N., "Preface" in "From Copenhagen to Brussels European Defence: Core Documents", *Chaillot Paper*, No. 67, Paris, Institute for Security Studies, 2003.

[11] Menotti, R., "European Security Strategy – Is it for Real", *ESF Working Paper*, No. 14, Brussels, Centre for European Policy Studies, 2003, p. 16.

[12] European Council, A Secure Europe in a Better World: European Security Strategy, Brussels, 12 December 2003, p. 1.

Previously, the ESDP's Helsinki Headline Goal,[13] which was essentially geared towards crisis management in the EU's immediate neighbourhood such as the Balkans, did not quite seem to address the emerging strategic realities of the new world order, especially post 9/11. Moreover, as François Heisbourg has argued, it "is in the interpretation and implementation of the Petersberg Tasks that the absence of a common European strategic vision becomes all too apparent",[14] and the EU's outlining of the Petersberg Tasks "does not provide even the roughest guideline as to the vision of the world in which European forces could be called upon to operate".[15] In a similar vein, another commentator asks, "Where will the Petersberg Tasks be implemented? Is a worldwide range of action imaginable or will the ESDP focus on just a few key areas? Which interests have to be defended? Which types and scales of threats might justify an EU operation?".[16] Therefore, those commenting felt the need for a framework spelling out the strategic objectives of the EU in a changed international context.[17]

Through its analysis of the external context of the EU's role and action, ESS seeks to provide a framework for future EU external action, and for the use of its external policy instruments towards that end. However, when it comes to defining actual goals and priorities for the achievement of policy objectives, the document is deficient as a strategy. Moreover, in a traditional sense, a strategy paper should "also describe which means can be used, and under what conditions to fulfil that specific purpose", and the ESS "falls short of these criteria".[18] It therefore reads more like an "inspirational sketch".[19] Considering the

---

[13] The Headline Goal formulated at the 1999 Helsinki Council set the objective for the EU to achieve by 2003 the capability to rapidly deploy within sixty days forces of up to fifteen brigades or 50,000-60,000 personnel which could be sustained for a period of at least one year. These should be militarily self-sustaining with the necessary command, control and intelligence capabilities.

[14] The Petersberg Tasks were outlined in the Western European Union (WEU) Ministerial Council's Petersberg Declaration of June 1992 whereby a set of potential roles for collective European action without necessarily involving the US were identified. These include humanitarian and rescue tasks, peacekeeping tasks and tasks of combat forces in crisis management, including peacemaking.

[15] Heisbourg, F., "Europe's Strategic Ambitions: The Limits of Ambiguity", *Survival*, Vol. 42, No. 2, Summer 2000, p. 8.

[16] Biscop, S., "In Search of a Strategic Concept for the ESDP", *European Foreign Affairs Review*, Vol. 7, 2002, p. 473.

[17] Haine, Y.-H., "ESDP: an Overview", *op. cit.*, p. 46.

[18] Toje, A., "The European Union Security Strategy: A Critical Appraisal", *European Foreign Affairs Review*, Vol. 10, 2005, p. 121.

[19] Duke, S., "The European Security Strategy in a Comparative Framework: Does it make for Secure Alliances in a Better World?", *European Foreign Affairs Review*, Vol. 9, 2004, p. 2, as quoted in *Ibid.*

purpose behind the EU's development of its military capabilities and the "hardships involved in pooling the EU Rapid Reaction Force and battle groups, it is notable how the document avoids references to the use of force", and "does not offer even the roughest guideline as to the situation in which EU forces could be called upon to operate".[20]

Nevertheless, despite perhaps failing to spell out the specifics befitting a traditional strategy paper, the ESS nonetheless provided a broad conceptual framework to guide future EU external policies and actions. An important characteristic of the ESS is that it is informed by a threat perception, "a dimension never addressed as such by the Union".[21] It identifies five key threats, namely international terrorism, proliferation of weapons of mass destruction, regional conflicts, state failure, and organised crime. What is also significant is that towards addressing these threats, the strategy emphasises that the EU's first line of defence would now lie abroad.[22] This is a marked departure from a traditional emphasis on territorial defence and therefore hints at the EU's global role. This however does not suggest a preference for any pre-emptive military action on the lines of US policy. A key concept not to be missed in this context is what the Strategy terms, "preventive engagement". It refers to the EU's approach to stability and nation-building which includes not only the rapid deployment of troops, but also humanitarian assistance, policing missions, enhancement of the rule of law and economic aid packages.[23] The EU policy is therefore to follow a more comprehensive approach which combines both long-term, essentially civilian measures that address the root causes of external threats, as well as short-term measures which may include both civil and military instruments such as those under ESDP.

The ESS also emphasises the need to build security in the EU's neighbourhood by securing "a ring of well governed countries"[24] to the East and South. The EU's policy towards the Western Balkans reflects this approach and it is in this region that the EU is the principal external actor. In the Western Balkans, the EU has made significant progress in pursuing its strategic objectives and in utilising all its available instruments of policy, including those under ESDP, especially in Macedonia and Bosnia-Herzegovina.[25] Post-enlargement, these EU strategies and

---

[20] Toje, A., "The European Union Security Strategy: A Critical Appraisal", *op. cit.*, p. 121.

[21] Haine, Y.-H., "An Historical Perspective", *op. cit.*, p. 50.

[22] European Council, European Security Strategy, *op. cit.*, p. 7.

[23] Haine, Y.-H., "An Historical Perspective", *op. cit.*, p. 51.

[24] European Council, European Security Strategy, *op. cit.*, p. 8.

[25] Bretherton, C. and Vogler, J., *The European Union as a Global Actor, op. cit.*, pp. 183-184.

policies are now focused towards the EU's new neighbours, especially Moldova, Ukraine and Belarus. The ESS further sets out the objective of the establishment of "an international order based on effective multilateralism". The EU's commitment to multilateralism is informed by the rules and principles of the UN Charter, and is regarded to be at the core of the Union's external actions. However the emphasis on "'effective' multilateralism seeks to promote both Member State consistency and a more robust approach to ensuring that international norms are adhered to".[26]

ESDP and EU External Action: Challenges Ahead

A significant challenge facing EU external action under ESDP is that it is not always easy to achieve consensus among the member states as regards the scope and direction of policy. Their differing attitudes towards ESDP policy formulations stem from differences of size, strategic tradition and orientation towards the difficult questions involving national sovereignty. This problem is compounded by the EU's latest enlargement which brought in additional viewpoints informed by varied national preoccupations. Difficulties in achieving coherence in decision making may seriously hamper the rapid deployment of forces in crisis situations. Also, problems with cross-pillar coordination continue to impede effective implementation of CFSP and ESDP decisions. Moreover, "the intergovernmental mode meant that dedicated Community funding was unavailable and that cross-pillar obstacles would have to be overcome, if the multifunctional aspirations of the ESDP were to be realised".[27]

Another important challenge for ESDP policy and action is related to its current and future relations with NATO and the United States. One contentious issue in this regard is NATO's insistence on its option of first refusal of any proposed operation. This invited reservations from the EU and especially France. It could also seriously compromise the EU's independence in deciding to carry out an external crisis management operation and thereby also undermine its aspirations to emerge as a global strategic actor. The Berlin-plus[28] arrangement facilitates independent EU action but, by using NATO assets, does not address the Union's aspirations for fully independent action. Hence the concept of "framework nation" had to be adopted whereby a fully autonomous EU

---

[26]   *Ibid.*, p. 186.

[27]   *Ibid.*, p. 199.

[28]   The Berlin-plus agreement which was finalised between the EU and NATO in December 2002 provides for autonomous EU action in the field of crisis management by utilizing NATO planning and military assets.

operation was possible without NATO assets by employing an existing national headquarters for command and planning purposes. The EU operation in the DRC was the result of such an arrangement.

The issue of acquiring and developing further military capabilities is another challenge for the ESDP, especially in the context of the changing dimension of its missions and ESDP's emerging global scope. At present the need is not so much to have more personnel under arms but to evolve the means to move and support them effectively.[29] The "headline goal 2010" seeks to address this deficiency by developing rapidly deployable specialised battalion size "battle groups" which are to be earmarked specifically for use under a UN mandate. But what the EU lacks most are capabilities for strategic lift, logistics, advance communication systems and independent command, control and intelligence facilities, which are indispensable for fulfilling any aim of global deployability.

Current Issues and Emerging Trends

The present strength of forces available and those being developed under ESDP "suggest that the scale of operations [will] continue to remain relatively small".[30] Future planning, however, "envisages ESDP forces that are much more rapidly deployable and capable of undertaking concurrent operations".[31] The ESDP continues to be formally committed to the Petersberg Tasks "but considerations of the future role of ESDP, in the ESS and elsewhere, reveal the emergence of a broader agenda".[32] The strategy emphasises the need to "think in terms of a wider spectrum of missions" that "might include joint disarmament operations, support for third countries in combating terrorism and security sector reform".[33] Moreover, the scope of the original Petersberg tasks was also broadened by the provisions of the EU's Lisbon Treaty in that it now includes "joint disarmament operations, humanitarian and rescue tasks, military advice and assistance tasks, conflict prevention and peace-keeping tasks, tasks of combat forces in crisis management, including peace-making and post-conflict stabilisation".[34] The treaty

---

[29] Bretherton, C. and Vogler, J., *The European Union as a Global Actor, op. cit.*, p. 205.

[30] *Ibid.*, p. 209.

[31] *Ibid.*

[32] *Ibid.*

[33] European Council, European Security Strategy, *op. cit.*, p. 12.

[34] Article 28 B(1), "Treaty of Lisbon amending the Treaty on European Union and the Treaty establishing the European Community (Extracts)" in "EU Security and Defence Core Documents 2007 Vol. VIII", *Chaillot Paper*, No. 112, Paris, EU Institute for Security Studies, October, 2008, p. 446.

provision also lays down that all of "these tasks may contribute to the fight against terrorism, including by supporting third countries in combating terrorism in their territories".[35] The ESS also hints at the use of military means to restore order in failed states.[36] As regards terrorism, instead of solely concentrating on a military response, the Extraordinary European Council convened in the wake of the eleven September terrorist attacks, called for "an in-depth political dialogue with those countries and regions of the world in which terrorism comes into being" and for "the integration of all countries into a fair world system of security, prosperity and improved development".[37] However, at the Seville European Council of June 2002, a declaration was adopted which "stressed the EU's determination to fight terrorism and indicated that both CFSP and ESDP means could be used to that end".[38]

In terms of the geographical scope of ESDP activity, the Balkans continue to remain an important area for the exercise of ESDP instruments, both civil and military. The EU's enlargement may have extended security to the new members but the expanded borders of the Union bring it closer to regions of instability and conflict. Hence the immediate neighbourhood comprising the South Caucasus in particular and the West Asian region are bound to sustain the interest of the EU and its ESDP. However, the EU's prospects for using its ESDP instruments, especially military means, in these two specific regions are likely to be limited by considerations of the geopolitical interest and the influence of Russia and the US respectively. With regard to West Asia "Washington still more or less claims a politico-military monopoly, regardless of the ambitions of the EU and its Euromediterranean Partnership".[39] Concentration on the EU's immediate neighbourhood does not exclude the Union's involvement in other parts of the world but the EU has to prioritise its options "because the available means are limited and because the ESDP's current early stage of development calls for modesty".[40] Beyond the EU's immediate neighbourhood, ESDP missions have already been active in Africa and more recently in the Asia Pacific. The EU is, however, as one commentator remarked, "[…] only

---

[35] *Ibid.*

[36] European Council, European Security Strategy, *op. cit.*, p. 7.

[37] Extraordinary European Council, *Presidency Conclusions*, Brussels, 21 September 2001, http://ue.eu.int/Newsroom/makeFrame.asp?MAX=&BID=76&DID=67808&LANG=2&File=/pressData/en/ec/140.en.pdf&Picture=0.

[38] European Council, *Presidency Conclusions*, Seville, 21-22 June 2002, Annex V, http://ue.eu.int/newsroom/makeFrame.asp?MAX=&BID=76&DID=72638&LANG=1&File=/pressData/en/ec/72638.pdf&Picture=0, p. 31.

[39] Biscop, S., "In Search of a Strategic Concept for the ESDP", *op. cit.*, p. 482.

[40] *Ibid.*, p. 483.

likely to intervene in areas of strategic and economic importance, and at a low cost of military casualties".[41] This opens up possibilities of the ESDP being more constructively engaged in Africa and the Asia Pacific, especially in evolving close security cooperation practices with some of the prominent regional organizations in these regions.

ESDP operations are likely to continue under the broad framework of the EU's preference for multilateralism and commitment to the UN system. Already several ESDP missions have been conducted under the aegis of UN Security Council resolutions, and its latest innovation of the "battle groups" concept is explicitly linked to UN operations.[42] However, in the words of one commentator, "the strong emphasis that the EU places on its political autonomy leads it to somehow distance itself from the UN".[43] For instance, "obtaining a UN mandate for ESDP operations does not appear to be a requirement as long as these operations are deployed in Europe, with the consent of the host state, and are of a non-coercive or civilian nature".[44] This said, a preference for a broad multilateral framework for ESDP is perhaps augmented by the fact that third countries have regularly been involved in ESDP operations. Detailed arrangements for third-country involvement were made at the Seville European Council of June 2002, but several questions regarding their participation remain, including: "How many troops are acceptable from third states in a EU-mandated operation? How involved may third states become in the development of a concept for operations? How heavy may a third party's role be in daily command and control?".[45] In the final analysis, the EU's use of military means is only complementary to its other instruments of policy, including development aid and civilian capacity-building, and this is evident especially in the Balkans where the majority of the ESDP's military and police missions have been undertaken and where Community instruments have been employed.[46]

---

[41] Gegout, C., "Causes and Consequences of the EU's Military Intervention in the Democratic Republic of Congo", *European Foreign Affairs Review*, Vol. 10, 2005, p. 429.

[42] Bretherton, C. and Vogler, J., *The European Union as a Global Actor*, *op. cit.*, p. 210.

[43] Tardy, T., "EU-UN Cooperation in Peacekeeping: a Promising Relationship in a Constrained Environment" in M. Ortega (ed.), "The European Union and the United Nations: Partners in Effective Multilateralism", *Chaillot Paper*, No. 78, Paris, EU Institute for Security Studies, June 2005, p. 51.

[44] *Ibid.*

[45] Missiroli, A., "The European Union: Just a Regional Peacekeeper?", *European Foreign Affairs Review*, Vol. 8, 2003, p. 502.

[46] Bretherton, C. and Vogler, J., *The European Union as a Global Actor*, *op. cit.*, p. 212.

The Implications of the ESDP's External Dimension for the Asia Pacific

The ESDP's external dimension received a fresh impetus in 2005 with the launching of the AMM in the Aceh province of Indonesia. After its involvement in Africa in 2003, the ESDP was once again active in a theatre of conflict outside and distant from the EU's immediate neighbourhood. ESDP's first ever foray into the Asia Pacific also marked another step in the direction of the EU attaining the status of a serious global actor and also introduced a new dimension to EU-Asia Pacific security relations. The robust mandate given to this new ESDP mission meant that the EU was now faced with new possibilities of emerging as an important security actor in the Asia Pacific. It is significant that the EU, in association with the ASEAN, was the only international body accepted by all the parties of the Aceh conflict to oversee the implementation of the Memorandum of Understanding between them. This is a pointer to "a telling recognition of the international credibility of EU intervention under ESDP".[47]

The Aceh Monitoring Mission: A Test Case for EU-Asia Pacific Cooperation in Civilian Crisis Management

Before the AMM got underway, it was felt in European circles that the EU "would do better to concentrate its efforts closer to home, notably in the stabilisation of the Balkans and in bringing order to Europe's backyard in sub-Saharan Africa and in the neighbourhood at large, tackling the urgent problems of migration and organised crime stemming from these areas".[48] But the ESDP mission in Aceh was regarded as potentially beneficial in the following respects.[49] Firstly, it would demonstrate that despite the rejection of the Constitutional Treaty and the budgetary stalemate, "ESDP was still upon its feet and able to deliver". Secondly, "a mission in Indonesia would match the vision of those who regarded the Union as a global player, not limited to stabilising its neighbourhood but nurturing more ambitious goals". And thirdly, "the mission would offer a test case for the functioning of the ESDP machinery for civil crisis management, and in particular of the newly established Civmil Cell". The AMM was an EU-led ESDP mission but it was conducted together with five ASEAN countries, namely Brunei, Malaysia, the Philippines, Singapore and Thailand, and with contributions from Norway and Switzerland. This involvement of outside part-

---

[47] Braud, P.A. and Grevi, G., "The EU Mission in Aceh: implementing peace", *op. cit.*, p. 36.

[48] *Ibid.*, p. 22.

[49] *Ibid.*

ners and third countries reflects the EU's preference and commitment to "effective multilateralism", a framework that also informs the Union's strategic engagement with the Asia Pacific. The partnership with ASEAN is a test case for the future security cooperation between the two organizations in the Asia Pacific, and reflects the EU's policy of support for regional organizations as effective partners in promoting peace and security across the world. The AMM was set in the context of the ongoing efforts to strengthen the civilian crisis management capabilities of the EU and demonstrated its potential of becoming the main provider of security in its neighbourhood and beyond.

The EU's Strategy and Approach towards the Asia Pacific

In its very first report on the CFSP in 1997, the Council made it clear that "Asia continues to constitute a key priority for the Union's Common Foreign and Security Policy".[50] The Union had a tradition of active engagement and economic and political cooperation with some Asian countries on its periphery under its Euro-Med Partnership (EMP) and its European Neighbourhood Policy. It had also consistently advocated a political settlement of the Middle East crisis which acts as a hurdle for all attempts to deepen Euro-Mediterranean security cooperation. However, given the prominence of the US in the region, it is difficult to foresee how far ESDP instruments can be exercised in the West Asian region. Civilian aspects of ESDP have, however, been applied in the form of the EU Coordination Office for Palestinian Police Support (EU COPPS) set up in April 2005, and the EUPOL-COPPS launched in November 2005, the first ever police mission in the Palestinian Territories conducted by third parties.[51] Mention may also be made of the integrated rule of law mission in Iraq of February 2005, named EUJUST LEX.

Apart from its engagement with its immediate Asian neighbourhood, the European Commission first produced an overall strategic approach to Asia (including Australasia) in 1994, in a document entitled: *Towards a New Asia Strategy*. Although much of this document is still broadly valid, the EU revised and updated its approach to Asia in 2001 with a new policy document entitled: *Europe and Asia: A Strategic Framework for Enhanced Partnerships*. This document signified a more robust EU approach because it emphasised the importance of the security dimension as well in relations with Asia. The document subdivides Asia into four sub-regions, South Asia, South East Asia, North East Asia and

---

[50]   Council of Ministers, *Annual Report CFSP 1997*, point 15a.

[51]   Grevi, G., Lynch, D. and Missiroli, A., "ESDP operations", Paris, EU Institute for Security Studies, http://www.iss-eu.org/esdp/09-dvl-am.pdf, p. 15.

Australasia.[52] Of the six broad objectives spelt out by the document, from the security point of view, mention may be made of the EU's aim to a) "contribute to peace and security in the region and globally, through a broadening of our engagement with the region"; b) "contribute to the protection of human rights and to the spreading of democracy, good governance and the rule of law"; and c) "to build global partnerships and alliances with Asian countries [...] to strengthen our joint efforts on global environmental and security issues".[53] These objectives are likely to provide the broad guidelines within which the EU's security policy and its ESDP instruments may be applied in the Asia Pacific. A European Parliament study of 1999 called for a more active "involvement of the CFSP in 'Asian' security issues, for instance in the areas of confidence-building, proactive and preventive diplomacy and conflict resolution".[54] The significance of real and potential conflict in some of Asia's prolonged flashpoints remains high for Europe. This is evident from "the indication, often heard in EP and in EU security circles, that the 1992 Petersberg Declaration [...] may well be worth emulating in connection with conflict resolution in Asia".[55]

Parameters of ESDP's Role in Asia Pacific Security

In the context of the broad objectives provided by the ESS, the interpretation of the future role of ESDP is unlikely to give rise to any threat perceptions in the Asia Pacific. This is due in large part to the fact that, in the conduct of its external relations, the EU has successfully maintained its civilian image of a responsible international actor, firmly committed to the norms of international stability informed by the principles of the UN Charter. In fact, "UN-centrism in European security cooperation in Asia could offer an alternative Western identity for Europe in Asia and strengthen the EU's image as a more independent security actor in the region".[56] It has also been argued that "Europe

---

[52] European Commission, *Europe and Asia: A Strategic Framework for Enhanced Partnerships*, Brussels, 4.9.2001, COM(2001) 469 final, http://europa.eu.int/comm/external_relations/asia/doc/com01_469_en.pdf, p. 3. One may note that West Asia and Central Asia do not find mention as it is more viable to approach these regions within the broad context of the EU's Neighbourhood Policy. Also, an increasingly active EU role would have to take into account the already active US-involvement in these regions, especially in West Asia.

[53] *Ibid.*, p. 15.

[54] Wiessala, G., "More than Distant Neighbours: CFSP and Asian Countries" in M. Holland (ed.), *Common Foreign and Security Policy: The First Ten Years*, 2nd edition, London, Continuum, 2004, p. 96.

[55] *Ibid.*, p. 97.

[56] "Executive Summary" in T. Kivimaki and J. Delman (eds.), *The Security Situation in Asia: Changing Regional Security Structure?*, Copenhagen, Nordic Institute of Asian Studies, 2005, p. xi.

should seek constructive involvement in Asian preventive diplomacy and try to utilise its expertise in the field of 'soft security' which uses civilian means instead of military means".[57] In fact, ESDP's experiences in conflict resolution and crisis management, together with its frequent use of civilian measures, can provide a comparative advantage to the EU to constructively develop a culture of security cooperation with the Asia Pacific in the field of crisis management. It has also been suggested that, rather than developing new structures, the EU's main policy in Asia "should be related to the strengthening of the development of the existing security institutionalisation in Asia".[58] The EU should "respect Asian methods of preventing conflicts and managing them in order to minimise violence"[59] and also "consider and acknowledge the value of the Asian institutions of conflict security cooperation and try to work with them".[60] To this end, the EU "should give sufficient priority to official Asian security dialogue forums such as the Asia-Europe Meeting (ASEM) and ASEAN Regional Forum (ARF)".[61]

The EU and the ASEM Process and the ARF

The ASEM process does provide an important forum for dialogue and cooperation between the EU and East- and South-East Asia. Nevertheless, although political dialogue and cooperation comprises one of the three pillars of the ASEM process, meaningful political and security dialogue have been hard to come by, as many of the topics for discussion are considered "out of bounds" or "too delicate".[62] The European side has, however, expressed its interest to pursue political dialogue and find common ground for joint action in areas such as terrorism, drug trafficking and regional security. Notwithstanding, the vital political dimension continues to be absent. Cooperation on security issues are therefore found to be more feasible in the framework of the EU's relations with ASEAN and in the ARF where the EU enjoys a full seat and participates as an organization. Although since the early 1990s the EU had expressed a strong desire in widening the security agenda in its relations with ASEAN, the non-compatible security cultures between the two organizations meant that "for most of the 1990s the EU and ASEAN could not find any common ground on conflicting issues such

---

[57] *Ibid.*, p. iv.

[58] *Ibid.*, p. v.

[59] *Ibid.*, p. iv.

[60] *Ibid.*, p. v.

[61] *Ibid.*

[62] Koellner, P., "Whiter ASEM: Lessons from APEC and the Future of Transregional Cooperation between Asia and Europe", http://www.iias.nl/asem/publications/koellner_whitherasem.pdf, p. 17.

as the liberalisation and democratisation of authoritarian regimes, human rights, sustainable development, and 'good governance'".[63] In recent times, there has been a growing acceptance of the importance of non-traditional security on the Asian side as a result of a changing security culture. This has resulted in an ongoing process of harmonisation of Asian and European security cultures.[64]

The ARF is the main focus of the EU's security and political dialogue with Asia. However, even within the ARF, all security discussions "have focused hitherto primarily on threat perceptions and confidence-building measures rather than on concrete management of regional security conflicts and conflict resolution mechanisms involving legal obligations and not just non-binding political declarations".[65] The ARF therefore remains as more of a consultative forum and it is too early to say that the EU could bring its instruments under ESDP to bear on ARF with a view to greater security cooperation. Until the ARF evolves mechanisms for preventive diplomacy, the EU could perhaps insist on cooperation on soft security issues, and the experiences of ESDP's civilian instruments may prove beneficial in this regard.

Notwithstanding the limitations of achieving more pro-active security cooperation with existing regional organizations in Asia, the EU is likely to continue to focus on evolving arrangements for security cooperation with regional organizations in keeping with its agenda of pursuing effective multilateralism. Where long-term cooperative structures at the inter-regional level are not possible, coalitions involving one or a group of Asian nations, as during the Aceh Mission, could be forged. For the EU therefore, Asia is the most challenging test case for building regional security arrangements.[66] The EU keeps its out-of-area ESDP missions open to participation by other regional and extra-regional states. "But to give meaning to ideas such as "African ownership" and "open coalitions", the EU needs to channel more resources and expertise to regional organizations in the developing world".[67]

---

[63] Dosch, J., "Changing Security Cultures in Europe and Southeast Asia", *Asia-Europe Journal*, Vol. 1, No. 4, December 2003, p. 494.

[64] *Ibid.*, p. 486.

[65] Umbach, F., "EU-ASEAN Political and Security Dialogue at the Beginning of the 21st Century: Prospects for Interregional Cooperation on International Terrorism", http://www.dgap.org/attachment/36292e5f08f727196eb4ca1f3d4df243/cd1d2a2bd8c 8006601338d8544b575b3/EU-ASEAN-Panorama+2004.pdf, p. 2.

[66] Acharya, A., "An Asian Perspective: Regional Security Arrangements in a Multi-polar World: the EU's Contribution" in M. Ortega (ed.), "Global Views on the European Union", *Chaillot Paper*, No. 72, Paris, EU Institute for Security Studies, November 2004, p. 93.

[67] *Ibid.*, p. 100.

The EU and Asia's Emerging Global Powers: India and China

The EU's aspirations for assuming a greater role in crisis management in Asia should also take into account the regional sensitivities and strategic aspirations of emerging global powers like India and China. On the other hand, ESDP's growing experience in civilian and humanitarian crisis management may prove beneficial for the EU in seeking to evolve common strategies with India or China towards addressing humanitarian crisis-like situations with regional implications. Any direct ESDP contribution on the ground may also introduce a multilateral dimension to any regional humanitarian crisis management operation and help in allaying fears and distrust among smaller nations, especially in the context of South Asia. However, it is perhaps too early to envisage any such scenario. As far as India's relations with its individual neighbours are concerned, its policy of seeking bilateral solutions to the contentious issues precludes any option of the involvement of external players.

It may be worthwhile to note that India has been at the forefront of UN peacekeeping and today ranks high among the most committed contributors to UN peacekeeping operations across the world. India's peacekeeping experiences in the former Yugoslavia and elsewhere, together with its commitment to multilateralism under the UN system, make it an attractive partner for the EU and its ESDP. In recent years, the emerging political relations between the EU and India have shown greater signs of maturity with the two sides increasingly exhibiting a greater understanding of each other's approach to the erstwhile difficult issues of terrorism and human rights. Both sides have expressed their desire to "establish an EU-India security dialogue on global and regional security issues, disarmament and non-proliferation".[68] The current political dialogue under the broad framework of the emerging India-EU Strategic Partnership may offer future possibilities to both India and the EU to evolve strategies of potential cooperation in the field of crisis management.

Conclusion: Australia between Europe and Asia

By way of conclusion, it is far from fanciful to foresee a meaningful and constructive role for Australia in any future EU and ESDP security engagement with the Asia Pacific. Given its historical and cultural links with Europe and its geographical proximity to Asia, together with its recent engagements with its Asian neighbours, Australia has the poten-

---

[68] European Council, "Political Declaration on India-EU Strategic Partnership" in *EU Security and Defence: Core Documents 2005*, Vol. 6, Brussels, 7 September 2005, *Chaillot Paper*, No. 87, (pub.) Paris, EU Institute for Security Studies, March 2006, http//www.weu.int/institute/chaillot/chai47e.html, p. 248.

tial of emerging as a cementing force in any security and strategic partnership between the EU and the Asia Pacific Region. In fact, Australia's opportunity lies in its potential ability to perhaps combine its European roots with its economic and political linkages with its Asian neighbours in order to foster a security community that could evolve mechanisms of regional security cooperation and management of conflicts. Australia's military capabilities and its peace keeping traditions, including its experiences in East Timor, may prove beneficial in this respect but the challenge would lie in projecting the image of a responsible power and in allaying among its neighbours any fears of an emerging regional hegemon. A fine balance between Asian values and European experiments may hold the key for the emergence of an effective Asia Pacific security community.

To sum up, the Asia Pacific Region offers both challenges and opportunities for the EU's ESDP. As far as security cooperation is concerned, the EU would do well to increasingly deal with the Asia Pacific at the level of both individual Asia Pacific security players as well as Asian regional security organizations. Relations for security cooperation may at times prove difficult, owing to the fact that a regional approach to security in Asia and the Asia Pacific is still a relatively new phenomenon. Security cooperation in Asia continues to be characterised by strong bilateral overtones. On the other hand, it may serve Asian nations well to emulate experiences of European security cooperation and conflict resolution in an effort to find solutions to some of Asia's intractable security issues and problems. This is easier said than done, because the realities of European security and Asian security are markedly different. Unlike the European efforts at arriving at a comprehensive and common approach to security, the Asia Pacific has yet to evolve such a common or regional approach to security. Moreover, the intricacies of Asian security issues make such a possibility arising in the future all the more remote. In the final analysis, however, the EU's adherence to a rule-based international order and its commitment to multilateralism would allay any fears or threat perceptions that might arise in the Asia Pacific regarding ESDP. ESDP's civilian instruments may continue to prove beneficial for the EU to approach security issues in the Asia Pacific while the application of the military means under ESDP will depend to a large extent on the EU's ability to co-opt Asian actors and regional organizations in arrangements of effective crisis management and preventive diplomacy.

CHAPTER 12

The Euro in the French Pacific Press

Yoon Ah CHOI

Introduction

This chapter aims to investigate the limits of identity and borders which are constrained by discourse and thus to examine the perception of the EU in the Pacific region. The French territories' relationship with Europe and the wider Pacific community is the subject of constant revision and redefinition on many levels, placing them in a somewhat anomalous position as an "in-between" entity, regarded as "self" as well as "other", depending on the context. The Pacific's increasing awareness of the importance of achieving integration and cooperation between its various island nations is bringing them closer to the wider Pacific community, while the territories' current EU status as Overseas Countries and Territories (OCT) ties them to the EU system. Consequently, the future path of the French Pacific territories as either increasingly "European" or "Pacific" remains uncertain.

David Held's theory of cosmopolitan democracy is a useful point of reference because it helps to understand the interplay between power and space. He views global order as being constrained by "multiple systems of transaction and coordination which link people, communities and societies in highly complex ways".[1] Held also discusses how power distribution, power relations, and power as concept and practice are closely correlated with spatiality, all of which are perceptible through discursive representations of space. Furthermore, he comments that regional integration "follows the same logic as globalisation. It aims to expand the realm of governance, primarily through [...] "intricately institutionalised and spatially dispersed activity".[2]

The study of political space helps to "recognise that political, economic and cultural exchanges take place in different forms of social space and, together with structural influences, contribute to how that

---

[1] Held, D., *Democracy and the Global Order: from the Modern State to Cosmopolitan Governance*, Oxford, Polity Press, 1995, pp. 101-2.

[2] Held., D., *Globalisation, Anti-globalisation*, Oxford, Polity Press, 2002, p. 121.

space is framed and perceived".[3] This statement reflects how boundaries can occur in layers and the fact that institutional processes such as economic agreements, constitutions and regional integration schemes determine the territories' identity and standing in the global context. The territories have access to certain rights of EU citizenship and, as OCTs, must partially abide by EU law. The French Pacific territories have the right to adopt the European single currency and partake in EU elections. Although they are affiliated with the EU customs territory, they are excluded from the Schengen zone and are the subject of external policies on development and trade.

Concepts such as sovereignty and governance come into play in shaping the conceptual boundaries within which states identify themselves. However, when these processes are inconsistent or ambiguous, as is the case for the French Pacific territories, it becomes harder to define identity and borders.

This chapter addresses the following questions: How is the European currency represented in the New Caledonian press media? Are there any linguistic structures exposing a power hierarchy established between certain actors? Is a new relationship between France and the French OCTs emerging in the media? How do the wider political theories about European integration correlate to the linguistic findings of this chapter? Where do individuals feature in the transitivity structure?

A critical discourse analysis of newspaper articles selected from a major local newspaper of New Caledonia, namely, *Les Nouvelles Calédoniennes* will be conducted.[4] With a "media frame",[5] news about the euro will be closely observed, focusing on syntactic and lexical features of the representations. Correlations between linguistic observations and political theories will also be made.

---

[3] Youngs, G., *International Relations in a Global Age: a Conceptual Challenge*, Malden, Polity Press, 1999, p. 97.

[4] Barker, C. and Galasinski, D., *Cultural Studies and Discourse Analysis: a Dialogue on Language and Identity*, London, Sage, 2001; Schiffrin, D., Tannen, D. *et al.*, *The Handbook of Discourse analysis*, Oxford, Blackwell Publishers, 2001; Way, E.C., *Knowledge Representation and Metaphor*, Boston, Academic Publishers, 1991; Weiss, G. and Wodak, R., *Critical Discourse Analysis: Theory and Interdisciplinarity*, New York, Palgrave Macmillan, 2003; Wodak, R. and Chilton, P.A., *A New Agenda in (Critical) Discourse Analysis: Theory, Methodology, and Interdisciplinarity*, Amsterdam, Philadelphia, J. Benjamins, 2005.

[5] The term "media frame" is used according to the definition given by Scheufele, D.A. in "Framing as a Theory of Media Effects", *Journal of Communication*, Vol. 49, No. 1, Winter 1999.

Context

The people of Tahiti, New Caledonia and Wallis and Futuna are French citizens and they have access to certain rights and benefits in member states of the EU.[6] With their close, on-going administrative ties, extensive trade and economic interaction with France and current agreements which affect the islands' trade, investment, labour mobility and tourism sectors, these territories have already become familiar with the euro. The dominating nature of the new currency and its possible introduction to the French Pacific territories, imply French control over this region, reinforcement of the territories' "European" identity and Europe's presence.

The Pacific territories of France, namely New Caledonia, French Polynesia and Wallis and Futuna, have been attached to the EU from the very outset. The three territories' status as an Association of the European Community was first defined by the Treaty of Rome in 1957 and subsequently under Articles 182 to 187 in the EC Treaty.[7] The EU's development policy grew out of the founding members' responsibility for their territories. European identity is extended to the territories as noted in the EU's new strategy on partnership with Pacific Islands:

> The four territories in the Pacific of EU member states (New Caledonia, French Polynesia, Wallis and Futuna and Pitcairn) represent a valuable and important European presence in the region. They also constitute an asset to be taken fully into account in the strategy in order to promote their integration in the region.[8]

The EU's relationship to the Pacific can be defined by the European Development Fund (EDF),[9] which primarily targets the African, Caribbean and Pacific (ACP) group. But the French territories, as OCTs, also benefit from this fund. Worth €23 billion, the Tenth Framework began in 2008, in the hope of bringing a stronger and more sustainable economy to the developing world. During the previous EDF period, New Caledonia received €13.8 million, which was mostly dedicated to pro-

---

[6]   French citizenship was extended to these territories in recognition for their contribution in fighting for France in the Second World War.

[7]   The Treaty of Rome was amended by the Single European Act, the Maastricht Treaty, the Treaty of Amsterdam and the Treaty of Nice, http://europa.eu/scadplus/leg/en/lvb/r12300.htm.

[8]   European Commission, "EU Relations with the Pacific Islands – A Strategy for a Strengthened Partnership", *Communiqué*, 29 May 2006, p. 5.

[9]   Holland, M., *The European Union and the Third World*, New York, Palgrave, 2002; Holland, M. and Koloamatangi, M., "Governance, Capacity and Legitimany: EPAs, EBA and the European Union's Pacific Regionalism after Cotonou" in J. Bryant-Tokalau and I. Frazer (eds.), *Redefining the Pacific?: Regionalism Past, Present and Future*, London, Ashgate, 2007.

fessional education. French Polynesia received €13.2 million which went towards water purification and housing in poor areas.[10] Wallis and Futuna received €11.5 million which was allocated to infrastructure projects.[11] The EU is an important trading partner for the territories and bilateral trade with France is still very prominent. For example, 97% of Wallis and Futuna's imports come from mainland France.[12] The interaction between the French territories and the wider Pacific region is growing and the territories have expressed their interest in a new Economic Partnership Agreement between the EU and the Pacific, and are official observers to the process. The EU encourages greater integration in the Pacific and regionalism is being extensively practised by the Pacific Islands Forum, which is an intergovernmental organization with sixteen independent Pacific nations. New Caledonia and French Polynesia are associate members and Wallis and Futuna holds an observer status in the Forum.

In addition, the advisability of adopting the euro has been debated in recent years. According to the Chamber of Commerce in French Polynesia, 70% of businesses are in favour of adopting the euro because it would allow cheaper transactions and greater stability.[13] Gaston Flosse and Oscar Temaru, former presidents of French Polynesia, have also expressed their desire to bring in the euro in French Polynesia. On the other hand, New Caledonia has mixed feelings about adopting the euro as it would entail a loss of control in economic and monetary matters.[14]

The roots of the euro are to be found in the fixed exchange rate system introduced in the late 1970s. A series of economic crises, notably the "Black Wednesday" crisis experienced by the UK in 1992, widened the currency bands and sounded the death knell of the fixed rate exchange system.

The Pacific is familiar with the concept of regional monetary integration, as the Australian and New Zealand currencies are used in certain parts of the Pacific region while the French Pacific territories have a common currency: the Pacific Franc (CFP).

---

[10] Europa website, *Development Policies*, http://ec.europa.eu/development/Geographical/ RegionsCountries/Countries/oct/oct_home_en.cfm?cid=polynesie-francaise.

[11] *Ibid.*

[12] Central Intelligence Agency, *The World Factbook*, https://www.cia.gov/library/ publications/the-world-factbook/geos/wf.html#Econ.

[13] Chambre de Commerce, d'Industrie, des Services et des Métiers de Polynésie française, http://www.ccism.pf/.

[14] Sovereignty, metropolitan power and independence are key, yet controversial, questions in these territories, notably for New Caledonia.

The European single currency is already present in the French Pacific region, due to its inseparable links with France and its intensive trade relations with Europe. The euro has a fixed parity with the local currency of the three territories, which is officially known as the "Pacific Franc Exchange (XPF)" (1,000 F CFP is equal to €8.38/1 F CFP = €0.00838).[15] The Franc is also legal tender in Vanuatu, a former British/French territory. The CFP coins show the French national symbol on one side and a regional symbol on the other.

The euro is a major symbol of the EU and a concrete manifestation of successful regional integration. The former president of the European Commission, Romano Prodi, has stated that: "The euro was not just a banker's decision or a technical decision. It was a decision which completely changed the nature of nation states".[16]

The common currency engaged Europe with the challenge of facing a single economy and had a strong psychological impact on European citizens. The introduction of such a powerful instrument to the French Pacific Islands could have a big impact on the identity of the French island nations.

Dave Peeble demonstrates how Pacific nations are cooperating to achieve greater economic stability and increased intra-regional trade relations.[17] The potential benefits of adopting the euro include facilitated trade, investment and tourism. Moreover, monetary union would allow more efficient economic data management and better regulation of monetary/fiscal statistical information. Furthermore, monetary union is a tool which can be used to prevent inflation and make transactions and fiscal transfers more efficient, as well as eliminating the costs associated with exchange rate volatility.[18]

On the other hand, the territories have not yet formally indicated their willingness to adopt the euro and the essential requirement for the adoption of this currency in the region is that all three French Pacific territories come to a mutual agreement. Holding a referendum on the adoption of the European currency is in the ambit of the authorities of each territory. Monetary policy is an area of jurisdiction of the French Republic under New Caledonia's constitutional status.[19]

---

[15] Institut d'Émission d'Outre-Mer, http://www.ieom.fr/

[16] Interview with Romano Prodi, *Financial Times*, 9 April 1999.

[17] Peeble, D., *Pacific Regional Order*, Canberra, ANU E Press and Asia Pacific Press, 2005.

[18] *Ibid.*, p. 145.

[19] Cameron Diver, Head of Office, Office of Regional Cooperation and External Relations, Gouvernement de la Nouvelle-Calédonie, Interview, 3 May 2007.

Methodology

The discourse studied here consists of press articles about the euro currency from *Les Nouvelles Calédoniennes*. Fifty-three news items were collected from September 2001 to December 2006.

Claes de Vreese's study on EU news coverage illustrated the importance of news about the launch of the euro in the news media. It evaluated the amount of attention given to EU news and the nature of the editorial approach.[20] It showed the way EU news is prone to cycles and that there are trans-national differences in the structure and organization of the news.

According to the post-structuralist theory on discourse, meaning is a socially conditioned product that carries ideological conceptions of power. Critical Discourse Analysis provides valuable tools for analysing discourses in relation to social and political issues.[21] Michael Halliday's ideational model of transitivity provides different categories of processes, namely Material, Mental, Verbal, Relational, Existential processes which can construe a single event in different ways.[22] This model is applied to dismantle the representations which contain an experiential centre consisting of a process and participants. Circumstantial elements occur outside this centre. The analysis also looks at metaphorical expressions. It is natural for the human mind to make a connection between separate concepts in order to facilitate the understanding.[23] Such metaphorical thinking can act as a vehicle for conveying ideological attitudes, amplifying the distinction between "us" and "them" with certain semantic implications. Linguistic findings are then linked to wider political theories.

George Lakoff and Mark Johnson's study of metaphors provide a useful guideline for interpreting the function of metaphorical representations with the understanding that the human conceptual system is largely

---

20 Schuck, A. and de Vreese, C.H., "Between Risk and Opportunity. News Framing and its Effects on Public Support for EU Enlargement", *European Journal of Communication*, Vol. 21, No. 1, 2006, pp. 5-32.

21 Fairclough, N., *Media Discourse*, London, E. Arnold, 1995; Fairclough, N., *Language and Power*, New York, Longman, 2001; Fairclough, N., *Analyzing Discourse: Textual Analysis for Social Research*, New York, Routledge, 2003.

22 Halliday, M.A.K., *An Introduction to Functional Grammar*, 3rd edition, London, Edward Arnold, 2004.

23 Such nature of metaphors is comparable to the way people observed language during the Renaissance period, perceiving it as already existing in nature in a secret form. It was up to human beings to discover and translate these divine and natural signs so that they may become intelligible. Michel Foucault gives a detailed account of how the notion of language developed throughout the different historical continuities in *The Order of Things* (1966).

governed by metaphorical thinking.[24] To identify metaphors, one must recognise the difference between "dead" metaphors and "live" metaphors.[25] The first variant refers to metaphorical expressions that have already been lexicalised. That is, metaphors which have lost their original sense over time. One of the examples offered by Hilary Wise in her book is the French verb *arriver* (to arrive).[26] Today, when people come across this word, they only understand it as a physical act of reaching a certain destination, instead of conceptualising a riverbank (*rive*) from which the verb is derived. As for "live" metaphors, they are productive and more creative in nature, which causes people to correlate two, often dissimilar concepts.

Petr Drulák's discourse study on metaphors of European integration is also an important reference.[27] Drulák demonstrates a comprehensive approach in combining political studies and discourse analysis. He shows that metaphors reflect political thinking and practices. The most frequently occurring metaphors in his analysis defined EU as Motion, as Containers and as Equilibrium, which corresponded to various theories of European integration. The Motion/Container/Equilibrium categories are relative to "Journey", "Spatial", and "Balance" observed in this study.

Observation

While certain newspaper articles from the corpus displayed linguistic features which betrayed their ideological leanings, others consisted of elements purely for stylistic or logical reasons. This analysis tested the objectivity/subjectivity of the representations and demonstrated the significance of certain structural or lexical choices made in the press representations of the euro.

Representations of the Euro: Metaphors

Euro news in the New Caledonian press were analysed according to its placement. The three separate sections where euro news occurred determined the angle of domesticity and they were categorised under "New Caledonia", "France" and "World".

---

[24] Lakoff, G. and Johnson, M., *Metaphors We Live by*, Chicago, University of Chicago Press, 1980, p. 4.

[25] Wise, H., *The Vocabulary of Modern French: Origins, Structure and Function*, London, Routledge, 1997, p. 136.

[26] *Ibid.*, p. 499.

[27] Drulák, P., "Motion, Container and Equilibrium: Metaphors in the Discourse about European Integration", *European Journal of International Relations*, Vol. 12, No. 4, SAGE Publications and ECPR-European Consortium for Political Research, 2006, pp. 499-531.

Placement	Articles	Metaphors	Date Frame
New Caledonia	18	34	14)12/01 ~ 01/02, 2)'04, 2)'06.
France	25	41	23)09/01 ~ 02/02, 2)'06.
World	11	42	11)09/01 ~ 01/02.

The local section ("New Caledonia") had domestic relevance, the "France" section gave a semi-local/semi-international angle, while the World section gave an international angle. The following table shows the most frequently occurring conceptual metaphors which were employed to represent euro news:

Placement/Metaphors	Journey	Spatial	Balance	Personification
New Caledonia	15/34 (44%)	16/34 (47%)	0/34 (0%)	3/34 (9%)
France	22/51 (43%)	6/51 (12%)	6/51 (12%)	17/51 (33%)
World	12/42 (29%)	12/42 (29%)	1/42 (2%)	17/42 (40%)

The most frequently occurring metaphors were grouped as journey, spatial balance and personifying metaphors, and the conceptual image of the euro differed according to the angle (domestic/semi-domestic/international) from which it was reported.

The dominant metaphorical image in the local New Caledonian news about the euro was represented in spatial terms: the euro taking up space, being *within* New Caledonia, and *within* the French territories, the euro is sheltered, a sense of space between the Pacific francs and the euro, the *euro zone*, the *heart of Europe*. According to Drulák, container metaphors are common in supranational discourses which acknowledge the EU as a constantly growing institution, becoming more wealthy and influential with enlargement. Container metaphors establish discursive space and create division between entities. Euro news represented from the domestic angle views the euro as a border-creating factor. The press shows how the local currency imposes a barrier and seems to suggest that, by adopting the euro, a common territory between Europe and the French Pacific region can be established. The space in which the euro exists is often shown in a positive manner.

As for euro news placed in the "France" section which provides a semi-local/semi-international angle, the dominant metaphor associated the euro with the concept of journey: The euro is shown as an entity which is in the process of *passing through*, in *a relay*; it is portrayed as *taking a new step*, its *first steps*. The possibility of it being *"derailed"* is mentioned, and the integration process is shown as a *passage*, act of *arrival*, a *quest*. The euro has also been represented as a *guest*. This category relates to metaphors of motion, which sheds a neo-functional view on European integration, representing it as an ongoing process rather than a product. The motion metaphors are identified as conventional and already sedimented images of the EU, and they are useful for illustrating neo-functional views of the EU because they share the same semantic grounds, specifically, movement and direction.

From an international angle, the image of the euro is often portrayed as having human qualities. The personifications of the euro were linked to representations of birth, life and health of the euro. The euro was given human attributes with the use of adjectives like "*young*". Moreover, the euro is depicted as a *star* and is also conceptualised as *seducing*, *hiding*, and *driving*. Balance/equilibrium metaphors were the ones that appeared least frequently with the exception of the euro news section about France. According to Drulák, this category is associated with intergovernmental theories regarding European integration.

Transitivity Structure: Agency

The transitivity structure of propositions that depict the euro issue manifests the semantic/syntactic status assigned to it. Agency can be increased or decreased depending on what position of the transitivity structure a particular element occupies. The Agent role implies more power and responsibility because it carries out the action depicted by the main verb. The Agent is also, plausibly, responsible for the impacts of such action.

New Caledonia:

When I examined the transitivity structures of euro images in the local section, I noticed that most of the agent-participants referred to a more general type of actor, such as France and the New Caledonian people. The agent participants of the following propositions are highlighted and in italics:

(1) "Si *les Calédoniens* ne passent pas à l'euro, ils auront malgré tout la fierté de dire qu'un peu de leur terre compose la monnaie unique européenne".[28] ("*If the Caledonians do not switch over to the euro [...]*")

(2) "Après la métropole qui a abandonné sa monnaie nationale pour adopter l'euro, *les Calédoniens* peuvent à leur tour manipuler la

---

[28] "Du nickel calédonien dans les pièces de 1 et 2 euros", *Les Nouvelles Calédoniennes*, 4 December 2001.

monnaie européenne".[29] (*"[...] the Caledonians can themselves handle the European currency"*)

(3) ***"Paris*** exige toujours l'accord des trois collectivités françaises du Pacifique [...] ***elle*** accepte de renoncer au franc CFP pour engager un processus d'arrimage à la zone euro".[30] (*"Paris still demands the agreement of the three French Pacific Collectivities [...] It accepts to [...]"*)

France:

In the euro representations placed in the France news section, there were relatively stronger and more frequent representations of agency. Most agent-participants signified technical, specific aspects of the monetary integration such as prices, the franc, banks and politicians. And thus, a sense of responsibility was discursively assigned to the concepts mentioned above. Here is the data that demonstrates this:

     1. Consumer prices

(4) *"**Certains prix** flambent avant l'euro"*[31] (*"Certain prices are going through the roof before the arrival of the euro"*)

(5) *"**Les prix de nombreux produits de grande consommation**, comme les lessives, le beurre ou le lait, ont flambé de juin 2000 à juin 2001, dans la perspective du passage à l'euro[...]"*[32] (*"The prices of numerous major products [...] went through the roof [...] in anticipation of the changeover to the euro"*)

(6) *"**Les prix** dérapent avec le passage à l'euro"*[33] (*"The prices are slipping with the changeover to euro"*)

     2. French/Pacific francs

(7) *"**Le franc** va mourir à 641 ans"*[34] (*"The franc is going to die at 641 years of age"*)

(8) *"**Le franc français** fêtait, mercredi, ses 641 ans"*[35] (*"The French franc celebrated, on Wednesday, its 641 years"*)

---

[29] "Les Calédoniens ont eux aussi découvert l'euro", *Les Nouvelles Calédoniennes*, 8 January 2002.

[30] "Passage à l'euro: une année décisive pour la Calédonie", *Les Nouvelles Calédoniennes*, 3 February 2006.

[31] "Certains prix flambent avant l'euro", *Les Nouvelles Calédoniennes*, 1 September 2001.

[32] *Ibid.*

[33] "Les prix dérapent avec le passage à l'euro", *Les Nouvelles Calédoniennes*, 5 September 2001.

[34] "Le franc va mourir à 641 ans", *Les Nouvelles Calédoniennes*, 5 December 2001.

[35] *Ibid.*

3. Banks

(9)   *"La Banque centrale européenne (BCE)* a grand besoin d'un passage à l'euro réussi pour redorer son blason [...]"[36] (*"The European Central Bank (ECB) needs a successful changeover to the euro to regild its coat of arms"*)

(10)   "A 130 jours du passage à la monnaie unique, *les banques* convertissent progressivement les comptes de leurs clients en euros"[37] (*"In 130 days of the crossover to a single currency, the banks are progressively converting the accounts of their clients into euros"*)

4. Government staff

(11)   *"Le ministre de l'Economie et des Finances Laurent Fabius* a lancé lundi un 'strict rappel à l'ordre' aux commerçants qui profiteraient du passage à l'euro pour augmenter leurs prix et a dévoilé un plan contre les éventuels 'dérapages'".[38] (*"The Minister of Economy and Finances, Laurent Fabius, issued a strict warning to businesses which might take advantage of the crossover to the euro to augment their prices"*)

(12)   *"le Premier ministre Lionel Jospin et son ministre de l'Économie Laurent Fabius* ont fait leur adieu solennel au franc [...] Mais *ils* ont surtout salué l'arrivée de l'euro [...]"[39] (*"the Prime Minister Lionel Jospin and his Minister of Economy Laurent Fabius have given their solemn farewell to the franc, but they have especially greeted the arrival of the euro"*)

(13)   "Depuis juillet, *tous les fonctionnaires* perçoivent leurs salaires en euros"[40] (*"Since July, all civil servants have received their salaries in euros"*)

In reality, the territories are already very exposed to the euro as there is a lot of mobility and interaction between France and the islands. The Pacific Francs have a fixed rate with the euro and the local banks are controlled by the metropolitan banking system. The *Institut d'émission d'Outre-mer* (IEOM) was established in 1966 and it controls monetary

---

[36]   "Euro: la BCE condamnée au succès", Economie/Monde, *Les Nouvelles Calédoniennes*, 27 Novembre 2001.

[37]   "Avec la rentrée, prix et services s'affichent de plus en plus en euros", Économie/Métropole, *Les Nouvelles Calédoniennes*, 4 September 2001.

[38]   "Les prix dérapent avec le passage à l'euro", *Les Nouvelles Calédoniennes*, 5 September 2001.

[39]   "Le franc n'a plus cours, l'euro seule monnaie des Français", *Les Nouvelles Calédoniennes*, 19 February 2002.

[40]   "Avec la rentrée, prix et services s'affichent de plus en plus en euros", *Les Nouvelles Calédoniennes*, 4 September 2001.

affairs including transfers to and from France in the territories. It issues CFP francs and supervises banking agencies in the French Pacific territories. French control over local monetary issues is beneficial in that the French territories are financially protected from any devaluation which may result from trade with France, or from other external constraints.[41] If the European Central Bank were to take over monetary powers in these territories, such privileges might be discontinued.

World:

The representations of agency in euro images from the international angle were noticeably more descriptive and dynamic than others. There was frequent use of adjectives, descriptive representations, and usually of critical nature by referring to the currency as *"this euro"*, *"these little bags [of euros]"*, *"the new currency"*, *"the first bags of euros"*, etc.:

1. Euro

(14) *"euro a engendré une flambée d'inflation"*[42] (*"the euro produced a blaze of inflation"*)

The occurrence below shows the euro as an Agent-participant:

(15) *"L'euro s'arrache dans les pays européens"*[43] (*"The euro is a sell-out in the European countries"*)

The euro is the direct cause of the inflation and the main verb of proposition, which is a Material process, has physical or even violent implications attached to the meaning. As for the following representations, they stress the novelty of the euro:

(16) *"Les sachets des premiers euros* ont remporté un franc succès samedi dans les six nouveaux pays européens"*[44] (*"The first bags of euros met with great success on Saturday in the six new European countries"*)

(17) *"La nouvelle monnaie* a déjà commencé à sortir de ses cachettes [...]"*[45] (*"The new currency has already started to come out from its hiding places [...]"*)

---

41 Dropsy, V., "La Polynésie française et l'euro", *The Pacific and Europe: The 50th Jubilee of the European Communities*, Vol. 7, Victoria University of Wellington Law Review and New Zealand Association for Comparative Law, 2007, p. 106.

42 "La grande distribution se défend de faire monter les prix", *Les Nouvelles Calédoniennes*, 28 August 2002.

43 "L'euro s'arrache dans les pays européens", *Les Nouvelles Calédoniennes*, 18 December 2001.

44 *Ibid.*

45 "Dans 100 jours, l'euro sera dans les poches des Européens", *Les Nouvelles Calédoniennes*, 18 September 2001.

2. The European Central Bank

(18) *"La banque centrale* a joué un rôle crucial [...] de coordination dans les préparatifs logistiques du chamboulement monétaire"[46] (*"The Central Bank played a crucial role in coordinating the logistic preparations of the monetary chaos"*)

(19) *"La jeune banque centrale* n'y peut sans doute pas grand-chose [...] à la glissade de la monnaie"[47] (*"The young Central Bank perhaps cannot do much about [...] the currency's slide"*)

3. People of the European Community

(20) "[...] *les Européens* ont partagé la même curiosité pour ces pièces rutilantes"[48] (*"The Europeans shared the same curiosity for these gleaming coins"*)

(21) "Dès l'arrivée de l'euro, à minuit, *de nombreux Européens* ont pris d'assaut les distributeurs pour se procurer des billets"[49] (*"Since the arrival of the euro, at midnight, numerous Europeans stormed the ATMs to obtain the notes"*).

(22) "Forts du succès de l'euro, *les dirigeants européens* veulent en faire un tremplin pour relancer la dynamique européenne"[50] (*"Emboldened by the success of the euro, European leaders want to use it as a springboard to boost the European dynamic"*)

(23) *"Les autorités européennes* font le pari que l'euro entrera ainsi un peu dans la vie des citoyens"[51] (*"The European authorities are betting that the euro will thus enter into the lives of the citizens"*)

(24) "Pas étonnant donc que *les Italiens* voient arriver l'euro et ses innombrables pièces"[52] (*"It's not surprising then that the Italians are seeing the euro and its countless coins arrive"*)

These representations of the euro show unity among European people by referring to them collectively.

---

[46] "Euro: la BCE condamnée au succès", *Les Nouvelles Calédoniennes*, 27 November 2001.

[47] *Ibid.*

[48] "L'euro s'arrache dans les pays européens", *Les Nouvelles Calédoniennes*, 18 December 2001.

[49] "Baptême du feu pour l'euro", *Les Nouvelles Calédoniennes*, 3 January 2002.

[50] *Ibid.*

[51] "Un kit pour les dirigeants de l'Union européenne", *Les Nouvelles Calédoniennes*, 18 December 2001.

[52] "2002, année de la redécouverte des porte-monnaie", *Les Nouvelles Calédoniennes*, 21 December 2001.

Transitivity Structure: Relational Processes

The linguistic findings from this analysis convey varying attitudes about the euro depending on the placement of euro news. Relational processes have an affirmative function, and they are normally signified by the verb "to be". Such representations have the function of identifying a participant by attributing certain qualities, and they can be factual or judgmental.

New Caledonia: Positive, Optimistic, Identity Constructed.

Relational processes in the local news turned out to be positive and optimistic:

(25) "L'euro sera une monnaie reconnue et appréciée dans le monde entier"[53] (*"the euro will be a recognised and valued currency in the whole world"*)

(26) "L'euro sera très certainement une valeur sûre"[54] (*"the euro will most certainly be a sure bet"*)

If the French Pacific territories were to switch to the euro, they would benefit from using an internationally recognised and secure currency. The euro is also denoted as an attribute to which the state is favourable:

(27) "L'État y est largement favourable"[55] (*"The State is very favourable to it"*)

France: More Negative Images, Nostalgic.

On the other hand, most of the relational processes signifying the euro in the France section revealed negative and nostalgic implications. The press stated that the introduction of the euro is a historical act, and there were a couple of statements which showed that people were worried about this event. The French franc was to come to a sad end, but another instance portrayed the franc as having "beautiful hours ahead".

(28) "Le passage à l'euro est un acte historique" (*"The switch to the euro is a historic act"*)

(29) "Le franc aura une triste fin" (*"The franc will come to a sad end"*)

(30) "le franc a encore de belles heures devant lui" (*"The franc still has beautiful times ahead"*)

---

[53] "Les Calédoniens ont eux aussi découvert l'euro", *Les Nouvelles Calédoniennes*, 8 January 2002.

[54] *Ibid.*

[55] "Euro et corps électoral au menu du comité des signataires", *Les Nouvelles Calédoniennes*, 3 February 2006.

World: Neutral, Factual.

There were comparatively few instances of relational processes representing news about the euro in the international section and the ones that were identified were of a neutral and factual nature:

(31)   "Les Européens vont avoir dans leurs poches des euros sonnants et trébuchants" ("*The Europeans are going to have real euros in their pockets*")

Transitivity Structure: Circumstances

Although circumstantial elements are peripheral features of the transitivity structure as they are situated outside the experiential centre, they are significant in that they add a different quality to the overall representation which exposes a certain degree of subjectivity of the discourse. Circumstances can justify the action denoted in the experiential centre which amplifies the responsibility of the agent- participant in the representation by providing adjunct information about the manner/cause/purpose of the action, therefore creating blame. Circumstantial features can also add a physical dimension to the representation which minimises the agency. The "locative" circumstances specify the temporal and spatial aspects of the event and make it seem more factual and static.

New Caledonia	France	World
à l'euro (x2) *entre* le franc CFP et l'euro	*avant* l'euro *dans* la perspective du passage à l'euro *durant* la période du basculement à l'euro *avec* le passage à l'euro *en cas de* dérapage des prix grâce à l'euro *pour* le lancement de l'euro *lors du* passage à l'euro *face à* cette mobilisation *à cause de* l'euro *avec* un nouveau venu, l'euro *pour* le lancement de la monnaie unique *dans* toute la zone euro	*depuis* sa naissance *à l'intérieur de* la zone de ses cachettes *à la glissade de* la monnaie *dans* l'inconnue de l'euro *dans* les pays européens *dans* les six nouveaux pays européens *dans* la vie des citoyens *dans* la petite histoire italienne *avec* l'arrivée de l'euro basculants à l'euro

The table above indicates the general nature circumstances located in different sections. When it occurred in the "French" news, the euro was accompanied by "how" and "why" the action took place which gave a rational dimension to the euro images.

France: Causal

Thanks to the euro [...]; [...] for the launching of the euro; Facing this mobilisation [...]; [...] because of the euro; [...] for the launching of the single currency in the whole euro zone.

On the other hand, the representations from the "World" section seem more factual as the circumstances tend to locate euro-related events in time or space. As for the occurrences in the local section, the transitivity structures seemed to lack circumstantial elements.

World: Locative

since its birth; Inside the zone; in its hiding places; in the unknown of the euro; in European countries; in the life of the citizens.

Euro news reported with a domestic angle lacked structures with circumstantial elements.

Conclusion

This chapter has demonstrated how the European monetary union is represented by the press media in the French Pacific region. By conducting a discourse analysis which deciphered internal linguistic structures of "euro" news and by critically observing these representations and correlating to various political theories, I revealed the discursive standing of the euro and the effects of the monetary integration as perceived by the French territories as well as exposing their current relations with the EU.

The press has given plenty of attention to the euro-related events and from the linguistic findings, we could conclude that New Caledonia is optimistic about the euro and wants to adopt the European currency although they acknowledge that it is causing France various economic problems. This perception shows the territories' welcoming and positive stance towards Europe while they separate themselves from France.

Through the study of transitivity structure, we showed that agency was more perceptive and targeted in the context of the French economy. The circumstantial features of the transitivity structure revealed how the euro was discussed critically, and in logical terms in the France section, while it had a more static, objective status in the representations with an international focus. Overall, the euro was represented as an entity, rather than a happening, and the analysis demonstrated that the most frequently occurring conceptual metaphors which were categorised as journey, spatial balance and personifying metaphors, were connected to supranational, neo-functionalist and inter-governmental thinking, respectively.

The metaphorical images attached to the euro in the local section, created a boundary, a conceptual border, which the territories can enter by adopting the euro. The euro images found in the "France" section treated the currency as a neo-functional phenomenon, while globally it seems to have an entertaining character. The journey metaphors depicted the euro as a destination for the New Caledonian people while certain container metaphors alluded to a sense of space defined by the euro. The press emphasised the changes, and novelty of the monetary integration, and provided a well rounded report, exposing negative consequences as well as positive ones. Euro images were mostly negative when they were associated with France and the images from the World section were represented in a dramatic manner. Euro news with a local focus tended to be more general and positive. Furthermore, the metaphors of the European monetary integration which reflected a sense of journey, space and balance were compatible with Drulák's discourse study linking metaphors with neo-functional, supra-national and inter-governmental theories.

CHAPTER 13

Europe's Act of Brinkmanship?
New Zealand and the EU Constitution

Natalia CHABAN, Sile SAMMON & John CONDREN

Introduction

An opinion that the European Union (EU) develops from "crisis to crisis"[1] seems to be supported by the EU's evolution in previous decades – examples being its failure to react in a timely fashion to the Balkan crises in the 1990s, the EU's inability to present a single position on the US-led war in Iraq in 2003 and, most recently, the rejection of the Constitutional Treaty by two of its founding member states, France and the Netherlands, in 2005, followed by a "no" vote in Ireland to the Lisbon Treaty in 2008. These critical developments are aggravated by a lack of popular support for the EU's actions – in particular, observers note a record-low voter turn out in the Parliamentary elections in 2004 and again in 2009; increasing emergence and development of anti-EU parties; and the public's lukewarm and indeed at times hostile reception of the EU's enlargement to the East and South (including the still sore issue of Turkey's proposed membership of the "club"). This chapter focuses on the EU's constitutional "crisis", with its peak in the rejection of the initiative by the people in two EU states, and, more specifically, on the external perceptions of this European political drama.

This particular focus is grounded in the assumption that the initial failure of the treaty spurred strong and controversial reactions not only *within* the Union, but had a peculiar and unwelcome influence on *external* perceptions of the EU as a global actor. This major EU internal event triggered outsiders' visions of the Union being increasingly divided internally. This fragmented impression complemented another very recent perception of the EU, as being unable to act cohesively externally (namely, the EU member states' disparate reactions to the US-led war in Iraq in 2003). Joschka Fischer, Germany's former foreign minister, noted that "the rest of the world will not wait for Europe while

---

[1]   Words assigned to Jean Monnet, as cited in A. Duff, "Plan B: How to Rescue the European Constitution", *Notre Europe: Etudes et Recherches*, No. 52, 2006, http://www.notre-europe.eu/uploads/tx_publication/Etud52-en_01.pdf.

it bickers over institutional reform and external policy issues",[2] and warned of a growing risk of Europe becoming a "playground for upcoming super powers".[3] In this context, the perception of the EU as a *disunited polity*, both in domestic and foreign affairs may impair international judgement on a capable, integrated Europe.

External perceptions of the EU are recognised to be an underresearched and frequently overlooked field in EU scholarship.[4] Yet, such studies may be the key when it comes to the investigation of the EU's roles as a global actor (namely, the EU's actual actions, goals and capabilities in the field of foreign policy)[5] and the Union's foreign policy identity as a distinctive international actor.[6] With 90% of EU citizens expressing a wish for the EU to play a more visible global role,[7] research on the EU's external perceptions may serve not only as a tool to sharpen the EU's maturing foreign policy, but as yet another mechanism to connect the EU with its citizens. Indeed, if the EU's actions are to be validated (or not) by the outsiders, the insiders may approve (or not) further integration attempts.[8] To ensure such critical reflections, a systematic identification on a wide geographic scope and regular report-

---

[2]   "EU Needs Reform or Fade away", *Europe Daily News*, http://www. europedailynews.com/2007/03/30/eu-needs-reform-or-fade-away/

[3]   *Ibid.*

[4]   Lucarelli, S., "The European Union in the Eyes of Other: Towards Filling a Gap in the Literature", *European Foreign Affairs Review*, Vol. 12, No. 3, 2007, Special Issue "Beyond Self-Perception: The Other's View of the European Union", pp. 249-270.

[5]   Smith, H., *European Union Foreign Policy: What It Is and What It Does*, London and Sterling, Va., Pluto Press, 2002; Holland, M., *European Union Common Foreign Policy: From EPC to CFSP Joint Action and South Africa*, London, MacMillan, 1995; Holland, M. (ed.), *Common Foreign and Security Policy: The First Ten Years*, London, Continuum, 2005.

[6]   Cederman, L.E. (ed.), *Constructing Europe's Identity: The External Dimension*, Boulder, CO., Lynne Rienner Publishers, 2001; Lucarelli, S., "Interpreted Values: A Normative Reading of EU Role Conceptions & Performance" in O. Elgström and M. Smith (eds.), *The European Union's Roles in International Politics: Concepts and Analysis*, London, Routledge, 2006; Lucarelli, S. and Manners, I. (eds.), *Values and Principles in European Union Foreign Policy*, London, Routledge, 2006; Smith, K., "Conceptualising the EU's International Identity: Sui Generis or Following the Latest Trends?", paper presented at the *First Pan-European Conference on European Union Politics*, Bordeaux, 26-28 September 2002.

[7]   US German Marshal Fund survey, September 2007, reported in *EUobserver*, http://euobserver.com/9/24717/?print=1.

[8]   Lucarelli, S., "European Political Identity and the Others' Image of the EU: Reflections on an Unexplored Relationship", paper presented at *GARNET-JERP 5.2.1 Final Conference, The Europeans. The European Union in Search of Political Identity and Legitimacy*, Florence, 25-26 May 2007.

ing of the EU's external perceptions to its citizens and policy-makers are needed.

To date, empirical studies of the EU's external perceptions in media and elite discourses have been rare. Several incremental studies of elite perceptions have included studies of EU perceptions among Australian MPs,[9] ASEAN political, business and civil society elites,[10] and international negotiators in three different multilateral settings.[11] The GARNET FP6 project "The External Image(s) of the European Union: A global survey" undertaken in 2005-2006 also attempted to tackle the deficit of research of the EU's external perceptions studies via surveying official discourses in eight countries and performing a rudimentary media analysis.[12]

The most comprehensive investigation of the EU's external perceptions is the study of the Asia Pacific visions of the EU conducted by the National Centre for Research on Europe, University of Canterbury, New Zealand (NZ).[13] It is a comparative empirical study of the EU's percep-

---

9   Murray, P., "Australian Perspectives on the European Union", *European Information*, No. 8, 1999; Murray, P., "Australian Voices: Some Elite Reflections on the European Union", *CESAA Review*, No. 29, 2002, pp. 5-18, http://www.cesaa.org.au/publications.htm; Murray, P., "Australian Views on Europe and the EU-Australia Relationship: An Assessment", paper presented at the *European Union-Australia Relations Workshop*, CERC, University of Melbourne, July 2002; Murray, P., "What Australians Think about the EU: Elite Perceptions and the Current Context", paper presented at the *Conference on The EU in International Affairs*, NEC, Canberra, July 2002, http://www.anu.edu.au/NEC/MURRAY-updated1July.pdf.

10 A.R.S. Prgetti S.r.l. Ambiente, Risorse e Sviluppo, *Final Report, Survey Analysis of EU Perceptions in South East Asia*, January 2003, Framework Contract AMS/451-Lot 7; *Perceptions of the EU's role in South East Asia*, Framework Contract Commission 2007, EuropeAid/123314/C/SER/multi, Lot No. 4.

11 The three settings being: the United Nations Forum on Forestry's fourth session in Geneva in May 2004; the 13th Conference on International Trade in Endangered Species of Wild Fauna and Flora, Bangkok, October 2004; the World Trade Organization (member states permanent representations in Geneva). See Elgström, O. and Smith, M. (eds.), *The European Union's Roles in International Politics: Concepts and Analysis*, London, Routledge, 2006; Elgström, O., *Leader or Foot-Dragger? Perceptions of the European Union in Multilateral International Negotiations*, Report 2006:1, Swedish Institute for European Policy Studies, www.sieps.se/publ/rapporter/bilagorf2006 I.pdf, p. 12; Chaban, N., Elgström, O. and Holland, M., "The European Union as Others See It", *European Foreign Affairs Review*, Vol. 11.No. 2, 2006, pp. 245-262.

12 GARNET Working Paper No. 17/07, *The External Image of the European Union*, http://www.garnet-eu.org/index.php?id=27; *European Foreign Affairs Review*, Vol. 12, No. 3, 2007, Special Issue "Beyond Self-Perception; The Other's View of the European Union".

13 Holland, M. *et al.* (eds.), *The EU through the Eyes of Asia*, Singapore-Warsaw, University of Warsaw, 2007; Chaban, N. and Holland, M. (eds.), *The European Union and the Asia-Pacific: Media, Public and Elite Perceptions of the EU*, London,

tions and images existing in the public discourses of mass media, the general public and national elites in nineteen countries in the region (as of 2009). A NZ case presented in this chapter is a part of this study. Specifically, this chapter investigates external media and stakeholders' framings of the constitutional process and the EU role in it. The chapter focuses on how the European Constitution "saga" was reported in five leading NZ newspapers and what perceptions of the EU dominated the opinions of the NZ national stakeholders (political, business and media cohorts) with regards to the EU Constitution "crisis".

The choice of the press as a medium for analysis is grounded in the fact that newspapers still remain one of the main sources of political information in New Zealand,[14] being preferred by more educated, cosmopolitan, and older audiences[15] – among those, national elites.[16] Five reputable national newspapers monitored in this study over the period of three years – 2004, 2005 and 2007 – produced a sample of eighty news items which reported the Constitutional Treaty with reference to the EU.[17] A methodology of intertextual discourse analysis was employed. Semi-structural in-depth face-to-face interviews took place in 2004 and 2005, and involved fifty-one NZ stakeholders (thirty in 2004 and twenty-one in 2005). Defined as being "in positions to make decisions having major consequences",[18] the stakeholders sample involved twenty-two business respondents – members of national business round tables, other official business networks and leading exporters; nineteen members of national parliament representing different parties (including the ruling party's members in key government positions); and ten national media "gatekeepers" – editors-in-chief, editors of special sections, news directors, and leading journalists. While the media component warranted an insight into a popular, leading and credible source of international information, inclusion of the elite component guaranteed

---

Routledge, 2008; Chaban, N. *et al. The EU through the Eyes of Asia: New Cases, New Findings*, Singapore, World Scientific, 2009. For more publications see www.euperceptions.canterbury.ac.nz.

[14] Mulgan, R., *Politics in New Zealand*, Auckland, Auckland University Press, 2004, p. 293.

[15] See Stempel, G. and Hargrove, T., "Mass Media Audiences in a Changing Media Environment", *Journalism and Mass Communication*, Vol. 73, No. 3, 1996, pp. 549-558.

[16] Schulz, W., "Foreign News in Leading Newspapers of Western and Post-Communist Countries", paper delivered at the 51st Annual Conference of the International Communication Association, Washington, D.C., 24-28 May 2001, www.kwpw.wiso. uni-erlangen.de/pdf_dateien/ica_fn2001.pdf.

[17] *New Zealand Herald, Otago Daily Times, Sunday Star Times* (only in 2007), *The Press, Dominion Post, Waikato Times*.

[18] Wright Mills, C., *The Power Elite*, Oxford, Oxford Press, 1956.

an account of the opinion of policy- and decision-makers and information "gatekeepers", when it came to foreign policy formulation and implementation.

Three research questions lead this investigation. First, how did EU external discourses (NZ media and stakeholders in this study) frame a major EU development in the project of European integration? Second, what are the pragmatic implications of this imagery to EU policy- and decision-makers and EU citizens? Finally, what are the consequences of a typical imagery of the EU, a key international counterpart, to NZ stakeholders?

Focusing on the images and perceptions of the EU's key event, the Constitutional Treaty, this chapter firstly provides an insight into the history of the treaty in order to establish the overall context necessary to understand the background of the Union's external imagery. Secondly, this chapter surveys the official NZ reaction to the EU's core evolution, grounding it within a broader context of EU-NZ relations. Within this angle, the chapter specifically focuses on the perceptions of the treaty by NZ stakeholders. Thirdly, it addresses the NZ media imagery of the treaty with reference to the leading and influential actors of the "saga". Finally, this chapter discusses the pragmatic implication of the dominant imagery of the constitutional process to the EU, NZ and NZ-EU relations.

Constitutional "Saga": Contextualising Research

The economic, social, political and military spheres of the EU turned their collective attention to forwarding, promoting and developing the formulation of a Constitution for Europe in 2001, during a much-debated and much-publicised ratification of the Treaty of Nice. This project (subtitled "Bringing Europe closer to its citizens") was intended and designed to be implemented by each member state (including the ten candidate members who eventually joined the "club" in 2004) by 1st November 2006. The text of the final draft of the Constitutional Treaty was agreed upon under Ireland's presidency of the European Council in June 2004, completing a two-and-a-half-year deliberation begun by the European Convention in December 2001. Representatives of each member state signed the Treaty Establishing a Constitution for Europe in Rome on 29 October 2004. From its inception, the Treaty aimed to enable the EU to progress as an essential body on the world stage and to further and protect European interests by giving the Union a more autonomous and unified identity. In the opinion of many optimists, the Constitutional Treaty could have promoted the project of European integration on a new, more cohesive level. However, sceptics cited deeply-rooted and ever-present sentiments of nationalism and patriotism as a possible counterbalance to the success of the treaty.

Spain was the first nation to test the public view of the new document in 2005. With a large majority voting in favour of the treaty, this positive outcome sent an encouraging message to other European leaders. Yet, despite this hopeful beginning, Europe was very soon plunged into confusion, when France and the Netherlands each rejected the treaty in national referenda in May and June 2005 respectively. The subsequent postponement of ratification procedures in a number of member states created uncertainty and fear for the Constitutional Treaty's future. Luxembourg pursued its plans for a referendum; yet, the treaty was given no more than a lukewarm endorsement by the popular vote. The United Kingdom (UK) presented an even more intriguing picture – although initially no public consultation was foreseen in the UK, a referendum was unexpectedly introduced and then, in a more surprising twist of events, it was cancelled. The *status quo* until October 2007 presented a rather complicated internal tableau – sixteen member states had ratified the treaty by means of a parliamentary vote, seven had postponed the ratification procedure, two had ratified the treaty by referendum, and two states had rejected the treaty by referendum.

The question on everybody's mind was why the French and Dutch voters decided to reject the new Constitutional Treaty. Concerns over the loss of national identity, fears for European security and the freedom to be involved in or absolved from conflict situations and misgivings over economic policies outlined in the Constitutional Treaty comprise some of the main reasons for the rejection of the new Constitution for Europe in the two referenda.[19]

The Constitutional Treaty was intended to replace the existing framework of treaties that had created the European Economic Community (Treaty of Rome, 1957) and the European Union (Treaty of Maastricht, 1992), as well as those treaties that had amended and altered the Treaty on European Union (Amsterdam, 1997 and Nice, 2001). This revision aimed to streamline the Union's laws and policies, as well as highlight the very essence of European integration and the need for cooperation. One encompassing basic document that could be examined and altered at various points in the future seemed to be a sensible option. Many states set out the framework of their legal, social and political systems in similar-style constitutions that are always subject to review and reform by internal referenda or other means. Strictly speaking, the EU's streamlining of the treaties should not have been classed as a "constitution", as those member states whose legal systems found their

---

[19]   Duff, A., "Plan B: How to Rescue the European Constitution", *op. cit.*

basis in a constitution were not expected to actually replace their means of asserting national identity with the new formulation. However, they would be required to verify and ensure that every article of their own constitution was in accordance with the EU's new creation. This, though, was seen by many as a trespass into the sovereignty of individual states.

There were too many new provisions in the Constitutional Treaty for them all to be alluded to here, but some of the more important aims and developments of the treaty included provisions that the "three pillars" system of judicial capability, customs and foreign policy and policing affairs established under Maastricht would be abolished, and such matters brought under stronger European Union control. The post of Minister Vice-President of the Foreign Affairs Commission was created with the aim of giving the EU a stronger and more efficient unified capability in negotiations with third parties, such as the United States, Russia, Middle Eastern countries or the United Nations. The principle of the supremacy of EU law over national legislation was reiterated.[20]

The final draft of the proposed Constitutional Treaty received stinging criticism from many political and media circles – it was frequently attacked for being overly liberal, undemocratic, promoting the US-style federal system of government, lacking in attention to social matters such as integration of minorities and of not going far enough to promote the essential battle against climate change and global warming.[21] However, it was always going to be difficult to produce an attentive, complex and carefully written document that appealed to every citizen of the Union.

In June 2007, under the German Presidency of the European Council, the idea of a Reform Treaty was proposed at the European summit meeting in Berlin as a means of addressing the failure of the Constitutional Treaty to win the support necessary for acceptance and ratification. On 18-19 October 2007, the European Council achieved final agreement on the Reform Treaty. On 13 December 2007, the Reform Treaty was signed at a summit in Lisbon, Portugal and subsequently known as the Treaty of Lisbon. The treaty incorporated many of the reforms of the ill-fated 2005 Constitutional Treaty, yet it has learnt its lessons of the failure of its predecessor. The Lisbon Treaty paid greater attention to, among other things, economic governance of the EU, social matters, and fundamental human rights (the Charter of Fundamental Rights now forms a key and undeniable component of the new treaty). The accusations of the "anti-democratic" nature of the European Com-

---

[20] This principle was first upheld by the European Court of Justice in the famous case of *Van Gend en Loos* in 1963.

[21] Duff, A., "Plan B: How to Rescue the European Constitution", *op. cit.*

mission have been analysed and addressed. Also, means of preserving fossil fuel stocks and cutting down on their usage, while simultaneously promoting the development and usage of renewable energy sources form important parts of the new treaty. Finally, the Lisbon Treaty addressed means of enhancing and protecting the EU's status as a major world power, while continuing to work in cooperation with other entities to preserve and promote peace in troubled areas, such as the Middle East and Sudan.[22]

The Reform Treaty was due to come into force by 1 January 2009, if successfully ratified by all EU member states in 2008. The Irish Republic was the only state where a mandatory referendum was held – the country's constitution would have to change in order to accommodate the Lisbon Treaty. In June 2008, 53.4% of those who voted in Ireland, or 862,415 voters, chose to reject the Reform Treaty.[23] The outcome of the Irish vote plunged the EU-27 into a difficult and confusing situation, which was only resolved by a second referendum in October 2009. The Lisbon Treaty entered into force on 1 December 2009.

External Echo of the Constitutional Debate: The EU in the Eyes of NZ's Stakeholders

This chapter considers one case in the study of the EU's external perceptions: images of the Constitutional Treaty in the media and stakeholders' discourses in one Asia Pacific country, New Zealand. Why New Zealand? The two distant locations, the EU and NZ have a long history to their relationship – NZ was one of the first countries to establish formal diplomatic relations with the European Commission in 1961.[24] This relationship, which used to be exclusively dominated by trade and agriculture, is increasingly including new facets, such as dialogue on the environment and cooperation in counter-terrorism. Moreover, NZ's relations with Europe go beyond the contacts with the EU – a common heritage and shared cultures (mainly due to the extensive contacts with the UK in the past) are the key.

The Joint Declaration on Relations between the EU and New Zealand (1999) formed the basis of the EU-NZ relationship.[25] It focused on strengthening the close ties between the two parties through a number of common goals, such as cooperation on development issues in the South Pacific region and the support of democracy. The Declaration outlined mechanisms for facilitating dialogue between the two entities, namely

---

[22] http://europa.eu/lisbon_treaty/index_en.htm.

[23] "Ireland Rejects EU Reform Treaty", http://news.bbc.co.uk/2/hi/europe/7453560.stm.

[24] http://www.delaus.ec.europa.eu/newzealand/EU_NZ_relations/politicalrelations.htm.

[25] http://ec.europa.eu/external_relations/new_zealand/intro/index.htm.

the EU-NZ Ministerial Consultations, which take place every six months in the capital of the EU member state holding the Presidency. The 1999 Declaration was followed by the Action Plan New Zealand and the European Union: Priorities for Future Cooperation,[26] which was adopted at the EU-New Zealand Ministerial Consultation in March 2004 and reviewed in 2007. The Action Plan translated the general objectives listed in the Joint Declaration into concrete cooperation activities. On 21 September 2007, a Joint Declaration on relations and cooperation between the European Union and New Zealand was adopted in Lisbon between the Portuguese Foreign Minister Mr Luís Amado (Portugal was a holder of the EU Presidency in the second half of 2007), European Commissioner for External Relations Mrs Benita Ferrero-Waldner and the NZ Foreign Minister Mr Winston Peters.[27] This document combined and replaced the 1999 Joint Declaration on Relations between the European Union and New Zealand, as well as the 2004 Action Plan. The new Joint Declaration is an important new document that will guide the EU-NZ bilateral relationship until 2012. It reiterates the strengths of the relationship and outlines specific and practical cooperation measures. The Joint Declaration sets out a detailed action programme for the EU and NZ in such areas as global and regional security, counter-terrorism and human rights, visas, development and economic cooperation, trade, climate change, science and technology.

The EU remains an important economic partner to NZ. As of December 2006, the EU has been NZ's second largest market after Australia, taking some 15% of NZ's total exports valued at NZ$5.296 billion (June 2007).[28] Agricultural products make up 67% of NZ's exports to the EU. The EU is the largest, highest value and in many cases, the fastest-growing market for NZ's key products like butter, sheep meat, apples and kiwi fruit. With tourism being NZ's single largest export industry, exceeding its dairy industry in earnings, visitors from the EU are an important source of NZ's income – in June 2006-June 2007 approximately 483,000 EU citizens visited NZ (20% of all arrivals to NZ).[29] The EU exports to NZ are made up mainly of medicine, cars, telecommunication equipment, machinery, transport material and chemicals.[30] Additionally, the euro has become an important trading currency for

---

[26] http://www.delaus.ec.europa.eu/newzealand/JointDeclaration2007/EU-NZJointDeclaration.pdf, p. 4.

[27] http://www.delaus.ec.europa.eu/newzealand/JointDeclaration2007/index.htm.

[28] http://www.mfat.govt.nz/Foreign-Relations/Europe/0-eu-overview.php.

[29] http://www.delaus.ec.europa.eu/newzealand/JointDeclaration2007/EU-NZ.pdf.

[30] http://www.ec.europa.eu/trade/issues/bilateral/.../newzealand/index_en.htm.

NZ. Approximately 40% of the foreign exchange reserves in the NZ Reserve Bank are held in euro.[31]

Cooperation between the EU and NZ is stable and growing and is to be seen in many spheres beyond the strictly economic sectors. The diplomatic relationship between NZ and the EU has continued to flourish.[32] In addition to its nine embassies in EU member states before the 2004 enlargement (Belgium, France, Germany, the Netherlands, Sweden, Italy, Portugal, Spain and the UK), NZ opened a new embassy in Warsaw, Poland, in 2005, after the latest EU enlargement. This embassy will represent NZ not only in Poland, but also in the three Baltic nations of Estonia, Latvia and Lithuania. Ten EU member states currently have embassies in NZ, namely, the UK, France, Germany, Italy, the Netherlands, Poland, Spain, Finland, Greece and Latvia.

Another important area of the EU-NZ political cooperation is joint action in Asia Pacific. In his speech given at the Netherlands Institute of International Relations,[33] the former NZ Foreign Minister Winston Peters talked about the growing EU involvement with New Zealand in their aid efforts in the Pacific. He specifically noted how NZ sees the EU as a "constructive, like-minded partner in the pursuit of democracy, security, good governance and sound development across the Pacific region". Echoing this sentiment, Benita Ferrero-Waldner,[34] European Commissioner for External Relations and European Neighbourhood Policy, in her speech at the Europa Lecture in Wellington in May 2007, outlined plans to "upgrade" the relations between the EU and NZ by boosting trade and investment; improving security in the Pacific region; and tackling the global issues of energy security and climate change.

In addition to economic and political contacts, the NZ-EU people-to-people relations are also on the rise. One of the examples of this trend is the EU-NZ Pilot Cooperation in Higher Education launched in 2006.[35] Active people-to-people contacts are supported by conducive visa regulations – from 1st April 2005, citizens from twenty-five EU states had visa-free status to enter New Zealand. This completes the reciprocity of visa arrangements already in place for New Zealanders travelling to all EU member states.[36] New Zealand currently has working holiday

---

[31] http://ec.europa.eu/external_relations/new_zealand/intro/index.htm.

[32] http://www.beehive.govt.nz/ViewDocument.aspx?DocumentID=22971.

[33] The Hague, 3.30pm, 15 October.

[34] Benita Ferrero-Waldner, *The European Union and New Zealand – New Perspectives*, Europa Lecture, Te Papa Museum, Wellington, 27 June 2007.

[35] http://ec.europa.eu/education/programmes/eu_others/nz/index_en.html.

[36] This means that New Zealand passport holders do not require a visa if their stay is no longer than 90 days in a six month period within the EU, http://www.delaus.ec. europa.eu/newzealand/eu_guide/faqsvisas.htm.

schemes in place with the following EU members: Belgium, Denmark, Finland, France, Germany, Ireland, Italy, Netherlands, Spain, Sweden, the UK – a boon for all those young Kiwis who want to broaden their horizons by working their way around Europe.

The NZ official reaction to the dramatic events surrounding the Constitutional Treaty rejection was rather limited and neutral. Former NZ Minister of Foreign Affairs and Trade Phil Goff, in his comments on the events in Europe,[37] noted that the failure to ratify the Constitutional Treaty will be of "limited importance to New Zealand", and will not affect the NZ "key economic relationship with the EU". In addition, he stated that the EU-NZ political relationship would continue as before. The only place that this relationship would be affected by the failure to ratify the Constitutional Treaty would be foreign policy. "What happens with the EU's common foreign policy over the next few years will be of far-reaching significance", he commented. In the same speech, while referring to the rejection of the Constitutional Treaty, Goff stressed that "the Common Agricultural Policy (CAP) is a more relevant prism through which to view relations with the EU", identifying perhaps that internal bickering of the member states is seen to be of lesser importance to NZ, when set against the urgent need to reshape the CAP – a policy which is seen as damaging to NZ agriculture producers.

In view of the cautious NZ official stance on EU constitutional development, this study attempts to seek a more detailed perception of the Union's major development among NZ stakeholders, as defined above.

When commenting on the NZ-EU relations in general, a number of the stakeholders shared the opinion that relations were "still growing".[38] Some interviewees felt that these relations were extremely important, specifically due to extensive historical and trade links. Echoing the statement by Goff, for many, the CAP was one of the main references in the context of EU-NZ relations. The policy's impact on NZ has been noted to be "vast".[39] Indeed, the CAP was seen not only as a policy which damages NZ agricultural producers, but also as a policy which damages the EU's international reputation – a "fortress Europe" , resistant to change, was not seen as an international leader. In addition, most of the interviewees noted the impact the UK's decision to join the European Community in 1972 had on NZ: that decision was noted to "still reverberate […] to this day".[40] It occasioned a major economic shock to the NZ economy as guaranteed markets for NZ produce in the

---

[37] http://www.beehive.govt.nz/ViewDocument.aspx?DocumentID=22971.
[38] Political "elite" respondent.
[39] Business "elite" respondent.
[40] Political "elite" respondent.

UK disappeared and NZ was forced to grapple with the world market on less than favourable terms.

Despite these close and intense links between the EU and New Zealand recognised by the majority of stakeholders interviewed, the Constitutional Treaty was mentioned only occasionally. In most cases, it was optimistically seen by the political actors as an "issue that has to be worked through".[41] Some politicians noted that "the EU Constitution got a little bit knocked down and does not fundamentally alter what actually happened".[42] The Constitutional Treaty was mentioned by political respondents when discussing EU enlargement changing the future of the EU. The Constitution was seen as instrumental in cementing a "tight group whose energies and efforts are inevitably going to be looking East and to Turkey".[43] Revealingly, disagreements between the member states, be it on Iraq or the Constitutional Treaty, led to rather colourful descriptions of the EU by the NZ politicians as a "constellation of stars, rather than a giant star"[44] or even as a "sponge with some solid bits".[45]

From the business stakeholders' perspective, the Constitutional Treaty was an attempt to make a "cohesive EU possible".[46] Some other interviewees felt that because of the derailment of the Constitution project, the EU did not find itself united, and this weakened its position as an international leader. Encouragingly, the EU was still believed to play a key role in a wide range of areas, even if some member states did not support the Constitutional Treaty. As with the political stakeholders, the NZ business interviewees scrutinised the Constitutional process through the enlargement prism – an opinion was expressed that ratifying the treaty is a "big hurdle"[47] that has to be overcome before Turkey can join the EU.

Representatives of the media cohort used the example of the Constitutional debate to illustrate a newsworthy event deserving NZ media attention. Indeed, the EU news was often seen to be "difficult to sell"[48] to the readers, mainly due to the lack of drama or easily recognised faces. Arguably, the failure of the Constitutional Treaty presented an attractive newsworthy information package with negativity, conflict, scandal and political celebrities, all entangled together. One of the

---

[41] Political "elite" respondent.

[42] Political "elite" respondent.

[43] Political "elite" respondent.

[44] Political "elite" respondent.

[45] Political "elite" respondent.

[46] Business "elite" respondent.

[47] Business "elite" respondent.

[48] Media "elite" respondent.

editors we interviewed was even considering the subject for an editorial. Interestingly, media "gatekeepers" were under the impression that their outlets had a "reasonable coverage"[49] of the constitutional process. Yet, it was pointed out that while New Zealanders are aware of EU enlargement and the on-going debate around the European Constitution, these topics seemed to be relatively irrelevant for the average NZ reader. The EU was called a "part of the world that they [New Zealanders] are interested in, not a focus".[50] Importantly, an opinion was shared that "anything that has a link with some relevance to New Zealand is not that hard to sell".[51] However, events surrounding the constitutional debate were not perceived by the newsmakers to affect New Zealanders directly.

Images of the EU Constitutional Project in the NZ Media Discourse

With national reputable newspapers being reported by the interviewed stakeholders to be one of their major sources of information on the EU, this chapter employs discourse analysis techniques to trace the print media imagery of the EU and its actors in the constitutional "saga". This approach to the study of the EU's image is supported in the relevant literature. According to Hakan Samur,

> [This] constructivist approach to international relations is especially appropriate in the case of the EU, because the EU aspires to be more than an international society: a supranational one. This means that the EU needs to create its own norms, values and practices to a greater extent than any international society.[52]

This investigation employed a longitudinal perspective and traced the media portrayals of the Constitutional Treaty in the daily coverage by five leading newspapers in New Zealand throughout three years, namely, 2004, 2005 and 2007.[53] In order to identify the media framings of the EU (one of the research questions), this analysis focused on the imagery of the actors profiled as the leading lights of the constitutional process. Three groups were considered in this inter-textual discourse analysis: firstly, the EU institutions and officials, secondly, the EU member states and their leaders, and finally, the citizens of the EU. The subsequent questions elaborating the main question concerning the

---

[49] Media "elite" respondent.

[50] Media "elite" respondent.

[51] Media "elite" respondent.

[52] Samur, H., "The Power of Discourse in the EU Playground", *Journal of European Affairs, EU Policy Network* 31/2, 2004, p. 31.

[53] 2008 was beyond the scope of this analysis.

media discourse were: Who were the most visible actors in the unfolding drama surrounding the European Constitution? Are the EU institutions seen as leading or supporting performers? Do the member states steal the limelight of media attention from the EU institutions and officials, even when the plot is about further inter-governmental integration? What were the portrayals of EU citizens in a conflict, which ultimately was triggered by the *vox populi*? In short, were they presented as leads or mere spear-carriers?

The three years of the media monitoring – 2004, 2005 and 2007 – traced the milestones in the constitutional debate. The year 2004 marked the conclusion of the Constitutional Convention; 2005 was the year when the voters of two members states, France and the Netherlands, rejected the Treaty and the UK faced the dilemma of whether or not to hold a referendum; and 2007 was the year in which the debate on the treaty resurfaced on the EU agenda and saw the signing of the Lisbon Treaty in December. The year 2006 was excluded from the analysis, as it was the so-called "period of reflection" in EU political discourse, necessary to process the failure of the treaty.

The coverage turned out to be highly uneven. The data set included nineteen articles in 2004 (twelve months of monitoring), forty-four in 2005 (six months of monitoring) and seventeen in 2007 (twelve months of monitoring). A peak in coverage in 2005 featured primarily the rejection of the treaty by France, one of the EU's "Big Three". The Netherlands' "No", coming from a smaller member state, attracted less comment. There were also extensive reports on the debate about whether or not the UK should hold a referendum on the treaty. The coverage in 2007 decreased dramatically in comparison to 2005 (and was slightly less than in 2004). Significantly, only a small number of articles exclusively focused on the Lisbon Treaty in 2007. This is puzzling as there were several major developments in the constitutional stalemate, such as the change of leadership within the EU's "Big Three" (the UK, France and Germany); the resurgence of the treaty discussion; and, finally, meetings of the EU leaders in October and December, resulting in a breakthrough agreement on the text of the treaty, leading to the Lisbon signing. The agreement on a text was reported in only one article, and the signing in only two. This preliminary overview suggests that the NZ newsmakers were more interested in featuring discord rather than accord within the EU.

One is struck by the fact that fully 65% of the EU-related articles were written overseas. A paltry 9% were written by New Zealand journalists, while 26% were non-attributed. Among the overseas items, British sources predominate (*Reuters*, as well as the UK newspapers *The Independent* and *The Guardian*), in all, 40% of the sample. In contrast,

9% originated from the *Agence France-Presse* (AFP) news agency, and almost 15% from other sources (*International Press*, *Bloomberg* and *Newsweek*). The EU's Constitutional Treaty was not marked by a major interest among local journalists. Fewer than one in eleven of the sampled articles was written by a NZ journalist.[54] In almost 83% of the articles, the EU and its constitutional debate were featured as a major theme, with news coverage focusing solely on the EU and its actors. In 4.4% of articles the treaty process was a secondary point of reference (more specifically, in the context of the reporting of Nicolas Sarkozy's election to the presidency of France). In 14.5% of articles the EU and its constitutional project were only a minor reference. Only 1% of news items positioned this major EU evolution in the local NZ context. A peculiar media framing of the Constitutional Treaty – a major topic in the external context – presented the Treaty evolution as a major, but external development for the NZ audience. This had the effect of conveying a message of distance and detachment of the event from the local context. A big fraction of the publications presented the treaty from a neutral angle (41.4%), yet negative evaluations accounted for a resounding majority over the positive ones (42.5% *vs.* 16.3% respectively). Negative evaluations were the most visible in the 2005 coverage of the rejection of the treaty by France and the Netherlands, as well as in the reports on whether a referendum would be held in the UK.

The content analysis of the news texts revealed that the most visible group of actors in the NZ press coverage was not the EU institutions or officials or the EU citizens, but the leaders of the member states. Consequently, this chapter focuses first on the media images of the leaders of the EU member states, then on media framing of the EU institutions and officials, and finally on the imagery of the EU citizens in the constitutional "saga".

EU Member State Leaders

The most visible, most colourful and controversial (read newsworthy) in the NZ coverage of the EU Constitutional Treaty were the leaders of the EU member states, more specifically, of the EU's "Big Three" – France, Germany and the UK. Previous research on the EU's external perceptions in the Asia Pacific revealed that the EU's "Big Three" – France, Germany and the UK – and their leaders were the most visible actors in the media coverage in the region. The NZ media coverage of the constitutional debate was not an exception – the most visible actors were the "usual suspects" again, namely, the UK, France and Germany (France with twenty-three articles, the UK with sixteen articles and

---

[54]   The rest of located news items (26%) were non-attributed.

Germany with seven articles). There was very little mention of the smaller member states, with the Netherlands being featured in eight articles and Luxembourg in three. This attention is obviously due to the Netherlands' rejection of the Constitutional Treaty around the same time as France, and the fact that Luxembourg held the EU Presidency from 1st January to 30th June 2005. A division of roles between the EU's "Big Three" and the rest was colourfully summed in one article as a division between those at the "top table" and the "Union's pygmies".[55]

In the coverage of the Constitutional Treaty "saga" in 2004-2005, former British Prime Minister Tony Blair, was the most visible (twelve articles in 2004 and fifteen articles in 2005). The second most visible actor was former French President Jacques Chirac (he appeared in four articles in 2004 and in eighteen articles in 2005). Former German Chancellor Gerhard Schröder was the least visible of the "Big Three" leaders, appearing only in four articles. In the 2007 coverage of the Lisbon Treaty, the visibility balance shifted – a new German Chancellor Angela Merkel was the most prominent actor, appearing in six articles (Germany held the EU presidency in the first half of the year) alongside the new French leader Nicolas Sarkozy (six articles). The other new Head of Government, UK Prime Minister Gordon Brown, was mentioned in just three articles, putting him on a par with his Dutch and Luxemburg counterparts. Portuguese Prime Minister José Sócrates and Portuguese Foreign Minister Luis Amado were mentioned in one article each.

Overall, Tony Blair was the most visible actor, appearing in 39% of the total coverage. Jacques Chirac was the second most visible actor with 32%. Blair's dominant media profile could be partially explained by the fact that most of the articles reporting the treaty came from the British news sources, as discussed above. Heightened visibility of Jacques Chirac could be ascribed to the presence of *AFP*, the French wire, the only European continental source consistently used by the NZ press. In contrast, low media visibility of Germany, the Netherlands, Luxembourg, Portugal, or for that matter, any other EU member state in the constitutional debate could be partially attributed to a virtual absence of continental European news sources in the sample.

Predictably, the imagery of the member state leaders was unique in each case, however, several common trends were observed. Namely, the leaders of the "Big Three" were repeatedly portrayed as being instrumental in Europe's movement forward (*drivers* of the European locomotive) and powerful actors playing with the fate of Europe (*gamblers* and

---

[55] Field, C., "Big Three Anger EU Also-Rans; EUROPE: Blair Joins the Top Table, Amid Disquiet among the Union's Pygmies", *New Zealand Herald*, 20 February 2004, World.

winners/losers). Occasionally, images of a *weaver* and a *circus performer* surfaced, too.

Drivers

Description of the constitutional process as Europe's move forward evoked a concept of member state leaders as drivers. Leaders' performance as drivers was assessed differently by the press. Blair, for example, was portrayed as a *driver in control of a situation taking a risky move* – his advocacy of a referendum was seen as the biggest "*U-turn* in his history".[56] The rationale behind this "U-turn" was reported to determine Britain's place in the EU, if it "wants *to be at the centre* and heart of European decision-making or not", and "to decide whether their [UK people] *position lies* as a *leading* partner and ally in Europe or on its *margins*". He manages to keep the constitutional debate on hold in the UK, so the EU "can debate its future *direction*".[57] A positive light was also cast by the NZ press reports on the British Foreign Secretary Jack Straw. Several articles described him as a skilful politician in the situation surrounding the Reform Treaty,[58] with strong leadership potential ("*driving force* for the referendum within the Cabinet").[59]

Yet, Blair's ability to be in control of such risky driving was sometimes questioned. Because of his dramatic change of mind, he was mocked by the opposition party, the Tories, and was even criticised by some of his own party.[60] It is important to remember that three out of five monitored NZ newspapers (the *Dominion Post, The Press* and the *Waikato Times*) belong to a subsidiary of the Murdoch media empire, Independent/Fairfax Ltd. Rupert Murdoch is said to have informed Blair that neither Murdoch's mass-selling *Sun* nor *The Times* would support Labour's re-election campaign, unless Blair bowed to calls for a referendum on the Constitutional Treaty in the UK.[61] Another publication acidly noted that Rupert Murdoch and his newspapers were better informed than most UK Cabinet ministers.[62] This fuelled the stories and

---

[56] Grice, A., "Let's Decide Britain's Place in EU: Blair; BRITAIN: Prime Minister Wrong-Foots Conservatives in What is Seen as the Biggest Gamble of his Political Career", *New Zealand Herald*, 22 April 2004, B03. Italics in this and other quotes are ours.

[57] "Constitution on Back-Burner", *New Zealand Herald*, 18 June 2005, B11.

[58] "Dutch also Vote 'No' on EU Treaty", *Otago Daily Times*, 3 June 2005, p. 7.

[59] Grice, A., "Let's Decide Britain's Place in EU: Blair", *op. cit.*

[60] *Ibid.*

[61] Espiner, C., "The Gent's for Turning", *The Press*, 23 April 2004, Features.

[62] Grice, A. and Russell, B., "Seven Years on, Great Control Freak may be Losing his Grip; BRITAIN: Iraq, Europe Potential Minefields for Tony Blair", *New Zealand Herald*, 30 April 2004, B03.

the impression that Blair acted out of weakness rather than strength in bowing to media pressure. Papers even suggested that the "Great Control Freak is *no longer in control* of events".[63]

In contrast to Blair, French President Jacques Chirac was described as failing to be the *"driver"* of the Constitutional Treaty.[64] Unsurprisingly, many EU leaders were reported in the NZ newspapers as welcoming Nicolas Sarkozy, the victor in the French presidential race in 2007, as yet another *driver to the stalled Treaty* – a *"driving force* for reform in the 27-country bloc".[65] Echoing this image, Sarkozy was quoted after the Lisbon Treaty summit in December as saying "Europe was *blocked*, without knowing how to *move forward* and we found the solution with this treaty".[66] Similarly, German leader Gerhard Schröder was presented as one of the *drivers* in the *"cab of the EU's political locomotive"*.[67] Schröder was also described as *"twisting and turning* for any kind of electoral advantage so he [was] prepared to *reverse* Germany's 54-year-long ban on the referendum, the populist tool used by Adolf Hitler to establish the Nazi regime".[68] Schröder was cited as calling the "no" vote, "a *setback* for the process of ratifying the Constitution but it is *not its end"*.[69] He was confident that the EU Constitution would go ahead despite this problematic initial development. Finally, when the Constitution was rejected in the Netherlands, the Dutch Prime Minister (PM), Jan Peter Balkenende noted that "the voters have given a *clear signal"*[70] to the drivers of the European engine.

Winners and Losers (gamble or battle)

The image of Blair as a *gambler taking a big risk* surfaced, as this complete change of mind was the "biggest political *gamble* of his career".[71] Blair was labelled a staunch pro-European,[72] who faced a

---

[63] Grice, A., "Let's Decide Britain's Place in EU", *op. cit.*

[64] Field, C., "Big Three Anger EU Also-Rans; EUROPE: Blair Joins the Top Table, amid Disquiet among the Union's Pygmies", *New Zealand Herald*, 20 February 2004, B03.

[65] "Leaders Welcome Sarkozy Victory", *Otago Daily Times*, 8 May 2007, p. 6.

[66] "New Treaty Embraces Ex-Communist States in Europe", *Otago Daily Times*, 15 December 2007, World.

[67] Field, C., "Big Three Anger EU Also-Rans; EUROPE: Blair Joins the Top Table, amid Disquiet among the Union's Pygmies", *New Zealand Herald*, 20 February 2004, B03.

[68] "Shaky Economies Threaten All European States. Political Crises Looming in France and Germany", *Otago Daily Times*, 13 September 2004.

[69] "Deafening 'Non' Shatters EU", *New Zealand Herald*, 31 May 2005, World.

[70] "Dutch Pile on Misery for EU Leaders", *New Zealand Herald*, 3 June 2005, World.

[71] Grice, A., "Lets decide Britain's Place in the EU", *op. cit.*, p. 3.

strong reaction after changing his mind on the Constitutional Treaty by introducing the idea of a constitutional referendum in the UK. Despite turbulent times and controversial decisions, Blair was still portrayed as a *winner* – he was noted to actually win "more *allies*, including the Dutch and Germans, for his call for the constitution to be put on hold so the EU could debate its future direction".[73] It seems that in the eyes of the NZ press, Blair came out of the constitutional crisis relatively unscathed compared to some of his European counterparts.

The new British PM, Gordon Brown, who came into office in 2007, was not very visible in the coverage of the Treaty "saga". Having inherited Blair's decision to hold a national referendum on the Constitution, Brown was reported to face a significant pressure from the British public. A reported poll for the *Daily Mail* found out that a quarter of Labour Party voters would likely abandon Brown, if he did not hold a referendum on the new EU treaty – according to the article, 82% of British voters wanted a referendum.[74] The NZ press reported a remarkable move by Brown who stood against pressure to hold a referendum on the treaty. According to him, Britain's sovereignty would not be undermined by the charter – he was quoted to be determined to "*protect* the British national interest and to ensure that the interests of the British people are *safeguarded*".[75]

In contrast to Blair, Jacques Chirac was portrayed as a weak leader and *looser*, who was demoralised, resigned to defeat, and disliked by the very people who voted him into power. He was even crudely called "a *lame duck*".[76] Chirac's UMP party was colourfully described in 2004 reportages as an inefficient (and even dangerous) body – a "*do-nothing regime* that is *fiddling* while the country *burns*",[77] a description that suggested that the French public were highly dissatisfied with their government. As a result, many French people were reported to believe the wildly exaggerated and widely circulated stories about how the new Treaty would undermine French independence and destroy the French welfare state. Chirac was presented in the NZ press as a reason for France's emphatic "no" to the Constitution project, a vote which re-

---

[72] Lovell, J., "European Future Hangs in Balance; EUROPE: Chris Patten Says 'No' Vote could Force UK out of the European Union", *New Zealand Herald*, 26 April 2004.

[73] "Constitution on Back-Burner", *New Zealand Herald*, 18 June 2005, B11.

[74] "Brits Want Treaty poll", *Otago Daily Times*, 21 August 2007, p. 8.

[75] "Europe Reaches Accord after Two Years of Wrangling", *Otago Daily Times*, 20 October 2007, p. 14.

[76] "Deafening 'Non' Shatters EU", *New Zealand Herald*, *op. cit.*

[77] "Shaky Economies Threaten All European States. Political Crises Looming in France and Germany", *Otago Daily Times*, 13 September 2004.

sulted in a "stinging *rebuff* to the *deeply unpopular* Chirac" since it "was more a case of voters showing what they thought of him rather than the constitution".[78] Unsurprisingly, Chirac was shown failing with his cajoling and heart felt pleas in trying to persuade the French public to vote "yes" on a referendum. With Chirac's hopes of securing another term in the office in the Elysée Palace vanishing, he was urged to "face the reality that France's political agenda was dominated by a sense of what was largely *his failure*".[79] Echoing rather negative portrayals of the French President Chirac, the images of the French Prime Minister Jean-Pierre Raffarin (another visible actor in the constitutional drama) were also unflattering. He was occasionally referred to as "hapless"[80] and "unpopular".[81] It seemed that the NZ media presented him to be the partial scapegoat for Chirac's defeat – the President had to "*deflect blame* by firing him".[82]

The German leader Gerhard Schröder emphasised that Germany and the other two major EU powers, France and the UK, "are not trying to *dominate* anyone, let alone Europe".[83] Yet, while being portrayed as a stronger player in international affairs, he was featured as a weaker leader domestically, similarly to Chirac, – Schröder was seen leading the "*wreckage* of the SPD, once the standard-bearer of European social democracy" and he was struggling to retain power in the upcoming elections. The NZ press noted his lagging-behind position in the election polls realistically describing a scenario if his party lost – control of the upper house would pass then to the Conservatives, which would make him a "'titular Chancellor', governing only that which his opponents permit".[84] The article also labelled him, along with Chirac, to be "*soft-option politicians* [who] find it easier to blame it [the EU] to help them out of their *political weakness*. In so doing, they lock themselves more tightly into the national discourses that are the source of their *problems*".[85] In contrast to Schröder, the new German leader, Angela Merkel, together with the new French leader, Sarkozy, was reported to "*win the*

---

[78]   "Shattering Impact", *The Press*, 2 June 2005.

[79]   Randall, C., "Humbling Vote for President who Put his Prestige on Line", *New Zealand Herald*, 31 May 2005, B01.

[80]   "French Vote Risks EU Gridlock", *New Zealand Herald*, 28 May 2005, World.

[81]   Randall, C., "Humbling vote...", *op. cit.*

[82]   "Dutch: Heed the People", *New Zealand Herald*, 4 June 2005, B11.

[83]   Field, C., "Big Three Anger EU Also-Rans; EUROPE", *op. cit.*

[84]   "Shaky Economies...", *Otago Daily Times*, *op. cit.*

[85]   *Ibid.*

overall EU support for a pared-down version of the bloc's dead constitution".[86]

A Weaver and a Circus Performer

The images of a *weaver* and a *circus performer* surfaced in the report
on Germany's new leader, Angel Merkel. Merkel was portrayed as a
capable and pro-active leader in the Constitutional stagnating drama
who took an active stance in persuasion of the member states to come to
a common agreement on the treaty, so the EU could move forward. She
was reported to host a two-day summit in Berlin in 2007 attempting to
reach agreement on the Constitutional Treaty. She was also reported to
"travel [...] to 18 member states to identify problems and tr[y] to resolve them".[87] During her trips, Merkel faced a mammoth, but still a
delicate task of trying to satisfy the eighteen countries, which had
already ratified the Constitutional Treaty. Unsurprisingly, she was
described by an unnamed diplomat as a leader "*picking threads out of a
fragile tapestry*, which could *unravel* at any point as countries revive –
or revise – their position".[88] Her actions were also described in terms of
a risky circus performance – "Merkel has a *tricky balancing act*", said a
European diplomat, mostly because she was showing favour to some
countries risking losing others.[89]

Importantly, a dominant theme of the lack of popular support to the
Constitutional Treaty suggested that from its inception the constitutional
project was an elitist idea. Unsurprisingly, when the treaty ratification
failed in the two member states, it was the leaders of the EU and its
members who faced the harshest criticism, both internally and externally. Predictably, the gallery of the EU member states' leaders featured
colourful, metaphorical and controversial portraits – on the one hand,
the images suggested energy to lead and skills to drive, to perform tricky
acts, to gamble and even to weave; on the other, the leaders were sometimes described as "lame ducks" and "soft politicians". A spectrum of
media descriptions, a sheer volume of colourful images and their frequency reveal that the member states' leaders captured the newsmakers'
attention as the leading and pro-active actors of the constitutional process, especially if we compare their visibility and profile to those of
communal institutions and the EU citizens.

---

[86] "Sarkozy-Merkel Honeymoon Over", *Otago Daily Times*, 15 September 20007,
p. 12.

[87] Field, C., "Treaty that Dare not Speak its Name", *New Zealand Herald*, 21 June
2007.

[88] *Ibid.*

[89] *Ibid.*

EU Institutions and Officials

In contrast to the EU members states' leaders, the EU's institutions and officials remained out of news limelight. The European Parliament (EP), the most represented EU institution, appeared in ten articles (12.5%), and actions of the European Commission were reported in only five news pieces (6%). Two other institutions – the European Central Bank (ECB) and the Council of Ministers – were mentioned only in brief. The most frequently mentioned EU official (six articles) was the President of the European Commission, José Manuel Barroso. Another official who was represented in the reportage, yet in a fleeting manner, was Javier Solana, High Representative for the Common Foreign and Security Policy.

When compared with the imagery employed in the reporting of the EU members states' leaders, a somewhat different portrayal surfaces in the media descriptions of the EU bodies and officials in the constitutional debate. The EU in general is compared to a *student facing a difficult task at school*, or even a *"test"*.[90] Despite the fact that the EU *"prepares* for national votes on Constitution"*,[91] a mere *"difficulty* and uncertainty"*[92] accompanying the initiative makes the EU *"grapple* [...] with hard questions"*[93] as its people prepare to vote. In this more general picture, the EU bodies and officials are compared to a person, who experiences *physical and emotional challenges*. Other occasional images included description of the process in terms of *advocate, performance on the stage* and *gambling* (with *winners* and *losers*).

Physical and Emotional Challenges

For the EP, whose members overwhelmingly voted for the ratification of the Constitutional Treaty, a positive outcome of the constitutional process would *"increase* and *strengthen* their powers".[94] Unsurprisingly, failure to ratify the treaty was "greeted with some *shock*"[95] in the EP. In contrast, the European Commission was reported to not benefit from ratification of the treaty, as it would *"trim* [...] the national

---

[90] "Another Test for Europe", *Waikato Times*, 14 June 2005.

[91] "EU Prepares for National Votes on Constitution", *New Zealand Herald*, 18 February 2005, World.

[92] "Difficulty and Uncertainty in Rescuing Compromise Constitution", *Otago Daily Times*, 31 May 2005, World.

[93] "EU Grapples with Hard Questions as Dutch Prepare to Vote", *New Zealand Herald*, 1 June 2005, B05.

[94] "EU Prepare", *New Zealand Herald, op. cit.*

[95] "Another Test for Europe", *Waikato Times*, 14 June 2005.

appointments to the executive Commission".[96] The European Commission's authority was called into question, since it was blamed by the treaty's French critics "for undermining social protection".[97] At that moment, the European Commission was seen as "a greatly *weakened* scapegoat".[98] The ECB appeared in the reports of the euro's day-to-day running, a process which had some connection with the constitutional "saga" – "separate national governments of the European Union could retain their sovereignty and in a *crisis* could override the ECB".[99]

Echoing this imagery of a body encountering physical and emotional challenges as a result of the constitutional crisis, Europe's foreign policy chief, Javier Solana, warned Europeans that "the Union's international role must not *suffer*" and he begged "not to plunge into 'a zone of *paralysis' psychologically*".[100] Indeed, the damage was palpable – "*deafening* 'Non' *shatters* [the] EU",[101] with rejecting voters "pil[ing] on *misery* for EU leaders".[102] Yet, on a more positive note, 2007 articles stated that the Treaty of Lisbon – a "*toned-down* version of the constitution" – would "give [the EU] *stronger* leadership [...] and a *more robust* foreign policy"[103] and will "make [...] the EU more democratic, more effective and *stronger*".[104]

Passionate Advocate

Contrasting more negative descriptions of the European Commission, its president, José Manuel Barroso, was portrayed as actively supporting and promoting the treaty, even when France voted "no" to the treaty – he "*urge[d]* member states to continue with ratification".[105] He called for a crisis meeting of EU leaders to discuss the matter after the treaty was rejected in France. A few days later, he was still pushing for the treaty to be accepted. He asked the EU countries "not to be hasty"[106] in abandoning it and warned the other EU leaders "that it would not be wise to come [to the talks] with new initiatives or unilat-

---

[96] "EU Prepare", *New Zealand Herald, op. cit.*

[97] "Difficulty and Uncertainty", *Otago Daily Times, op. cit.*

[98] *Ibid.*

[99] Dyer, G., "Infant Euro Struggles in Homelands", *Otago Daily Times*, 4 August 2005, Opinion, p. 15.

[100] "EU Grapples with Hard Questions as Dutch Prepare to Vote", *New Zealand Herald*, 1 June 2005, B05.

[101] "Deafening 'Non' Shatters EU", *New Zealand Herald, op. cit.*

[102] "Dutch pile on Misery for EU Leaders", *New Zealand Herald*, 3 June 2005, World.

[103] "New Treaty", Otago Daily Times, *op. cit.*

[104] "Dutch Pile on Misery for EU Leaders", *New Zealand Herald, op. cit.*

[105] "Difficulty and Uncertainty", *Otago Daily Times, op. cit.*

[106] "Dutch Also Vote 'No' on EU Treaty", *Otago Daily Times, op. cit.*

eral decisions that could make it more difficult to reach a consensus".[107] Commenting on the success of the Lisbon summit in December 2007, he enthusiastically noted that the treaty was there for the benefit of the enlarged EU. "For the first time, the countries that were once divided by a totalitarian curtain, were now united in support of a common treaty that they had themselves negotiated", he said.[108]

Show/Performance on the Stage

The leaders of the two main political groups in the EP (European People's Party-European Democrats (EPP-ED) and the Party of European Socialists (PES)) united to declare that "the *show must go on*"[109] and failure should not hinder European affairs.

Gamble (with Winners and Losers)

In 2007, when talks to reform the Constitutional Treaty re-emerged, Barroso was again reported pushing for agreement on the treaty – "if we don't get the *deal*, we will all be *losers*".[110]

As analysis shows, some images in the description of the EU institutions and officials paralleled the ones ascribed to the EU member states' leaders – e.g. performance on the stage and gamble (with winners and losers). Yet, those were occasional metaphors. Strikingly, the most visible was not the imagery of capable actors observed in the case of the member state leaders, but of a body experiencing physical and emotional crisis due to shocking external influences. The only exception was the European Commission's President, who remained in the eyes of the NZ press a passionate advocate of the treaty. Thus, it is suggested that portrayal of the EU institutions and officials in the constitutional "saga" created an image of a reactive, predominantly invisible, temporarily incapable communal arrangement, where individual members were more vocal, strong and resolved to action.

EU Citizens

Dutch Prime Minister Jan Peter Balkenende's reaction to the constitutional crisis was that it was "time politicians paid greater attention to their voters' views on Europe".[111] Since the EU Constitution is some-

---

[107] Nel, P., "Don't Write off the European Union yet, writes PHILIP NEL from Germany. The European Idea is Still a More than Worthwhile Notion", *Otago Daily Times*, 27 June 2005.

[108] "New Treaty Embraces Ex-Communist States in Europe", *Otago Daily Times*, 15 December 2007, World.

[109] "French 'Non' stings EU constitution", *Otago Daily Times, op. cit.*

[110] "Showdown Looms over New EU Treaty", *Waikato Times*, 22 June 2007, World.

[111] "Dutch: Heed the People", *New Zealand Herald, op. cit.*

times argued to be an "elitist" project, this study examined the framing of the EU citizens in NZ reports of the Constitutional Treaty. Predictably, the French and Dutch citizens were the most frequently reported. The most visible imagery coming out of the NZ press is the one of *opposition, fight* and *battle*.

Opposition / Fight / Battle

A negative result of the French referendum was called "French *resistance*".[112] A "no" meant that people of France got "the opportunity to vote *against* EU bureaucracy",[113] as well as to "*punish* the government over France's economy and high unemployment".[114] The NZ media reported that one of the main reasons standing behind the French voters' choice was a problem with Turkey's membership in the EU – opinion polls were reported showing "two-thirds of the French *opposing* Turkish accession to the Union".[115] A "*sting*"[116] and a "*knockout blow*"[117] to the constitution was a resounding 54.87% against the treaty. By this vote, the NZ newsmakers admitted that the French "committed their country and Europe to a fresh spell of turbulence and uncertainty after rejecting the treaty".[118]

The second rejection to the treaty came from the Dutch. The NZ press listed several factors outlining a "no" vote, among these

> growing political and social problems and anti-immigrant sentiment [which] has undermined the EU in the Netherlands and a range of issues has driven treaty *opposition*, from deep Dutch *dislike* of the Euro, *opposition* to Turkey's bid to join the bloc and concerns Brussels might undermine liberal Dutch policies on gay marriage and abortion.[119]

More than 63% of the electorate voted "no" – a vote, which "*fired a second shot to the heart* of the European project".[120] In the Netherlands, analysts said the vote was "less a *slap* at the country's politicians than worries that the ever-bigger EU *threatened* the Dutch way of life".[121]

As it turned out, an overwhelming rejection of the Constitutional Treaty by the citizens of two of the six founding member states was a

---

[112] "Mixed Media: French Resistance", *New Zealand Herald*, 28 May 2005.

[113] *Ibid.*

[114] "French 'Non' Stings EU Constitution", *Otago Daily Times, op. cit.*

[115] "France to Hold EU Referendum", *Otago Daily Times*, 2 January 2005, World, p. 12.

[116] "French 'Non' Stings EU Constitution", *Otago Daily Times, op. cit.*

[117] *Ibid.*

[118] "Humbling Vote…", New Zealand Herald, *op. cit.*

[119] "'No' Expected as Dutch Go to Polls", *Otago Daily Times*, 2 June 2005, World.

[120] "Dutch also Vote 'No' on EU treaty", *Otago Daily Times, op. cit.*

[121] "Dutch pile on Misery for EU Leaders", *New Zealand Herald, op. cit.*

major setback for the EU. Citizens' decisions were framed by the NZ media as an opposition and fight against the bureaucracy, inefficient governance and ignorance of public preferences at both the national and supranational levels. It became obvious that the voters were not happy with the current situation in the EU and in their countries, and that is why they used this opportunity to express their dissatisfaction much to the disappointment of their respective governments. Indeed, the voters' decisions shocked the EU, but, at the same time, it forced the Union to review the treaty and reflect on hurdles on the road to further integration.

Discussion and Conclusions

According to Steve Marsh and Hans Mackenstein,[122] the importance to the EU of international perception is arguably higher than for a state actor, as the Union does not possess any of the traditional advantages of statehood. Respectively, this study attempted to trace the perceptions of the EU and its major development – the Constitutional Treaty – in one *external* case, namely among the visions of the EU among the NZ national stakeholders, as well as images of the Union and its actors surfacing in the NZ national press.

The first angle in this study focused on how external-to-the-EU public discourses frame a major EU development in the European integration project. The NZ media monitoring in 2004, 2005 and 2007 coincided with the milestones of the constitutional process – the treaty was created, voted on and reformed. New Zealand media stakeholders admitted in interviews that the constitutional "saga" (especially, the 2005 rejections) was a truly newsworthy event (i.e. full of conflict, prominence and scandal). It seemed to have all the necessary ingredients to raise the EU's visibility in the NZ news media. Respectively, one of the most important findings was that the press visibility of this key development on the European continent varied dramatically over the three years, with the coverage peaking in 2005 (a year of rejection of the treaty by the two member states, full of negative and full of conflict information) before falling steeply in 2007 (a year of peaceful reintroduction and successful signing of the Lisbon Treaty). Evidently, good news on Europe does not sell!

It was also found that a selected few EU member state leaders were the "celebrities" in the constitutional "drama". This was usually to the detriment of other groups, such as the EU institutions and officials, or EU citizens. As a result, an average NZ reader might have had difficul-

---

[122] Marsh, S. and Mackenstein, H., *The International Relations of the European Union*, Harlow, Pearson, Longman, 2005, p. 247.

ties forming a general picture of the EU as a communal entity in the constitutional process. As discussed above, Tony Blair was reported in relation to the constitutional process in twenty-three articles, while the EP's contribution to the same process got attention in ten articles, and European Commission President Barroso was mentioned in only six articles. These findings seem to imply that the NZ reputable newspapers were mostly concerned with the actions of a select few in Europe, rather than the Community as a whole. Moreover, the most frequent imagery suggested that while the EU member state leaders were portrayed as skilful leaders (albeit to varying degrees), the portrayals of the EU institutions and officials often featured imagery of physical and emotional challenge and even incapability. Such depictions suggest that the news media assigned distinctly different roles to the national and communal actors in Europe – the latter being proactive and the former being reactive in the constitutional process.

The striking visibility of the UK and its leaders in the constitutional "saga" constitutes yet another finding. A reason for this attention by the NZ media could be the extensive cultural links between the UK and NZ. Yet, the nature of news sourcing should not be neglected (e.g. business arrangements for most NZ media outlets to tap into the news items made by their British counterparts). It comes as no surprise that the actions of the UK in general and a British PM in the Constitutional Treaty process received very close attention from the NZ press. Importantly, an EU-sceptic position typical of some of the British media explains the preference for certain Euro-sceptic framings of the treaty in the NZ coverage and perceptible negative evaluations of the process. Consider the pro-Conservative and Euro-sceptic *Telegraph* newspaper, quoted in a NZ newspaper, which gloomily commented on Blair's involvement in the constitutional process, "a fading Blair is embracing a cause with the smell of death upon it: European integration".[123]

A consideration for sources in media framings of the EU Constitutional Treaty seems to be supported by other findings. Media visibility of French matters in the treaty coverage could be attributed to the fact that French news wire *AFP* is among popular sources of EU news in the New Zealand press. On the other hand, a low media visibility of Germany in the constitutional debate could be partially explained by virtual absence of German news sources in the sample. It is interesting to note that even though the Netherlands also rejected the Constitution in a very dramatic referendum, there was only modest reporting of the Dutch result in the NZ print media. This media choice is even more puzzling,

---

[123] Lovell, J., "European Future Hangs in Balance; EUROPE: Chris Patten Says 'No' Vote Could Force UK out of the European Union", *New Zealand Herald*, 26 April 2005.

given that there is a sizable Dutch population in NZ,[124] who could relate to the reports about their historic motherland. This media preference could again be attributed to the sources' profile – the NZ press does not use the Dutch news sources, relying instead on British and, occasionally, French ones.

Another important finding was the NZ media vision of the changing distribution of roles in the treaty process within the EU. Germany's new leader, Angela Merkel, was portrayed as a capable leader of the constitutional reform in the present, in contrast to relatively invisible newcomers in the UK and France (Gordon Brown and Nicolas Sarkozy, respectively) when it comes to the constitutional matters. She was also depicted as a more influential and pro-active politician, when compared with Germany's previous leader, Gerhard Schröder.

Yet another finding was the NZ press's relative indifference towards those most affected by any changes made in the EU – citizens of the Union. With exception of the news pieces on the decision by the French and the Dutch, who in their majority were portrayed as fighting and opposing the national and communal bureaucracies, there were no articles that sought to express the sentiments of the voting public of the EU as a whole, or even reactions to the ongoing "saga" among the citizens of the remaining member states. The treaty had, in fact, been accepted by other EU states but this was not covered in the NZ media. This finding seems to provide yet further proof that the NZ news media follows a universal media pattern – it prefers to feature dramatic events that threaten to disrupt the EU and to ignore events that show a sense of unity and focus on agreement and compromise. The second consideration of this study was a pragmatic implication of the typical *external* imagery of the treaty process to the EU's internal stakeholders, i.e., policy- and decision-makers, as well as the EU citizens. Internally, the success of the Lisbon Treaty marked the "end to the institutional uncertainty"[125] the EU experienced in 2005-2007. According to the President of the EU Council in the second half of 2007, José Sócrates, an agreement on the Lisbon Treaty will allow the EU "to focus more efficiently on the issues that most concern its citizens".[126] Externally, Europe's Constitutional and Lisbon Treaties are major, but remote and complicated developments of the integration process. According to the European Commission President Barroso, the treaties aimed to equip the citizens of Europe with strong and effective institutions that enhance the

---

[124] http://www.stats.govt.nz/analytical-reports/concerning-language-2004/appendix.htm?print=Y.

[125] "European Leaders Approve EU Treaty", *EU Review*, 3/2, November 2007, p. 1.

[126] *Ibid.*

EU's capacity to act, and specifically, to succeed in the age of globalisation.[127] In this context, external validations of the EU's internal developments become a crucial element in legitimising the Union's on-going integration process with its citizens. However, this study revealed that the constitutional "drama" brought to the surface a peculiar profile of the EU in external discourses. The perception of the EU as an entity of unity and compromise seems to fade in competition to an internally divided, quarrelling and wrangling organization. Moreover, in the constitutional crisis, the national actors were portrayed as the controversial, but still leading actors of the process, while the communal institutions and officials were portrayed as less visible and less active (thus conveying an image of less important and less powerful?). The European public was featured to be in opposition to the establishment (either national or supranational).

The consequences of such imagery (both internally and externally) are insignificant, if the imagery is sparse. However, our research indicated that these *typical* media images found in the most respected and reputable press outlets may trigger *stereotypical* perceptions among the international public. Could such representations affect the EU's external reputation as a decisive and strong international leader in world affairs? Interviews with decision- and policy-makers in New Zealand probing on the impacts of the Constitutional Treaty illustrated that the overall attitudes were the ones of relative indifference to the major Union's evolution. Yet, many of those interviewed noted that, as a result of the constitutional crisis, the EU was seen as more of a divided, rather than a united, entity and thus, not an international political leader. This vision seems to support Joschka Fischer's argument cited above that Europe is "fading away" for its many international partners. On a cautious side, this study examined only one case study – NZ's visions of the constitutional "saga" – and more comparative research is needed. However, a heavy dominance of international news sources (65% of the sample) identified in the media analysis suggests that similar imagery could be found in other places around the globe, where popular British and French international wires and other sources are widely used.

The final consideration of this study was the consequences of the typical imagery and leading perceptions of the Constitutional Treaty for the EU's external partners (NZ, in our case). With the EU being the second largest trading partner for NZ, the Union's major internal developments are to be watched closely by the small Pacific nation. The successfully adopted Lisbon Treaty features important outcomes for the EU's external counterparts – consider the Union's ambition to forge an

---

[127] *Ibid.*

even closer Europe, as well as the EU's aspirations to progress as a major actor on the world stage, to further and protect European interests, and to establish a more autonomous and unified identity for the Union. With the EU being among NZ's most important economic and political partners in a globalising world, it is crucial not only to possess the most accurate and rapid information on the Union, but also to analyse what this information means, how the meaning was created and endorsed, and how the meanings were communicated to various publics.

In our case study, the news media's search for drama and scandal, as well as their long-established preferences for a limited number of news sources, resulted in a peculiar image of the EU in the NZ news discourses – overrepresented national actors and underrepresented communal and public actors; dominant negative evaluations; and relative invisibility of unifying processes inside the European Union in opposition to the visibility of dividing and destructing developments. Such imagery, projected of the EU, presented to the NZ readers an elitist, fragmented and bickering entity, seemingly easier to deal with on a bilateral, rather than common basis. Should such perceptions persist, they could be of real detriment to EU-NZ relations. After all, it was Albert Einstein who once famously noted, "Imagination is more important than knowledge".

Index

"European Policy"

"European Policy" is an interdisciplinary series devoted to the study of European integration in a broad sense. Although mostly focusing on the European Union, it also encourages the publication of books addressing the wider, pan-European context, as well as comparative work, including other forms of regional integration on the world scene. The core disciplines are politics, economics, law, and history.

While being committed to high academic standards, "European Policy" seeks to be accessible to a wide readership, including policymakers and practitioners, and to stimulate a debate on European issues. Submissions will normally undergo a thorough peer-review process. The series publishes both in English and in French.

Series Editor: **Pascaline WINAND**,

Professor/Director, Monash European and EU Centre
(Monash University, Australia)

Recent Titles

- No.47: *New Europe, New World? The European Union, Europe and the Challenges of the 21ˢᵗ Century*, Alfonso MARTÍNEZ ARRANZ, Natalie J. DOYLE & Pascaline WINAND (eds.), 2010, 283 p., ISBN 978-90-5201-604-7

- No.46: *Switzerland – European Union. An Impossible Membership?*, René SCHWOK, 2009, 155 p., ISBN 978-90-5201-576-7

- No.45: *The EU in the Global Political Economy*, Finn LAURSEN, 2009, 352 p., ISBN 978-90-5201-554-5

- No.44: *America, Europe, Africa / L'Amérique, l'Europe, l'Afrique. 1945-1973*, Éric REMACLE & Pascaline WINAND (eds./dir.), 2009, 329 p., ISBN 978-90-5201-529-3

- N° 43: *Le paysage européen de la sécurité intérieure*, Pierre BERTHELET, 2009, 573 p., ISBN 978-90-5201-473-9

- No.42: *In Pursuit of Influence. The Netherlands' European Policy during the Formative Years of the European Union, 1952-1973*, Anjo G. HARRYVAN, 2009, 284 p., ISBN 978-90-5201-497-5

- N° 41: *Les États-Unis et l'unification monétaire de l'Europe*, Dimitri GRYGOWSKI, 2009, 472 p., ISBN 978-90-5201- 489-0

- N° 40: *Le Traité de Rome : histoires pluridisciplinaires. L'apport du Traité de Rome instituant la Communauté économique européenne*, Sandrine DEVAUX, René LEBOUTTE & Philippe POIRIER (dir.), 2009, 210 p., ISBN 978-90-5201-500-2

- No.39: *European Integration from Rome to Berlin: 1957-2007. History, Law and Politics*, Julio BAQUERO CRUZ & Carlos CLOSA MONTERO (eds.), 2009, 286 p., ISBN 978-90-5201-464-7

- No.38: *European and Turkish Voices in Favour and Against Turkish Accession to the European Union*, Christiane TIMMERMAN, Dirk ROCHTUS & Sara MELS (eds.), 2008, 149 p., ISBN 978-90-5201-428-9

- N° 37: *Centre et centrisme en Europe aux XIXe et XXe siècles. Regards croisés*, Sylvie GUILLAUME et Jean GARRIGUES (dir.), 2006, 288 p., ISBN 978-90-5201-317-6

- N° 36: *Vers une Europe fédérale ? Les espoirs et les actions fédéralistes au sortir de la Seconde Guerre mondiale*, Bertrand VAYSSIÈRE, 2006 (2nd printing 2007), 416 p., ISBN 978-90-5201-353-4

- N° 35: *Institutionnaliser l'évaluation des politiques publiques. Étude comparée des dispositifs en Belgique, en France, en Suisse et aux Pays-Bas*, Steve JACOB, 2005, 271 p., ISBN 978-90-5201-078-6

- No.34: *Visions, Votes and Vetoes. The Empty Chair Crisis and the Luxembourg Compromise Forty Years On*, Jean-Marie PALAYRET, Helen WALLACE & Pascaline WINAND (eds.), 2006, 344 p., ISBN 978-90-5201-031-1

- No.33: *Networks of Empire. The US State Department's Foreign Leader Program in the Netherlands, France, and Britain 1950-70*, Giles SCOTT-SMITH, 2008, 516 p., ISBN 978-90-5201-256-3

- N° 32: *Le droit institutionnel de la sécurité intérieure européenne*, Pierre BERTHELET, 2003, 324 p., ISBN 978-90-5201-193-6

- N° 31 : *La crise autrichienne de la culture politique européenne*, Jacques LE RIDER & Nicolas LEVRAT (dir.), 2004, 241 p., ISBN 978-90-5201-188-2

- N° 30: *Les opinions publiques face à l'Europe communautaire. Entre cultures nationales et horizon européen /Public Opinion and Europe. National Identities and the European Integration Process*, Anne DULPHY & Christine MANIGAND (dir./eds.), 2004, 228 p., ISBN 978-90-5201-186-8

- N° 29: *Droit et souverainetés. Analyse critique du discours européen sur la Yougoslavie*, Barbara DELCOURT, 2003, 487 p., ISBN 978-90-5201-179-0

- N° 28: *L'Europe et ses collectivités territoriales. Réflexions sur l'organisation et l'exercice du pouvoir territorial dans un monde globalisé*, Nicolas LEVRAT, 2005 (2nd printing 2008), 304 p., ISBN 978-90-5201-174-5

P.I.E. Peter Lang – The website

Discover the general website of the Peter Lang publishing group:

www.peterlang.com